Human Resources

Human Resources
Mastering Your Small Business

Jill A. Rossiter

 UPSTART
PUBLISHING COMPANY
Specializing in Small Business Publishing
a division of Dearborn Publishing Group, Inc.

Chicago, Illinois

Publisher and Acquisition Editor: Jere L. Calmes
Editorial Assistant: Becky Rasmussen
Production Manager: Karen Billipp
Cover Design: Joni Doherty
Cover and Interior Illustration: Timothy Gibbons

Published by Upstart Publishing Company,
a division of Dearborn Publishing Group, Inc.

Printed in the United States of America
96 97 98 10 9 8 7 6 5 4 3 2 1

Author: Jill A. Rossiter

Creative Writer: Mary G. Shuter

Produced under the direction of: Richard O. Schafer, Ph.D., Director, Distance Learning, Wisconsin Small Business Development Center, University of Wisconsin-Extension and Jeannette McDonald, DVM, Research Assistant

Content Advisors: Richard O. Schafer, John Mozingo, Sandy Lewandowski, and Fred Waedt

Contribution by: William H. Pinkovitz, Past Director; Erica McIntire, Director, Wisconsin Small Business Development Center, University of Wisconsin-Extension, Donald E. Hanna, Chancellor

Library of Congress Cataloging-in-Publication Data

Rossiter, Jill A.
        Human resources : mastering your small business / Jill Rossiter.
            p.   cm.
        Included index.
        ISBN: 1-57410-018-1
        1. Personnel managment. 2. Small business--Personnel management. I. Title.
HF5549.R633 1996
658.3'03--dc20   95-51287
                                                                                              CIP

Contents

Preface

Welcome to the
Business Mastery Certification Series

Human Resources: Mastering Your Small Business is one of five units from the **Business Mastery Certification Series**.

- **Human Resources**

- Finance

- Marketing

- Quality Management

- Business and Legal Issues

These materials have been designed to lead the learner through the process of mastering the business concepts necessary to a successful small business owner or manager. The structure of the materials; the Challenges and Personal Workshops, coach the learner through the decision-making and growth process that is the basis for the mastery of these concepts. It is anticipated that the self-paced learner will take about 12 hours to complete the Challenges included in each unit. The flexibility of these materials also makes them a perfect instructional tool for use in classroom or distance education alternatives to independent study. If you are interested in the possible pursuit of either of these options, please contact the Business and Economics Section of the Independent Learning Program at the University of Wisconsin—Extension, at (608) 262-4876 or write to them at 432 North Lake Street, Room 201, Madison, WI 53706-1498 for more information.

The *Small Business Mastery Certificate* is awarded to the learner by the University of Wisconsin—Extension Department of Continuing Education upon satisfactory, accredited completion of the five courses in the Small Business Mastery series, signifying their proficiency in the management skills necessary to the successful small business owner and manager in the 21st century.

Your Challenge Begins

The purpose of the course is to help you develop sound policies and practices for managing your most important resource—your employees. This course will provide you with information pertinent to the hiring and development of your employees, and it will introduce you to the tools and resources that will help you make sound human resources management decisions every day.

To guide you in your learning process this course is organized into four learning Challenges:

Challenge 1: Hiring the Right Employees

Challenge 2: Developing Your Employees through Education and Training

Challenge 3: Developing Personnel Policies

Challenge 4: Managing for Peak Performance

Mastery Learning

This course has been designed for you to master human resources management concepts outside the classroom. The Personal Workshops that you find in this guide encourage a different type of learning. You are no longer just reading a book. *You* will be actively involved in the learning process of what it takes to develop a sound human resources management system. Your mastery of these concepts will prove beneficial as you apply your newly acquired knowledge and skills to *your* business.

Human Resources: Mastering Your Small Business is designed for you to apply your learning to your own business. This is your personal project. Enjoy!

What Are Personal Workshops?

Personal workshops are not tests, simply exercises and information-collecting forms designed to assist you in applying newly acquired techniques to your specific business.

You're Not Alone

As you work through your Challenges, you will be joined by other small business entrepreneurs, whose personal experiences with human resource management will illustrate key points in your learning sessions.

 PCB Corporation/Candace and Tony Washington: Candace and Tony Washington own PCB Corporation, a small manufacturer with 36 employees in a rural midwestern town. PCB operates as a job shop, assembling printed circuit boards to the specifications of its customers, who are manufacturers of televisions, stereos, automobiles, and computers. PCB's thirty assemblers operate three different lines, each set up to meet the technical specs for circuit boards ordered by a particular customer. They currently operate only one shift.

Pegasus Computer Systems/Jean Watson: Pegasus Computer Systems sells a wide range of computers and auxiliary equipment, including monitors, printers, modems, disc drives, etc., as well as a good assortment of software for the machines it stocks. Jean Watson, who started the retail business ten years ago, primarily serves small business and home computer customers. Jean has developed a reputation for providing excellent service to her customers, something the larger computer retailers cannot offer. Pegasus provides on-site set up and repair services, as well as free "workshops" in the store to introduce customers to its new hardware and software.

Neighborhood Medical Clinic/Dr. Carole Stein: Neighborhood Medical Clinic is a one-year-old family practice clinic owned by Dr. Carole Stein. The clinic currently employs a nurse, a receptionist/office manager, and a physician's assistant. Dr. Stein feels the practice has grown sufficiently in the past year to take on an additional full-time physician and professional staff members. She hopes to expand the clinic's hours and services, as well as to double the number of patients over the next two years.

Champy Athletic Company/Terry Rawl: Champy Athletic Company is a wholesaler of athletic uniforms and equipment based in Texas and serving a four-state area. Terry Rawl owns Champy, which employees six sales representatives for each of six territories. Sales for the past two years have been relatively flat, and Terry has decided that some changes need to be made. He has just added two new lines of athletic equipment to Champy's product mix, and he has realigned the sales territories to make them more equitable.

Learning Aids

The following icons are your learning aids. Highlighted in the margins of the page, these icons will provide you with study tips and valuable, interesting information on the topic of human resources.

FYI: Notes, quotes, and noteworthy information are located in an FYI box at the bottom of the page.

Call Out: Information worth pointing out or remembering is called to your attention.

Technology Tip: Advances in computer and telecommunications technology are already bringing rewards to the companies using them wisely. Useful applications are highlighted with this computer icon.

Resource Tip: Others probably already know what you want to know. You will discover valuable resources where you see this resource book.

Key Words/Phrases: Words and phrases that are considered business terms and are important to the understanding of the topic at hand are defined in the glossary.

Step Back: Occasionally you will be asked to refer to an earlier step or workshop for purposes of review or to take a second look at material.

Legal Notes: Throughout the Human Resources series, you will find "Legal Notes," that are included to alert you to the possibility that there may be state or federal laws which relate to particular decisions you will make in the process. The legal notes included in this material are not intended to convey legal advice nor to answer specific legal questions. As an employer, you should become aware of the basic legal issues related to employment in your state, and you should rely on an attorney for the specifics.

Challenge Summary: At the end of each Challenge, you will find a summary of what you learned in four key areas. These designations are used throughout the four Challenges so you can systematically build on each technique.

Information: This guide will provide you with pertinent business information as it relates to you on day-to-day matters as well as for strategic plans for your business.

 Tools: Personal Workshops are the tools you will use to help you test and analyze your business ideas and strategies.

 Learning: Running a business successfully involves you in ongoing learning. This learning will be selective and appropriate, fitting your business's needs and your skills, prior knowledge, experiences, and resources.

 Networking: You will not be alone as you make your business decisions. You will be given access to additional outside resources to contact for support and assistance.

Self-Assessments

You are encouraged to complete the Self-Assessments that are located at the end of each Challenge. Self-Assessments are tools designed to help you check your understanding of the materials covered. If during your self-check, you find that you do not fully understand something, you will be directed to take another look at the material you have read. The guide will direct you to specific pages for review or to additional resources for help.

How to Read this Guide

Spend a few minutes previewing all of your materials before you begin. Become familiar with the guide and the accompanying Personal Workshops. Begin formulating questions in your mind that you want answered as you complete this guide.

Acknowledgments

Many thanks and a great deal of appreciation goes to Shelly A. McLaughlin at the University of Wisconsin SBDC. She labored tirelessly to give this book its "look" and freshness.

We would also like to extend our gratitude to Barbara Harmony, Director of the Mid-Ohio Small Business Development Center in Mansfield, Ohio and Rita Friberg, Director of the Colorado SBDC at the Pueblo Community College in Pueblo, Colorado.

an opportunity for rethinking your organizational structure. Do not get caught in the trap of hiring based only on your immediate needs. Instead, think about your business plan and your vision for the company, and ask yourself the following questions:

- Do I currently have the right number of employees with the right kinds of skills to get the work done?

- Am I properly utilizing my employees? Are there new or different things they could learn or do to enhance the business?

- Do I have the people and talent needed to satisfy future needs?

If you answered "no" to any of these questions, you probably need to make some different decisions about your human resources. This still doesn't necessarily mean you should hire someone. Actually, there might be several options. You could:

- Reorganize the work load that currently exists to better take advantage of employees' talents and skills.

- Delegate, and provide training, if needed, to develop the people you have.

- Re-focus the efforts of your employees on the immediate needs of the company and drop low priority activities.

- Contract out excess work, hire temporary workers through an agency, or allow current employees to work overtime (especially if the need is seasonal or short term).

If, after careful consideration, none of these solutions seems reasonable, you should consider hiring a new employee. But, again, ask yourself these questions:

- Can the business support a new employee?

- Will the business's growth be limited without a new employee?

- Do I need a full-time or part-time employee? Permanent or for some limited term? Would two part-time employees be preferable to one full-time employee?

Legal Notes

Be aware that there are numerous federal and state laws which regulate hiring and employment, and know that they change frequently. New laws are passed; old laws are modified or deleted. Courts interpret the law and apply new meanings on an almost daily basis. To get an overview of employment law which might affect your business, check your local library for books or articles on employment law, or contact the Small Business Development Center in your state and ask about resources available, such as courses or counseling. Consult as necessary with your attorney, with your state's department of labor, the United States Department of Labor, the United States Department of Justice, Immigration and Naturalization Service, or other federal and state government departments.

- What level of increased production is needed to cover the costs of a new employee?

You should hire only when the business's growth can support a new employee or the business cannot grow without additional help. If that is your situation, then it is time to decide exactly what job the new employee will do.

PCB Corporation/Candace and Tony Washington: We received an order for 10,000 circuit boards from Kiddie Komputer Company (KKC), an account we had been trying to win for two years. If PCB could meet the delivery and quality specifications set by KKC, we were promised additional orders which would virtually double our annual production. To determine our strategy, we evaluated our situation and came to the following conclusions:

- We did not currently have enough employees to meet the KKC deadline without possibly sacrificing quality, which was an unacceptable option.

- Our future needs were unknown, since the KKC account depended upon our success with this order. On the other hand, our future growth could definitely be jeopardized if we couldn't meet KKC's specs.

- Hiring and training an entire second shift did not seem reasonable, since an increased future level of production was not yet guaranteed.

- Contracting out excess work or hiring temporary employees were not reasonable options, since the work of an assembler requires special skills, technical training and training in PCB's special quality control process.

Based on this information, we decided not to hire new employees, but rather to (1) focus all production activity on the KKC order immediately; and (2) offer assemblers time-and-a-half wages to work overtime in order to meet the specifications set by KKC. If we succeed and future contracts with KKC double our production as anticipated, we will consider hiring and training an entire second shift of assemblers within six months.

Legal Notes

Whatever decision you make about how to meet your employment needs (new hire, offer overtime, hiring "temps," etc.), you may be regulated by various federal or state laws. For example, immigration and child labor laws regulate who you can hire and under what terms. The Federal Fair Labor Standards Act and various state laws regulate minimum wage and overtime pay. If an outside contractor is hired, the employer may be required to prove non-employee status in the event of a liability claim or a claim for Worker's Compensation or Unemployment Compensation benefits. To protect yourself, always check with an attorney about which laws and regulations apply to your business.

Describe the Job and the Type of Employee You Need

Key Word

Job Analysis: Before you can hire the right employee with the right skills, you need to understand exactly what the job will be. You accomplish this by doing a **job analysis**. With the information you gain, you can write a job description and specifications for the skills, knowledge and abilities needed to do the job. These tools will help you locate and attract the best qualified applicants to your business. The information gained through job analysis will also help you determine the appropriate job title or classification, pay and benefits.

Job analysis involves studying the job to understand exactly what needs to be done. At this point in the process, do not be concerned about what characteristics the right employee should have. In fact, if you are analyzing an existing job, try to forget the characteristics of the person currently in the job. The goal of job analysis is to identify what duties any person in the job will have, what tasks will need to be done, and to clarify the conditions of the job, such as reporting relationships, travel requirements, etc.

If the position you are analyzing is a new one, you can essentially design the job from scratch through this process. If it is an existing job, you should observe and talk to the current employee. Or, you may find that other employees can be helpful in analyzing a job. If they have similar tasks, they can help you determine the time and skills needed to do the job, whether your expectations are realistic, and how the position fits in with the total operation.

Pegasus Computer Systems/Jean Watson: Recently, my business sales manager, Matt Glenner, negotiated a lucrative contract with the local college. The college agreed to purchase all of its personal computer hardware and software from Pegasus. Pegasus would, in turn, offer a 20 to 30 percent discount on its products to students, faculty, and staff of the college.

We both agreed that the current sales staff would be able to handle the increased business from the college. But when I spoke to Susie Morales, the service manager, we decided that an additional service technician would need to be hired if Pegasus was to retain the same level of customer service offered in the past. We felt the increased business from the college would easily support a new hire.

Our store had employed three service technicians who reported to Susie and were trained to provide technical support for each of the products Pegasus carries. I asked Susie to prepare a job description and a position announcement so we could begin our search. Susie realized that the current service technicians really didn't have job descriptions—their jobs had just sort of evolved over time into what they were today. She decided that before she could write a position announcement, she needed to get on paper exactly what the job involved and what qualifications the employee should have. Susie started by meeting with her service team; together, she believed, they could analyze the job, the first step in the hiring process.

Personal Workshop Preparation #1: Job Analysis

Job analysis is the first step in understanding what any job involves. The information you gather will be used to write both a job description and job specifications for the individual to be hired. To complete this workshop, you must select a job to analyze—it can be either an existing job (maybe your own) or a new one. Remember to think in terms of what the job *should* be, and not necessarily in terms of how someone might currently be doing it. On the other hand, it is important to involve other employees in the job analysis process, as they may have the best understanding about how much time certain tasks take and how the position relates to other positions in the company.

Susie Morales and her service team got together to analyze exactly what a Service Technician does. Here is how Susie and her team completed this Personal Workshop.

THE PURPOSE OF THIS WORKSHOP IS TO IDENTIFY WHAT DUTIES THE PERSON IN THE JOB WILL HAVE, WHAT TASKS NEED TO BE DONE, AND TO DESCRIBE THE WORKING CONDITIONS OF THE JOB.

Personal Workshop #1
Job Analysis

Job Title: Service Technician, Pegasus Computer Systems

Reports to: Service Manager

Supervisory Responsibility for: n/a

Major Duties/Responsibilities	Percent of Total Time
Sets up computer hardware systems	50%

Specific Tasks:	How Often:
a) assembles component parts according to specs	daily
b) tests and corrects defects	daily
c) dismantles, delivers and sets up on site	daily
Demonstrates basic system on site	10%

Specific Tasks: **How Often:**

   a) explains hardware system   daily

   b) demonstrates how to load software   daily

   c) provides customer with workshop/class info   daily

Repairs systems   35%

Specific Tasks: **How Often:**

   a) makes on-site diagnosis   daily

   b) repairs on site or in shop   daily

   c) sets up temporary replacement systems   weekly/as needed

Keep technical skills updated   5%

Specific Tasks: **How Often:**

   a) attend technician training programs
   as needed   quarterly/as needed

   b) read manuals & practice assembly   weekly

   c) consult with other service technicians or service
   manager as needed   daily

What special equipment or tools does the person in this position use?

Computer hardware; software; specialty tools for computer repair

What is the relationship of this position to other positions in the business?

Works closely with sales representatives to meet customer specifications on new systems; works closely with service technicians in diagnosis and repair; communicates directly with customers during set up and repair on site.

Describe the working conditions for the position:

Usual hours: A monthly rotating schedule based on the following:
Mon. - Fri., 8 A.M. - 5 P.M. for 3 weeks;
then Tues. - Sat., 8 A.M. - 5 P.M. in week #4

Overtime required: On-call duty rotates among service technicians
for evening and weekend emergency repairs

Travel required: Local only

Special conditions or requirements of position:
Digital dexterity; ability to lift up to 70 lbs.;
good eyesight; valid driver's license

THE PURPOSE OF THIS WORKSHOP IS TO IDENTIFY WHAT DUTIES THE PERSON IN THE JOB WILL HAVE, WHAT TASKS NEED TO BE DONE, AND TO DESCRIBE THE WORKING CONDITIONS OF THE JOB.

Personal Workshop #1
Job Analysis

Job Title:

Reports to:

Supervisory Responsibility for:

Major Duties/Responsibilities: **Percent of Total Time**

Specific Tasks: **How Often:**

Specific Tasks: **How Often:**

Specific Tasks: **How Often:**

Specific Tasks: **How Often:**

What special equipment or tools does the person in this position use?

What is the relationship of this position to other positions in the business?

Describe the working conditions for the position:

Usual hours:

Overtime required:

Travel required:

Special conditions or requirements of position:

Workshop Follow-Up

 By completing this workshop, you will have a better understanding of the job you are analyzing. You can now use this information to develop a clear description of the job and the qualifications needed to successfully do the job. Your job analysis can also help you determine the appropriate classification or job title, pay level, etc.

Key Word

A *job description* typically includes these basic elements: job title; a paragraph overview of the job, a list of primary duties and responsibilities, reporting relationships, and working conditions. A *good* job description, however, goes a step further to describe the results you expect from the person in the job. By including performance expectations for the duties and key activities of the position, you minimize the chances that the person hired misunderstands what the job is all about and what you expect the results to be. Defining your expectations also will help you write clear and valid specifications for the job, which is the next step in the process. The clearer your expectations are up front, the better the odds that the right person will be selected for the job.

You will be most likely to find the right person for the job if you give the applicants a realistic job preview—a clear idea of what it would *really* be like to perform this job in this company. A realistic job preview begins with a clear job description which includes the results you expect from a successful employee. It continues throughout the selection process by accurately describing, in writing and during the interview, what the job entails. Don't make the mistake of over glorifying the job and promising things you cannot deliver, or your new employee may come in with some unrealistic expectations. Remember that your goal is to find a good person-job fit—and that means no surprises. You want the employee's expectations to be congruent with your own, right from the start.

Personal Workshop Preparation #2: Building a Results-Oriented Job Description

Use the information gathered on your job analysis worksheet to write a job description. Add statements regarding your performance expectations for each of the major duties or responsibilities listed. Remember that you want the employee to know by reading this document exactly what the job is and the results you expect. Be as specific as possible in your description. For each duty, write at least one measurable result you expect. If it is a new position and you are not sure how realistic your expectations are, that's okay. Most jobs evolve over time, and most job descriptions need to be changed frequently, as the needs of the company change. Think of this job description as a starting point; and, if you would feel better, note on the job description that it is a draft or that it is subject to change.

As a preview of this workshop, observe how Susie Morales from Pegasus completed this exercise.

Pegasus Computer Systems/Jean Watson: After Susie and the service technicians analyzed their jobs, Susie found it fairly easy to sit down and construct a job description. She was confident that the performance expectations she had identified would be helpful both for the new employee and the current employees.

THE PURPOSE OF THIS WORKSHOP IS TO DESCRIBE THE JOB AND YOUR PERFORMANCE EXPECTATIONS

Personal Workshop #2
Building A Results-Oriented Job Description

Job Title: Service Technician, Pegasus Computer Systems

Reports to: Service Manager

Job Summary: The Service Technician assembles, repairs, and provides setup of computer hardware systems for business and personal computer customers, both on-site and in the service shop.

Major Responsibilities and Duties	Performance Expectations

• Setup of computer hardware systems:
  a. assembles component parts according to specifications
  b. tests & corrects all defects
  c. dismantles, then delivers and sets up on site
	Will ensure that all systems are set up according to customer specifications and free of defects by delivery date specified.

• Demonstration of computer systems on-site:
  a. provides explanation of system for customer and answers questions
  b. demonstrates how to load software
  c. provides information on workshops and classes
	Will ensure that each new customer receives appropriate manuals, an orientation to the system, and information about opportunities for classroom training on software and systems management.

• Repairs hardware/systems:
  a. makes on-site diagnosis of problems
  b. repairs hardware on-site or in shop
  c. provides temporary replacement equipment as needed
	Will promptly handle all customer hardware problems in a satisfactory manner, assisting the client on-site whenever possible.

• Develop and keep technical skills current:
  a. attend technician training programs;
  b. read manuals and practice repair and assembly techniques
  c. consult other service technicians as needed
	Will keep current on all equipment carried in the store; share expertise with other service technicians; and work closely with the service team to assure customer satisfaction.

• Other duties as assigned.	

Supervisory Responsibilities: None; this is an entry level position.

Working Conditions: Service Technicians are based in the Pegasus Service Center but do frequent work at the business and/or personal residences of customers for setup and repair services. Usual hours are Monday - Friday, 8 A.M. - 5 P.M. The service team rotates Saturday duty and emergency service on-call duty.

Special Requirements/Other Relevant Information: Service Technicians must have a valid driver's license.

THE PURPOSE OF THIS WORKSHOP IS TO DESCRIBE THE JOB AND YOUR PERFORMANCE EXPECTATIONS.

Personal Workshop #2
Building A Results-Oriented Job Description

Job Title:

Reports to:

Job Summary:

Major Responsibilities and Duties	Performance Expectations
(note: take this information from the job analysis worksheet)	(note: for each duty, write at least one measurable result you expect)

Supervisory Responsibilities:

Working Conditions:

Special Requirements/Other Relevant Information:

Workshop Follow-Up

✔ Check the job description you have written. Does it clearly describe the job and your performance expectations for any employee in that job? To be sure it is clear, ask a few employees who are close to the job to read it over and give you feedback. Does the description accurately describe what the job entails? Are your performance expectations reasonable and workable? When you are confident that you have clearly described the job, you are ready to think about the type of person needed to fill the job.

B e sure each job description includes a general statement that the employee may have other duties assigned by the supervisor, as needed. This is important so that the job can evolve and be flexible enough to meet the needs of your company. As a small business owner, such a statement will greatly increase your flexibility in making work assignments.

FYI

Key Word

Most *job specifications* include both *required* (or absolute) qualifications and *desired* (or preferred) qualifications. The required qualifications should include the *minimum* levels of education, work experience, skills, and personal characteristics needed to do the job. Later, in the selection process, applicants who are missing a required qualification will usually be eliminated from the pool.

It is often said that the best predictor of what a person will accomplish in the future is what she or he has accomplished in the past. This suggests that work experience should be an important consideration in selecting employees. Many positions advertised will specify the need for a certain number of years of experience. But is it quantity or the quality of the work experience that really counts? In developing job specifications, clearly state the work accomplishments you consider important for success in this position, and don't get hung up on the number of years someone might have warmed a seat or carried a business card with an impressive-sounding title. Later, when you review the work histories of applicants, look for evidence of track records or progressive experience which suggests an applicant has actually made some significant accomplishments.

Desired qualifications are like topping on the ice cream—nice but not necessary. Desired qualifications should be so noted and might give a particular applicant an edge over the others in the selection process. In fact, you might want to think about the relative value of different desired qualifications to your business—is it more important to have chocolate sauce or whipped cream on your ice cream, considering your immediate and future needs? Desired qualifications are not minimum requirements, however, and it would be unusual for an applicant to have all of the desired qualifications listed.

In writing job specifications, keep in mind that no matter how great an individual's education or work experiences are, he or she won't be working in a vacuum. Every business has a personality, its culture or business climate, which is a reflection of the mission and philosophy of the company, as well as the personalities and attitudes of the people who work there. Although different positions in the company call for different skills and abilities from employees, all employees should share certain traits and values which are consistent with the personality and philosophy of the business.

Legal Notes

In writing specifications for any job, keep in mind that all qualifications listed must be relevant to the job (that is, Bona Fide Occupational Qualifications, or BFOQ's) and not arbitrary. There are both federal and state laws prohibiting discrimination on the basis of race, religion, ethnic origin, gender, age (40 - 69), or disability. If any of the job qualifications disproportionately limit access to people in any one of these protected groups, you could be in violation of the law. For example, requiring that applicants be taller than 5'8" would disproportionately eliminate more women than men from consideration. Unless you can prove that this requirement is an absolute necessity for doing the job, a BFOQ, you could be in violation of the law.

This is not to suggest that all employees need to be alike. In fact, lack of diversity will limit any company. It is to suggest, however, that if an employee does not share the values of the company, does not believe in what the organization is doing or how it is doing it, then that individual is probably a poor "fit" for that company, and employment may not be a rewarding experience for either party.

Personal Workshop Preparation #3: Writing Job Specifications

Job specifications describe what type of person is qualified for the job. It is important that both *required* and *desired* skills and qualifications are clearly noted. This will help assure that only qualified applicants apply for the job, and it will help you in making selection decisions later. All skills and qualifications need to be valid indicators of job success. In other words, you cannot require that an applicant have a certain qualification or personal characteristic if there is no relationship between that characteristic and the ability to do the job. Use the headings in Personal Workshop #3 to build a set of specifications for your job.

 Pegasus/Jean Watson: Once Susie Morales had the job description and her performance expectations on paper, we got together to talk about the type of person we wanted for the job. We decided that a high school diploma would be a sufficient educational requirement, since we would do extensive training in-house, but of course it would be great to find someone with some formal technical training and/or experience. One thing we both agreed on: since the person we hire will be representing us on service calls, he or she must be good with customers. We also know that we need someone who will work well independently and who has good communication skills, since a service technician needs to work closely with both the sales representatives and the other service technicians.

Here are the job specifications we came up with, after much discussion about what Pegasus is all about.

If you aren't sure which skills or values are shared by all successful employees of your company, take a minute to reflect on the following questions:

FYI

• What is the mission of this organization?

• What is its vision?

• What are we committed to in this business? What do we value most?

• What skills and personal characteristics do all employees need to possess to be successful in this business? (examples might include honesty, written communication skills, the ability to meet deadlines, a positive disposition, a commitment to quality, etc.).

THE PURPOSE OF THIS WORKSHOP IS TO IDENTIFY THE SKILLS, KNOWLEDGE, ABILITIES AND EXPERIENCES AN INDIVIDUAL SHOULD HAVE TO FILL THIS POSITION.

Personal Workshop #3
Writing Job Specifications

Job Title: Service Technician, Pegasus Computer Systems

Education:

Required: High School Diploma

Desired: Some technical training in computers

Experience:

Required: None — will train

Desired: Experience in assembling and repairing computer hardware; experience reading and following technical manual specifications

Special Skills or Abilities:

Required: Ability to solve problems, individually and as part of a team; ability to communicate effectively and to give clear directions; ability and willingness to learn technical skills and apply learning

Desired: Some computer skills; feel comfortable using a computer

Personal Characteristics:

Required: Honesty and integrity; self-motivated and willing to learn; commitment to excellent customer service; outgoing and friendly; flexible; willing to work some evenings and weekends

Desired: Well-organized; enthusiasm for computers; high energy level

Physical Requirements: Must be able to lift up to 70 lbs.; have good eyesight and digital dexterity; able to drive with valid driver's license.

THE PURPOSE OF THIS WORKSHOP IS TO IDENTIFY THE SKILLS, KNOWLEDGE, ABILITIES AND EXPERIENCES AN INDIVIDUAL SHOULD HAVE TO FILL THIS POSITION.

Personal Workshop #3
Writing Job Specifications

Job Title:

Education:

Required:

Desired:

Experience:

Required:

Desired:

Special Skills or Abilities:

Required:

Desired:

Personal Characteristics:

Required:

Desired:

Physical Requirements:

Workshop Follow-Up

Congratulations! You now have a job description and specifications for the type of employee you need. Before you begin your search, however, you might want to get some additional feedback on what you have prepared. Ask a few people (employees or business associates) to read the job description and specifications and ask them the following questions:

1. Is the description clear? Does it give you a basic understanding of what the job entails?

2. Do the duties and tasks required sound reasonable? Are the performance expectations realistic? Is there anything that should be added or deleted?

3. On the job specifications, are the required and desired skills and characteristics reasonable? Is there anything that should be added or deleted?

Based on comments and suggestions received, revise the job description and specifications as necessary.

You are now ready to begin your search for the right person. Before you do, however, you need to have an idea about what it might take to attract an employee with the qualifications you have described. That means doing some serious thinking about what salary and benefits you can offer.

What Will this New Employee Cost You?

There is more to employee compensation than the wage or salary paid. You need to decide on a compensation package that will attract a qualified applicant to your business. The package should be fair and equitable to your other employees, and shouldn't cause you to go bankrupt.

There are literally hundreds of possibilities for designing a compensation package. A package could include any of the following:

- Wages, commissions, salary

- Benefits mandated by law: social security tax payments, unemployment and worker's compensation insurance

- Bonuses, incentive pay, gain sharing, profit sharing, employee stock ownership plans (ESOPs)

- Opportunities for promotion or raises

- Employee discounts on company products or services

- Paid benefits, such as vacation leave, sick leave, health or life insurance, travel and expense reimbursements, cost of living allowances, child care allowances, personal time off, etc.

- Professional development opportunities and specialized training

- Perquisites (or "perks"), such as memberships, a company car, subscriptions, etc.

In developing a compensation package, be creative and flexible. Keep in mind that different employees value different benefits, and so you may want to allow choices among benefit options up to a certain total value. This is called a **cafeteria plan**. Even if you are unable to offer any paid benefits or a high salary, your employees might be attracted by certain relatively inexpensive "perks," such as flexible working hours, a better title, or an annual buying trip to New York.

Key Word

Depending on where you live and what type of employee you need, the cost of hiring a new employee will vary greatly. To help you determine the right compensation package, take the following steps:

1. Do an **internal comparison**: if you have other employees, compare the job description and specifications for this position to others in the company. Considering the position and your performance expectations, where should the salary for this job be, relative to the others?

2. Do an **external comparison**: research compensation rates in your market area for similar positions. You can get this information by looking at ads in the newspaper, checking with industry and professional associations, searching the library for labor market and salary data, or by simply networking with other business people, including your competitors. Your area Small Business Development Center, Chamber of Commerce, Job Service, or state business development agencies might also be helpful in determining market rates for various jobs. Also find out what benefits are usual for this type of position and business in your area.

Pegasus Computer Systems/Jean Watson: Considering the wages of the more experienced Service Technicians, the market rates for similar positions in the area, and the fact that most skills required will be developed on the job, Susie and I decided that a new Service Technician should start at $6.00 per hour. Evening and weekend overtime work pays 1½ the hourly rate. At the end of the six month basic training period, the hourly wage will increase to $7.00 per hour and the service technician will

Legal Notes

There are numerous federal and state laws which regulate the administration of wages and benefits. For example, the Federal Fair Labor Standards Act stipulates the minimum wage and regulates overtime pay. Employers are required by federal and/or state law to withhold FICA (social security), Federal income taxes, and state and local income taxes from payroll checks. Other laws specifically regulate the administration of retirement programs, withholdings for child care, etc. Finally, there are tax laws regarding what payments are and are not deductible as normal business expenses and what benefits might be taxable to the employees. You are advised to consult an attorney and/or tax accountant for specific information.

earn one share of the store's profit. While opportunities for advancement in the service department at Pegasus are somewhat limited, a service technician could conceivably move into sales or become service manager some day, if that position becomes open. All employees earn two weeks of paid vacation each year, one week of paid sick or personal leave, and they get a 30 percent discount on all store products. We pay all training costs for service technicians, but we do not currently offer any health, life, or disability insurance benefits.

Recruitment: Where Do You Find Qualified Applicants?

To find the right employee, you need to recruit a pool of qualified applicants. The goal of recruitment is to attract a good number of applicants who possess all of the required qualifications for the job and some of the desired qualifications. If your applicant pool is too small, you might be forced to compromise what you consider to be a necessary skill or characteristic. That might result in a poor selection or, at least, an employee who will require a good deal of additional training and/or time from you. Do not be concerned about attracting too large an applicant pool. The job specifications you completed will be used later to help you screen candidates, allowing you to have a manageable number of qualified applicants to interview.

Start by writing a position announcement for the job, using the job description and specifications you have created. Most position announcements are relatively brief (no more than one or two paragraphs), and include instructions for getting more information or how to apply for the position.

Should You Use an Application for Employment Form?

Many employers require all applicants to complete an application for employment form when they apply for a vacant position. Other employers do not use a standard application form, but ask applicants to submit a letter, a resume, and perhaps a list of references, copies of transcripts, or other supporting paperwork. The advantage of requiring an application form is that you can gather the specific information you need in an order that will be most useful to you in screening applicants. The disadvantage is that you must be careful when developing the application form to ask only legal questions.

FYI

Make sure that the questions you ask applicants are legal questions. For counsel on this topic, review the government pamphlet entitled, *Avoiding Loaded Employment Application Questions Which May Lead to Discrimination* (Publication ERD-4825), prepared by the Equal Right Division of the Department of Industry, Labor and Human Relations.

If you decide to use an employment application form, author Fred Safer ("Personnel Laws: Are You in Compliance?" in *Small Business Legal Issues,* 1993, University of Wisconsin-Extension Small Business Development Center), recommends you consider the following:

- Use an up-to-date application blank.

- Do not take an application unless you are hiring.

- If hiring, give an application blank to anybody who asks for one.

- Do not promise to use the application blanks at a future date; for example, do not state that you will keep applications on file and screen them before you hire.

- Keep completed application blanks for one year, unless you are an affirmative action employer. In that event, other rules apply and applications must be kept for a longer period of time.

- Do not write comments on the application blank.

Personal Workshop Preparation #4: Writing a Position Announcement

Review the job description and specifications to help you write the position announcement. The position announcement should include a brief summary of the job and the qualifications needed, in addition to general information about how to apply for the position, application deadlines, and in some cases, salary information. Position announcements often also include some general information about the company and/or the community where it is located. What you include should depend upon the position and the breadth of your job search. For example, if the position requires specific technical skills, it is acceptable to use the jargon specific

Legal Notes

All employers must consider the principles of Equal Employment Opportunity (**EEO**) at every stage of the hiring process. Employers need to be aware of the federal fair employment laws which may apply to their businesses, such as the Americans with Disabilities Act of 1990 (ADA), Title VII of the Civil Rights Act of 1964, the Age Discrimination in Employment Act (ADEA), the Equal Pay Act, etc. Most states also have fair employment laws which impact small business hiring decisions. Owner/managers whose hiring decisions are challenged may have to demonstrate that their decisions are objectively based. If you have thoughtfully gone through the job analysis, job description, and job specification workshops, then you should have valid criteria for selecting an employee, which is the first step in establishing an objective hiring procedure. As always, though, you should check with an attorney regarding which laws apply to your business and what you must do to comply.

Key Word

to that field, since you can assume that anyone who doesn't understand the announcement doesn't have the skills needed. Likewise, if you are going to do a regional or national search for a position, it would be wise to include a bit of information about the location and character of the business and the community.

Pegasus/Jean Watson: We decided a local search for a new service technician would be sufficient. Susie designed an attractive flyer to be distributed around town announcing the job opening. Susie used the following workshop to guide her as she created the position announcement.

THE PURPOSE OF THIS WORKSHOP IS TO DEVELOP AN INFORMATIVE AND ATTRACTIVE ANNOUNCEMENT OF THE AVAILABLE POSITION IN YOUR BUSINESS.

Personal Workshop #4
Writing a Position Announcement

Write an announcement for the position in the space below. As a minimum, always include the following information in the position announcement:

☑ The position title and a brief descriptive overview of the job
☑ Required qualifications
☑ How to apply
☑ Application deadline
☑ The name of the company
☐ Equal employment opportunity statement, if applicable
☐ Affirmative action statement, if applicable

In addition, you may choose to include the following information:
☑ Descriptive information about the company or organization
☑ Desired qualifications
☑ Salary and/or benefit information
☐ Information about working conditions, hours, etc.
☐ Information about the community
☑ Anticipated start date, or other special information
☑ Our business logo
☑ Letter and/or resume required

Using the checklist as your guide, write your announcement in the space below.

Go back and review your checklist. Did you include everything in the announcement that you noted on your checklist? Is your announcement clear and easy to understand? If no, you will want to revise your copy, as necessary.

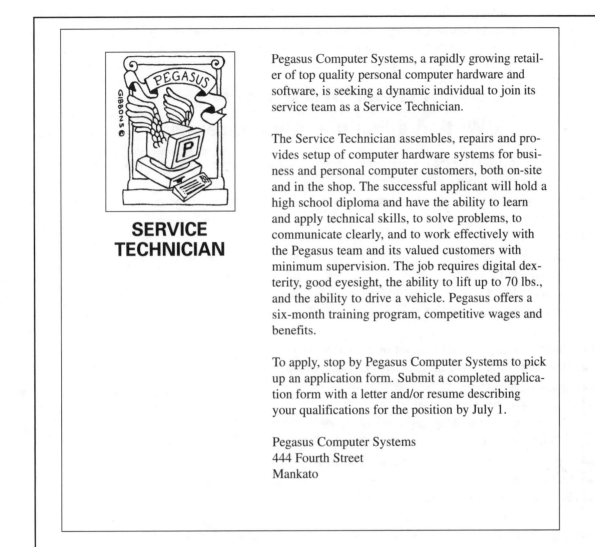

**SERVICE
TECHNICIAN**

Pegasus Computer Systems, a rapidly growing retailer of top quality personal computer hardware and software, is seeking a dynamic individual to join its service team as a Service Technician.

The Service Technician assembles, repairs and provides setup of computer hardware systems for business and personal computer customers, both on-site and in the shop. The successful applicant will hold a high school diploma and have the ability to learn and apply technical skills, to solve problems, to communicate clearly, and to work effectively with the Pegasus team and its valued customers with minimum supervision. The job requires digital dexterity, good eyesight, the ability to lift up to 70 lbs., and the ability to drive a vehicle. Pegasus offers a six-month training program, competitive wages and benefits.

To apply, stop by Pegasus Computer Systems to pick up an application form. Submit a completed application form with a letter and/or resume describing your qualifications for the position by July 1.

Pegasus Computer Systems
444 Fourth Street
Mankato

Legal Notes

In addition to outlawing discrimination in employment, certain companies contracting with the federal government must adopt an **affirmative action** program for the employment of women, minorities, handicapped, and Vietnam Veterans. Affirmative Action means the employer must actively seek out applicants from these protected groups. It does *not* mean that you must hire anyone who is not qualified for the position. To learn if you are required to have an affirmative action program and what that involves, contact your area Small Business Development Center, your regional Job Service center, the Equal Employment Opportunity Commission (EEOC), or check with your attorney.

Key Word

THE PURPOSE OF THIS WORKSHOP IS TO DEVELOP AN INFORMATIVE AND ATTRACTIVE ANNOUNCEMENT OF THE AVAILABLE POSITION IN YOUR BUSINESS.

Personal Workshop #4
Writing a Position Announcement

Write an announcement for the position in the space below. As a minimum, always include the following information in the position announcement:

❏ The position title and a brief descriptive overview of the job
❏ Required qualifications
❏ How to apply
❏ Application deadline
❏ The name of the company
❏ Equal employment opportunity statement, if applicable
❏ Affirmative action statement, if applicable

In addition, you may choose to include the following information:

❏ Descriptive information about the company or organization
❏ Desired qualifications
❏ Salary and/or benefit information
❏ Information about working conditions, hours, etc.
❏ Information about the community
❏ Anticipated start date, or other special information
❏ Our business logo
❏ Letter and or resume required

Using the checklist as your guide, write your announcement in the space below.

Go back and review your checklist. Did you include everything in the announcement that you noted on your checklist? Is your announcement clear and easy to understand? If no, you will want to revise your copy, as necessary.

Workshop Follow-Up

Check the announcement you have written to be sure your application instructions are clear. You may find it helpful to have other employees review it as well.

When you have a final copy of your announcement, you are then ready to proceed to the next section of this Challenge where you will learn where you can post your announcement and how you should continue with your search for an employee.

Methods of Recruiting

You should consider both internal and external candidates to fill a position in your company. In many instances, owner/managers assume no one in their organization is interested in or qualified for an open position. You cannot know, however, unless you ask. Some employers may limit their search to external candidates because they fear that promoting one worker will cause others to be disgruntled. Hiring is indeed a sensitive process, and hard feelings may result no matter what decision an employer makes. In many cases, however, employees want to be considered for an opening, even if they may not be fully qualified. Employers need to consider the advantages of both approaches.

Why it Might Be Better to Promote an Insider

- Promotion from within tends to be less costly than hiring an outsider. By promoting from within, you could eliminate recruiting expenses such as advertising, travel, search firm fees, and relocation costs, not to mention the indirect costs of lost productivity by the manager to locate, hire, and familiarize an outsider with the business.

- Employees tend to work harder when they know there are opportunities for promotion and a commitment by management to hire from within. On the other hand, employees who believe they are in dead-end jobs may lack motivation and commitment to the business.

- When you promote an insider, you are hiring a proven performer, a "known entity." You know the employee's accomplishments, work habits, and personal characteristics. And the employee knows the business and your performance expectations. Even though this knowledge alone cannot guarantee success in the new position, it is based on your direct observation and not on the impressions of other people, such as former employers.

The Advantages of Hiring an Outsider

- In some situations you may not be able to hire an insider with the proper qualifications to fill a position. In this case, you may find it advantageous to hire an outsider who is a more qualified individual; in other words, someone who already knows the job and can just step in and take over without extensive training and costs.

- An outsider can give your business some "new blood," a term which refers to fresh perspectives and new, creative ideas. Sometimes that new perspective and energy is lost when an individual is promoted from within and is too close to "the way it's always been done."

- Hiring from outside will give you the opportunity to diversify your work place, to keep it fresh, and to avoid the type of organization where everyone thinks and acts alike.

Whatever you decide, your decision should be based on what is best for the business in the long run. If you decide to look outside, be sure to let current employees know your reasons for opening the search. And keep in mind that opening the search certainly does not eliminate qualified internal candidates. Once a search is opened, however, your evaluation of internal candidates should be on the same basis as external candidates.

How Should You Recruit Applicants?

To develop a pool of qualified applicants, you should consider using several different methods to announce your job opening. The effectiveness of different sources depends primarily on the type of job. The costs of recruiting also vary with the method and scope of your search. Typically, the higher the level of the position, or the more specialized the skills required, the greater the need to recruit beyond your local area, and the higher the costs.

Possible sources of qualified applicants include the following:

Former and Current Employee Referrals

Post the job announcement and ask your employees to tell any qualified people they know about the job vacancy. In some cases, employers offer "finder rewards" to an employee who refers the individual hired, although such rewards should not be paid until the new employee has been with the company for a reasonable period of time

FYI

If you are committed to promoting from within, you might consider **cross-training** your employees so they can step into a co-worker's position on a temporary or permanent basis.

Cross-training can be time consuming, since it involves one employee teaching another how to perform all or parts of his or her job. The rewards, however, can be invaluable in the long run, especially in a small business. Cross-trained employees can pitch in to help co-workers during a busy period or take over for a co-worker on leave. If an employee leaves the company, a co-worker can step in to take on at least some responsibilities, relieving you of the need to hire and train a temporary employee or to hire quickly and perhaps compromise on some job specifications.

(perhaps one year). Employee referral should never be the exclusive method of recruiting, however, since it could result in illegal discrimination against women, minorities, and people with disabilities who were not given an opportunity to apply for the position.

Networking

Get the word out by taking every opportunity to tell others about your job opening. Call friends and professional associates. Pay a buck and announce it at a Kiwanis, Lions, or other service club meeting. Send a copy of the position announcement to your professional or technical association and ask that it be posted in the next newsletter. Or take the announcement to a professional conference and post it on the message board. Don't be afraid to call up people you think might be qualified to tell them about the position. Even if they aren't personally interested, they may know someone with similar skills who is. Most of these recruitment strategies are free, and they could result in some excellent, highly qualified applicants.

Employment Agencies

Employment agencies can be either public or private. Job Service is a local public agency that provides services to employers and job applicants for all types of employment. Its placement service is computerized, so your job opening will be entered quickly into an area job bank. Employers can expand the search by asking Job Service to list its opening in surrounding counties. Job Service also can provide you with local labor statistics, information about fair employment practices and affirmative action, and personalized recruitment assistance. Finally, check on special programs such as the Targeted Job Tax Credit Program (TJTC), a federal project offered through Job Service that offers employers tax incentives to hire people who may experience barriers to employment. The services of Job Service are free to employers.

There are two types of private employment agencies: retainer search firms and contingency recruiting firms. Employers generally hire retainer search firms to locate highly specialized people or top-level managers. These agencies require an up-front fee and typically handle only positions that pay more than $50,000 annually. You can expect to pay approximately one-third of the position's annual salary for this service. Contingency search firms, on the other hand, make their money in volume, collecting fees from employers only when they place a candidate. You can expect a contingency search firm to want to fill the position as quickly as possible, even if it means compromising your job specifications, so beware. Some temporary employment agencies also serve as contingency search firms. If you find that you need to hire temporary help until a permanent employee is found, check with the agency to find out the terms and conditions of hiring someone permanently that they may have placed with you as a "temp." The advantage of this approach is that you get to try out the employee without obligation, perhaps even while you are conducting your search.

Advertising in the Newspaper

Placing a classified ad in a newspaper can be costly, but can be a good source for finding qualified applicants, depending upon the type of job advertised. Before placing an ad, look at some samples in the "help wanted" section. Larger newspapers tend to list classified ads by job category. Also note which ads grab your attention and which ones get lost on the page. It might be worthwhile to pay a little more and run a well-designed display ad one time than to run a smaller, nondescript classified ad several times.

Newspapers tend to run more ads on certain days of the week, especially Sundays, which means that people looking for a job make a point to read the ads that day. Contact your newspaper to find out the best days to advertise, the costs (ask if they offer special rates for running an ad for a minimum number of days), and what services they offer to help you design an attractive ad. Costs of newspaper advertising depend upon the size of your ad and the circulation of the paper.

Keep in mind that any advertisement placed in the newspaper will be read by thousands of unqualified applicants. To avoid receiving thousands of unwanted applications or inquiries, be as specific as possible about the required qualifications in the ad. If you definitely don't want telephone calls or applicants dropping by your business without an appointment, say so in the ad. You might even consider asking job applicants to send a letter and resume to a post office box and not even list the company's name in the advertisement.

Advertising in Professional Trade Journals

If the skills required for the job are highly specialized or technical, or if you need to do a regional or national search, you might consider placing an advertisement in a professional association or trade journal, or an association newsletter. For example, if you need to hire a veterinarian, you may have greater success advertising your position in the various trade journals that veterinarians read, rather than the local newspaper. There are thousands of professional and trade associations, some statewide, some regional, some national and international; and most of them have a newsletter, at least. To find out the names of appropriate trade and professional associations, talk to people in the field, or go to the reference section of your local library. Costs for advertising in professional trade journals and newsletters range from free to very expensive, depending upon the association and the circulation of the publication.

School Placement Services

Most colleges, trade schools, and vocational schools have placement offices for their students and graduates. Just call the school or send them your job announcement, and they will include it in their job bank or place it on a job bulletin board. Needless to say, the educational requirements and skills needed for the job will help you decide which schools to contact. If the position can be filled by a high school student, also contact your area high schools. This service is typically free.

"Help Wanted" Signs in Your Window

This is an inexpensive way to get the word out and is especially effective for retail and food service businesses. Your sign should be large, easy to read, and specify times when applicants should stop in, if appropriate. For example, if your business is a restaurant, it might be in your best interest to specify that applicants drop by only between 2 P.M. and 4 P.M. daily.

Your Recruiting Plan

You have been introduced to various methods and sources for recruitment. As you prepare your recruiting plan, you will want to choose those areas which work best for you and your situation.

Take a look at the recruiting plan that Pegasus Computer Systems prepared.

Pegasus Computer Systems/Jean Watson: Susie Morales came to me with the following recruiting plan:

1. Post the position announcement on the employee bulletin board.

2. Develop a small display advertisement and run it in the local newspaper on Sunday, June 15.

3. Announce the opening at her next Kiwanis Club and Breakfast Club meetings.

4. Send a copy of the position announcement to the placement services of the local technical school, university, and community college; also ask their computer science departments to post the announcement.

5. Contact Job Service.

6. Post the position announcement in the front window of the store.

When to Use a Search Committee or Team to Select an Employee

Search committees are more commonly used in larger companies and for positions which require a good deal of interaction with other positions at any level in the company. A search team, in these cases, is typically made up of individuals

FYI

If you are doing a local search, a two week application period may be sufficient time to attract a good pool of applicants. If you are recruiting applicants regionally or nationally, you will need to allow more time for people to learn about the opening and to apply. Finally, if you are an affirmative action employer, you may be required to recruit applicants for a specified period of time. In some cases, employers will not list an application deadline date, but will state, instead, when the review of applications will begin. This strategy gives you some flexibility, in case a great looking application comes in a little late.

who represent those units which will work most closely with the new employee. In some cases, a search team may include a non-employee who has a special interest in finding the right person for the position. For example, if hiring a salesperson, you might want to ask one of your valued customers to assist in the selection process; if hiring a psychologist for a clinic, you might invite an advisory board member to help you out.

A search committee or team should be carefully guided through the selection process, trained regarding fair employment issues, and told of its role in the process. For example, will the members of the search team serve as advisors only, or will they make the final decision? Whether or not you choose to use a search committee or team, you should involve other employees in the selection process. At the very least, give future co-workers and subordinates an opportunity to meet the final candidates for the position. If, however, you want to be sure the new employee will fit into the organization and become part of the team, you should seriously consider involving other employees throughout the selection process, especially those who will work most closely with the individual.

Selection: How to Screen and Evaluate Job Applicants

Now that you have a pool of applicants to consider for your job opening, your next task is to screen those applications. Never assume that everyone who applies is qualified for the job. In fact, as you read through the application materials, you are likely to be amazed at the breadth of backgrounds and experiences represented, no matter how precise your job specifications were!

Before you begin your review of the applications, you might find it helpful to develop a screening worksheet. Use the worksheet as a tool to help you determine if an applicant has the required and/or desired qualifications for the job, and make a few notes about the applicant. A screening worksheet will be particularly useful if you have several applicants for the vacant position. It can also serve as a record of your decision-making process, which could be especially useful should anyone ever make a discrimination charge against you.

FYI

When reviewing candidates for employment, pay attention to how the application materials are presented, as well as to the content. If an application is full of errors, messy, or poorly written, consider whether these weaknesses would affect the applicant's ability to effectively do the job. For example, would you want to hire a secretary whose application letter is full of typos? Also consider how long the applicant has stayed with previous employers—job-hopping is usually considered negative, unless the applicant has been steadily moving up.

Personal Workshop Preparation #5: Developing a Screening Worksheet

Design a screening worksheet to fit your needs. You may choose to use the format provided for you in the next workshop or design one on your own. Use the job specifications you established to customize the worksheet to the position. Just a reminder—allow space for note taking on your worksheet as this will be helpful to you as you screen applicants.

 Pegasus Computer Systems/Jean Watson: We received over 50 applications for the Service Technician position. I asked Susie to design a screening worksheet to help us review each application, and we soon discovered that this tool really helped us stay focused on the job specifications. We also discovered, though, that we couldn't really get all of the information we needed by simply reviewing the written application materials. So we left room on the worksheet for us to take notes as we interviewed and checked references. Following is the screening worksheet that Susie designed.

THE PURPOSE OF THIS WORKSHOP IS TO DESIGN A TOOL TO HELP YOU SCREEN APPLICANTS.

Personal Workshop #5
Developing a Screening Worksheet

Screening Worksheet 1

Applicant Name:_____

Required Qualifications/Skills	Yes	No	Comments
1. High school diploma or equivalency	❑	❑	
2. Problem solving ability	❑	❑	
3. Effective communication skills	❑	❑	
4. Willingness to learn	❑	❑	
5. Honesty and integrity	❑	❑	
6. Outgoing and friendly	❑	❑	
7. Flexible	❑	❑	

Desired Qualifications/Skills	Yes	No	Comments
1. Some technical training in computers	❏	❏	
2. Experience in computer assembly/repair	❏	❏	
3. Experience using technical manuals	❏	❏	
4. Computer skills and comfort	❏	❏	
5. Good organizational skills	❏	❏	

Notes:

Overall Impression:	*Not Qualified*	*Marginal*	*Unsure*	*Highly Qualified*
	❏	❏	❏	❏

Initials:_____**Date:**_____

THE PURPOSE OF THIS WORKSHOP IS TO DESIGN A TOOL TO HELP YOU SCREEN APPLICANTS.

Personal Workshop #5
Developing a Screening Worksheet

Applicant Name:_____

Required Qualifications/Skills	Yes	No	Comments
1.	❏	❏	
2.	❏	❏	
3.	❏	❏	
4.	❏	❏	
5.	❏	❏	
6.	❏	❏	
7.	❏	❏	

Desired Qualifications/Skills	Yes	No	Comments
1.	❑	❑	
2.	❑	❑	
3.	❑	❑	
4.	❑	❑	
5.	❑	❑	
6.	❑	❑	
7.	❑	❑	

Notes:

Overall Impression:	*Not Qualified* ❑	*Marginal* ❑	*Unsure* ❑	*Highly Qualified* ❑

Initials:_____**Date:**_____

Workshop Follow-Up

Review the worksheet that you have designed. Does it include all of the required and desired qualifications and skills you noted in the job description? Did you allow room for notes? If so, your screening worksheet is ready to be used for your initial screening purpose.

Screening Applicants

Use the worksheet that you created to make notes as you quickly review the application materials that have been submitted. If you have any questions about an application, jot them down so you will remember to ask the candidate about them later. As you screen the applicants, you should make three or four piles of applications: one with applicants who lack a required qualification; one with applicants who have all the required qualifications, but look marginal; and one with people who look good, but for whom you have unanswered questions regarding their application. If you are using a search and screen committee or team, each person who will be screening applicants should use the same worksheet. This will help ensure that everyone is applying the same criteria to the candidates, and it will help keep everyone organized for the discussions which typically follow each step in the selection process.

If you are reviewing many applications, it might be helpful to go back and review the first few once you get to the bottom of the pile. This will help assure that you have been consistent throughout the process—those early applications might look very different to you now that you have seen what else is in the pile.

Pegasus Computer Systems/Jean Watson: Susie did the initial screen and ended up with ten applications in her "hot" pile; this consisted of people she wanted to examine more closely. An example of one of Susie's completed worksheets after the initial screening process completed is shown on page 35.

Doing a Second Screen: Sifting and Winnowing

Whether you need to do a second screen depends upon the results of the first screen. First, put the pile of "Not Qualified" applicants somewhere out of the way. Do *not* throw them away, and do not notify the applicants that they are out-of-the-running until you are absolutely sure that they will not be considered further for the job. Wait until you have hired another applicant, or at least until you are sure the selection process is going smoothly and you have several qualified applicants to choose from, before notifying less qualified candidates that they are no longer being considered.

Set the pile of marginal applicants aside as well, but be prepared to take a second look at this batch if none of your top applicants work out. Review again the pile of applicants you have questions about. If any of them look really intriguing, put them in with the pile of top candidates and make a note to ask the questions needed to get the additional information. Otherwise, add them to the marginal pile for now.

You need to decide at this point how many candidates you are willing to interview. Interviewing requires a good deal of time and energy. You should narrow the field to two to five top candidates before conducting interviews for most positions.

Here are some approaches to narrowing the field further.

Consider Desired Qualifications

Since everyone on the top pile has the minimum qualifications for the job, you might want to narrow the field by looking at the desired qualifications. For example, if fluency in Spanish would really be helpful to your company, you could eliminate those candidates who lack this desired qualification. If you would like to find someone who can just come in and take over the job, then pull those applicants who have the work experiences and accomplishments that most closely resemble this job and the results you desire. Or, if a few applicants have four out of five desired qualifications, you might select them over applicants with only one or two of the desired qualifications.

THE PURPOSE OF THIS WORKSHOP IS TO DESIGN A TOOL TO HELP YOU SCREEN APPLICANTS.

Personal Workshop #5
Developing a Screening Worksheet

Screening Worksheet 1

Applicant   **Name:** #1

Required Qualifications/Skills	Yes	No		Comments
1. High school diploma or equivalency	☑	☐		
2. Problem solving ability	☑	☐		
3. Effective communication skills	☑	☐		checked yes—check verbal if interviewed
4. Willingness to learn	☑	☐		
5. Honesty and integrity	☐	☐	?	determined if
6. Outgoing and friendly	☐	☐	?	interviewed
7. Flexible	☐	☐	?	

Desired Qualifications/Skills	Yes	No		Comments
1. Some technical training in computers	☑	☐		
2. Experience in computer assembly/repair	☐	☑		
3. Experience using technical manuals	☑	☐		
4. Computer skills and comfort	☑	☐		
5. Good organizational skills	☐	☐	?	determine in interview

Notes:
Looks like a good possibility—excellent technical training from SWTCC.
Good experience in problem solving and working independently.
Call for telephone interview.

Overall Impression:	*Not Qualified*	*Marginal*	*Unsure*	*Highly Qualified*
	☐	☐	☑	☐

Initials: SM   **Date:** 7/2

Ask Someone Else to Review the Applications

Assuming you are *not* using a search committee or team, remove your screening worksheets and ask a trusted employee to review the applications in the top pile. Be sure to give him or her worksheets to use and to describe specifically the criteria for selection. You will find that another person's reactions to the applications might be very different than your own. In fact, someone who looked great to you might have something in his or her application that raises "red flags" for someone else. On the other hand, the reader might confirm your assessment of who the top candidates are. You should find another perspective very useful.

Conduct a Preliminary Telephone Interview

Telephone interviews are especially useful for those applicants whose qualifications aren't clear on paper. It also gives you a great opportunity to see how effectively each individual communicates verbally. Use this first contact as an additional screening method by asking a few key questions related to your most important selection criteria. Ask candidates why they would consider leaving their current positions, if currently employed. Ask if your basic salary range is acceptable. Try to clear up any questions you have based on the information provided in the application. Finally, let applicants know that you will be making a decision regarding interviews in the near future and thank them for their interest in the position. One caution: if you call applicants at their current places of employment, ask if it is a convenient time for them to answer a few short questions, and if not, schedule another time to call back. You certainly do not want to do anything that might jeopardize their current employment.

Conducting the Interview

The basic purpose of a job interview is for both parties to assess how well the candidate and job match. Both parties need to come out of the interview with more information, therefore time should be allowed for the applicant to ask questions about the company and the job, as well as for the employer to ask questions about the applicant. Set the interview format and develop an interview agenda accordingly.

The Interview Questions

Using the job description and specifications as a guide, develop a set of interview questions to ask each candidate. These questions should cover the important aspects of the candidate's work experiences and accomplishments, education and training, and career goals or aspirations, as they relate to the position. Questions unrelated to the job should be avoided. Questions should primarily be open-ended, requiring more than a "yes" or "no" answer. Open-ended questions force candidates to think, to organize and to express their thoughts. They also allow candidates to say as little or as much as they want about a topic; but as each candidate talks, look for openings to ask clarifying and probing questions, that will help you learn a little more about that person. For example, if a candidate mentions having accomplished a certain goal, ask how she or he went about achieving that goal, overcoming obstacles, or what was learned from the accomplishment. The answers to such questions can give you insight into the candidate's work style, organizational skills, conflict management skills, determination, motivation, and/or values. This information will be useful in deciding whether this person is a good fit for your company, as well as whether she or he has the appropriate skills and abilities to do the job.

The Interview Format

Depending on the type of position open and the number of people involved in the hiring process, an interview could be as short as 30 to 40 minutes or as long as one or two days. Multiple interviews are typically scheduled for higher level

---

Legal Notes

Employers obviously need to ask a number of questions of applicants to decide who is best qualified for the position available. Many employers, however, are not aware that some of the questions they ask could be illegal or interpreted as discriminatory under certain federal or state fair employment laws. To protect yourself, ask only about those areas which provide information about the person's previous work experience and ability to do this job.

You **cannot** ask for the following information from job candidates:

- Age, date, place of birth, birth certificate or naturalization records
- Nationality of the candidate or of the candidate's close relatives
- Color of skin or race
- Religious affiliation or denomination
- Club, society and lodge memberships
- Photograph
- Citizenship, native language, or original name, if it has been changed by court order
- Marital status, maiden name, or information about a spouse
- Number and ages of children, or child care arrangements
- Whether the candidate has ever been arrested

It is **okay** to ask:

- The applicant's place of residence and length of residency
- If the candidate is a U.S. Citizen or has a legal right to remain permanently in the U.S.
- If the candidate has been in the U.S. Armed Services
- If the candidate has ever been convicted of a crime
- Information regarding any physical or mental impairments which would interfere with the candidate's ability to perform the job

positions and involve the candidate meeting with several different people in the business. More than one interview gives both you and the candidate better information to make your decisions. Candidates tend to be more relaxed in a second or third interview and are more likely to volunteer information. For most positions, however, one to two hours is adequate to get a general feeling about the potential employee, as well as to assess the candidate's skills, abilities, and suitability for the job. Be sure to allow plenty of time between interviews to reflect and make notes about the prior applicant and to prepare for the next interview. Just prior to the start of each interview, review the candidate's application materials and check to be sure you have everything you need to conduct the interview without interruption such as paper for taking notes, a copy of the job description, organizational chart, or whatever else you want to share with the applicant. Start the interview on time and adhere, as much as possible, to the interview agenda for each candidate. This will help assure that you get all the information needed to make a good selection decision. If you are an affirmative action employer, it is particularly important that you follow the same format for every candidate interviewed. Legally, in this instance, you must treat all candidates the same. As an example, if you take one candidate to lunch, you must take all of the candidates to lunch.

The Interview Agenda

Each interview should contain the following elements:

• **Greeting and Introductions:** Introduce yourself, welcome the candidate, and introduce any other members of the interview team. Try to help the candidate relax by being friendly and engaging in a bit of small talk; you might even want to offer the candidate a cup of coffee or other refreshment. Most people, no matter how confident, come into job interviews a little on edge. A candidate is more likely to open up in an interview if you are relaxed, friendly, and approachable. Preview the structure of the interview, and invite the candidate to ask any questions that come to mind throughout the process.

• **Body of the Interview:** You want to ask each candidate a set of prepared questions that relates specifically to required qualifications and skills. You want to learn whether the candidate can do the job, will do the job, and will fit into your organization. The basic topics you should cover include work history and experiences, education and training, and career goals or aspirations. Throughout this portion of the interview, the candidate should do at least 80 percent of the talking. You should be listening, taking notes, and asking follow-up questions for clarification. Also, pay attention to how the candidate communicates and presents him or herself to you. Try to get a sense of how this person would fit into the organization, might relate to other employees and customers, and the level of enthusiasm for your company and the position. Since job candidates usually look and act their best at job interviews, decide whether this candidate's behavior, personal hygiene, and dress are appropriate for this job.

• **A Job Overview:** Give the candidate a brief overview of the company, its goals and its philosophy. Using the job description as a guide, summarize the most important facts about the job, including information about the major duties and responsibilities, the reporting relationships, and your performance expectations. A brief description of wages or salary range, benefits, and working conditions is also appropriate here, although negotiations and details regarding benefits should be saved for later, when an offer is made. Your goal is to provide enough information to "sell" the company and job to the candidate without being exhaustive.

• **Conclusion of the Interview:** Invite the candidate to ask any remaining questions. Ask for a list of references from the candidate, including names, addresses, telephone numbers, and relationship to the candidate. Finally, state how you expect the search to progress and when the candidate can expect to hear back from you. Thank the candidate for interviewing for the position.

Pegasus Computer Systems/Jean Watson: Susie Morales and I ultimately narrowed the pool of candidates to five finalists. From the ten applications Susie had in her "hot" pile, she first narrowed the list to seven by eliminating those candidates who had no technical training in computers and no experience in reading and following technical manual specifications. Then she called each of the seven semi-finalists to ask them a few questions about their experience with computers, their reasons for wanting the job, and to get a feeling about how well they communicated by telephone. We eliminated two more applicants based on this additional information, and decided to invite the remaining five in for interviews. I decided to have Susie conduct each interview on her own, and she decided to involve the other service technicians when it was time to give each candidate the job overview. That gave them an opportunity to meet the applicants and to help her answer any questions that might be asked about the job. To close the interview, she gave the applicants a quick tour of the facility and introduced them to any other Pegasus employees who were around at the time. She allowed two hours for each interview and conducted a maximum of two interviews each day. Once the interviews were complete, Susie checked references and discussed the finalists with the members of the service team. Then she invited their top choice back for a final interview with me.

Personal Workshop Preparation #6: Developing Valid Interview Questions

Using the Job Description and Specifications you have prepared as a guide, develop a set of open-ended interview questions to ask each job candidate. Ask questions that relate to the individual's work experiences, education and training, and job-related characteristics, as outlined below. Do not ask any question that is not job-related or that might be illegal. Try to tie at least one question to each major job responsibility listed on the description, and to each of the performance results you expect.

In preparation for the interviews, Susie Morales completed Personal Workshop #6. She reviewed the job specifications and developed the following list of questions to ask each finalist.

THE PURPOSE OF THIS WORKSHOP IS TO DEVELOP A LIST OF LEGAL AND OPEN-ENDED INTERVIEW QUESTIONS WHICH WILL HELP YOU GAIN INFORMATION ABOUT AN APPLICANT'S SUITABILITY FOR THE JOB.

Personal Workshop #6
Developing Valid Interview Questions

Questions related to work experience:

1. Please give me a brief overview of your work experience.
2. What are some examples of skills or abilities you have developed that you think will help you in this job?
3. How much and what type of contact have you had with customers in your current job? Have you ever had to deal with an angry customer? How did you handle it?
4. What do you like about your current job? What would you like to change? What reasons do you have for seeking this position?

Questions related to education and training:

1. Please tell me about your formal education, including any training you have had that might be helpful in preparing you for this job.
2. What is your favorite way to learn?
3. Can you describe a situation for me where you had to teach something to someone else and how you went about it?

Questions related to personal work characteristics, style, attitude, values, etc.:

1. How would you describe the way you work? In other words, do you like to have a lot of supervision or little supervision; to work on your own or to be a part of a work group or team; to work on one project at a time, or to have lots of things going on simultaneously?
2. How do you think your current (or most recent) employer would describe your work and work habits?
3. What is there about this job that makes you think you would enjoy it and be good at it?
4. Can you describe for me a situation where you had a difficult work problem to deal with and how you solved that problem?
5. How do you feel about copying someone else's computer software? Do you think it should be legal or illegal and why?

Other Questions:

1. Do you have any questions about the job responsibilities or the performance expectations for the job?
2. May I contact your previous employers? Will you please provide me with three professional references?
3. If you are selected for this position, when could you begin work?

THE PURPOSE OF THIS WORKSHOP IS TO DEVELOP A LIST OF LEGAL AND OPEN-ENDED INTERVIEW QUESTIONS WHICH WILL HELP YOU GAIN INFORMATION ABOUT AN APPLICANT'S SUITABILITY FOR THE JOB.

Personal Workshop #6
Developing Valid Interview Questions

Questions related to work experience:

Questions related to education and training:

Questions related to personal work characteristics, style, attitude, values, etc.:

Other Questions:

Workshop Follow-Up

Double-check to be sure the questions you want to ask do not relate to the candidate's age, sex, race, color, religion, national origin, disability or marital status. If any of the questions can be answered with just a "yes" or "no" response, go back and revise it so that it is "open ended"—requiring more explanation from the interviewee. Use the questions you have developed in each interview, and take notes on each candidate's responses. After each interview, take a few minutes to reflect on the candidate's answers, and jot down your impressions about his or her suitability for the job on a note pad or the screening worksheet.

Checking References

Don't skip this step!! Check a few of the applicant's references, both those offered directly by the candidate and those developed in the interview. Ask the applicant's permission before calling anyone. Sometimes, understandably, a candidate will ask that you not contact the current employer. However, if a candidate declines to authorize any reference checks, or if the candidate still won't allow you to call the current employer even though you are ready to make an offer, you should beware. These situations suggest the candidate may be trying to hide something negative.

Past supervisors and co-workers are usually the best sources for objective job-related information about the candidate. Call the candidate's former supervisors,

---

Legal Notes

Candidate Testing

Company policies on pre-employment testing and drug screening vary widely because of state laws, company size, philosophy and other factors. The key to legal testing is that a test should validly predict job performance. For example, candidates for a secretarial position might be asked to take a typing test. Candidates for a job as bus driver for a day care center might legally be asked to take a drug test. For a position requiring strong business writing skills, a company might require applicants to produce a writing sample. If you wish to use a psychological assessment or a pre-employment test to learn more about an applicant's intellectual abilities, you had better be prepared to prove the test is a statistically valid predictor of job performance, in case it is legally challenged. The bottom line is, check with your attorney before requiring any pre-employment test.

FYI

When checking references, pay attention to the content of the answers, but especially note whether the person giving the reference seems enthusiastic about the candidate. Also realize that some companies have a policy against providing work references, other than verifying that the individual's dates of employment. If this is the response you receive when you call, do not automatically interpret it as a negative reference. Just try to get more information from the other references you contact.

identify yourself and the purpose of your call, verify the candidate's length of employment and position(s) held, and then ask a few key questions about the candidate's work performance and job-related characteristics. Take notes during each call. As in the candidate interview, do not ask questions which might be illegal or interpreted as discriminatory.

Making Your Final Selection

You should now have all the information needed to select the best candidate for the position. It might be helpful to put this information into some standard format. For each of your final job candidates, review the screening worksheet, your notes from the interview and reference checks, and all other application materials that you have gathered. Compare each candidate's strengths and weaknesses to the written job specifications. If it would be helpful, develop some sort of worksheet to compare the qualifications of the different candidates. Be cautious, though, about assigning "points" to different candidate qualifications and coming up with some sort of numerical total score—such systems tend to oversimplify the selection process and do not necessarily make the final decision any less subjective.

The important point is that you try to be as fair and objective as possible as you determine which candidate will be the best fit for the job. Document your decision-making along the way, noting your evaluation of applicants' job-related criteria only. Never, ever write down such subjective and inappropriate comments as "she was a knock-out," or "he looked like he might be lazy."

Making the Offer

Sometimes an offer is pretty straightforward, but sometimes it involves negotiations. Before contacting your top choice for the job, determine what you believe to be a fair and reasonable offer for this person in this job. Have some salary and benefit limits in mind, if you are interested in negotiating. Never make an offer during the employment interview—you both need some time to think about whether the situation is right. Invite your top candidate to come in, or make a verbal offer by phone. Follow any verbal offer with a letter stating the general terms of the offer, but do not imply that the letter is an employment contract. Give the candidate a reasonable period of time to make a decision, and invite him or her to

---

Legal Notes

Information obtained during reference checks is confidential. Employers should not share facts or impressions gathered during reference checks with other employees or the candidates themselves. Divulging that information has resulted in candidates suing former employers and former employers suing the company that asked for the references. Because of the threat of lawsuits, many companies will only release name, title and dates of employment of former workers.

call you if any questions come to mind. If you and the candidate cannot come to terms, then make an offer to your next choice on the list of acceptable candidates.

So Are You Finally Finished?

At this point you should feel terrific about finding a well-qualified new employee, but your work isn't done. Notify the other applicants that "a qualified person was selected for the job." **You have no obligation and should avoid telling any applicant why they did not get the job, and you have no business telling any other applicant anything about the individual who was selected.** Simply thank other applicants for their interest in the job, and repeat, as many times as necessary, that "a qualified person was selected for the job."

When your new employee begins work, he or she must complete an IRS W-4 Form (to claim tax exemptions) and a Form I-9 to establish eligibility to work in the United States. As the employer, you are responsible for checking the new employee's documents specified on the I-9 to verify identity and eligibility to work. You need to be prepared to produce the I-9 in the event of an inspection by the Immigration and Naturalization Service (INS) or the Department of Labor (DOL).

The new employee's supervisor and/or co-workers should assist you in setting up an orientation and training program for the new employee. And, of course, as owner/manager, you have a continuing responsibility to the personal and professional development of this and every other employee in your business—no small task. The good news is, though, that the "Challenges" which follow will help you develop the other human resources management skills needed to keep your business and your employees dynamic!

You Have Completed Challenge 1

By completing this Challenge, you have developed the skills needed to hire the right employees for your small business. From assessing your need for a new employee to making an offer to the top candidate, you now know the steps and have practiced using the tools which will help take the fear and guesswork out of the hiring process. You also have learned that certain employment decisions may be regulated by federal or state laws. Whether hiring your first or fiftieth employee, this Challenge can serve as your guide to sound hiring practices.

FYI

> If you are an affirmative action employer, or if you are ever charged with unlawful discrimination because of a selection decision you made, you may need to prove that your selection process was unbiased and valid. Careful documentation of the search and your decision-making process can help. Keep in mind that the application form and/or resume may become part of an employee's permanent record. As you go through the selection process, do not write comments on these documents.

You Leave Challenge 1 with the Following

Information: By working your way through this Challenge, you are now well-equipped to make hiring decisions, one of the most important tasks any owner/manager faces. You have been given many bits of advice and tips for success along the way, and you have been alerted to the possible legal pitfalls associated with employment. While all of this information cannot guarantee that every new employee will become a productive employee, it certainly minimizes your chances of making the wrong choice. The Challenges which follow will help you develop those employees so that they are productive and can help your business realize its mission.

Learning: This Challenge has been set up cookbook-style to guide you through each step of the hiring process, by providing examples and giving you an opportunity to develop your own tools. You will find that much of what you have developed by completing the Personal Workshops can be applied to other types of management decisions you need to make. For example, conducting job analyses for all positions in your company will help you develop a more efficient organizational structure, avoid redundancy, and come up with an equitable system for rewarding employees. Clear job descriptions which specify your performance expectations will help your employees know what is expected of them and allow them to perform

To stay current on employment laws and trends in human resources management for small business, check your local library for journals, such as the *Small Business Forum, Inc.*, and the *Harvard Business Review*. If these are not available locally, ask your librarian about getting them through interlibrary loan.

Legal Notes

The "Employment at Will Doctrine" is a historical "right" of employers to terminate an employee at any time for any reason, with or without cause. This also means that an employee may resign at any time with or without prior notice. However, over the past 50 years, legislatures and courts at both the state and federal level have developed many exceptions to this "right." Throughout the selection process, you could risk your "at will" employer status by writing or saying anything that might imply the existence of an employment contract or promise of future employment. Therefore, application forms, offer letters, employee handbooks, etc., should contain express statements confirming the at-will relationship, such as: "Either party may terminate the employment relationship at any time without cause. This document is not a contract. It may be changed or withdrawn by the company at any time," (Bordwin, p. 47). For more information, contact your attorney. You may also find it helpful to review the following article:

Bordwin, Milton. "Firing 101: Before, During and After." *Small Business Forum.* Winter 1994/1995.

accordingly. This Challenge has, in effect, provided you with skills and information that will help you be a better small business manager overall.

Tools: The Personal Workshops in Challenge 1 have given you an opportunity to practice using many of the tools needed to effectively manage human resources, whether in a large or small business. Those tools include job analysis, the job description and specifications, the position announcement, screening worksheets, etc. The formats used in this Challenge are only samples—you should revise and refine them to meet your needs. And, as noted above, you can use these tools for much more than just hiring new employees. They can be key to the strategic growth and effective decision-making of your small business.

Networking: Resource tips and case studies have been included in this Challenge to provide you with ideas and suggestions to guide you through the hiring process. For more guidance on human resources management for small business, contact the Small Business Administration, the Small Business Development Center (SBDC) in your state, Job Service, or the agency in your state which assists small businesses, usually part of a department of labor or economic development. Also, throughout this Challenge you have been encouraged to include your other employees in the process of hiring new people. Unless yours is a very small business, your current employees are often your best resource for understanding the work that goes on. You will recognize many rewards from implementing a team concept in your small business.

Challenge 1 Self-Assessment

After completing this Challenge you should be able to assess your need for new employees, and you should be able to take the steps necessary to hire a qualified individual who will be an asset to your company. Check your understanding of the concepts and the hiring process presented by using the following checklist. If needed, go back and review the steps of the process where you feel you need more practice.

**Pages
1 - 4**

Assessing Your Need for a New Employee

( ) I have a vision: I know what needs to be done, and I have a plan for hiring new people to move the business forward.

( ) I know the skills and talents of my current employees and am properly utilizing them in the business.

( ) I have explored the various alternatives available to me to meet my human resource needs.

( ) I can evaluate whether my businesses growth can support a new employee.

Describe the Job and the Type of Employee You Need

( ) I can conduct a Job Analysis for any position in my company with the involvement of my employees.

( ) I can describe the organizational structure of my company and how each employee fits into that structure.

( ) I can develop results-oriented job descriptions to guide my employees.

( ) I can develop a list of required and desired qualifications for a job which can be legally justified by the requirements of the job and which do not discriminate against any protected group.

( ) I can describe the values of this company and the personal characteristics shared by all employees.

Pages 5 - 18

Determining the Cost of a New Employee

( ) I have determined my budget for the new position.

( ) I have completed an internal comparison study to compare the job description, specifications, and salary to other positions in the company.

( ) I have done an external comparison to compare the position with similar positions in my market area.

( ) I have developed a compensation package which is equitable and will help me attract and retain good employees.

Pages 18 - 20

Recruitment and Selection

( ) I understand the benefits and limitations of using an employment application form.

( ) I understand that I cannot discriminate on the basis of age, sex, race, national origin, religion, color or disability, and I know how to document my efforts to avoid discrimination in the hiring process.

( ) I can design an attractive position announcement.

( ) I know where to find qualified applicants.

( ) I can develop a screening worksheet to organize the candidate selection process.

( ) I can organize and conduct a meaningful candidate interview.

( ) I can develop valid, open-ended interview questions.

( ) I can justify the use of any employment test required by my company.

( ) I can explain the importance of checking references.

Pages 20 - 43

Record anything from Challenge 1, your Personal Workshops, or your personal reflections that you want to remember.

Take Another Look

Review the results of your checklist above. If you feel you need more work in some areas, go back into the text and challenge yourself again. If you feel nervous about the legal issues mentioned in this Challenge, look for a class on legal issues for small business, or jot down your questions and check with your attorney to be sure you are in compliance.

Challenge 2
Developing Your Employees through Education and Training

"Lifelong learning is not a privilege or a right, but a necessity."

—Pat Cross

Your employees are your company's lifeblood! They can mean the difference between success and mediocrity. How they interact with customers, how they handle day-to-day operations and how they treat each other determines whether your business will flourish or fail.

Hiring good people with strong qualifications is *not* enough to assure you will have good employees. As owner/manager, you need to be sure that your employees have the information and skills they need to help your company succeed. Orientation and training delivers that information and teaches those skills. By implementing an effective employee development program, you can protect the investment you made in finding and hiring the right people in the first place. Simply put, employee education needs to be the business of your small business.

Challenge 2 is about developing employees in your small business through orientation and training. You are invited to participate fully in this Challenge. That is, don't simply read through the material, but try to see how things are done by following the case study examples, and develop an understanding of the material by completing the workshops, applying what you are learning to your own business. Try out the tools to see if they work for you. Try to become conscious of how you learn, because that information will help you to design an employee development program that will help all of your employees become as productive as possible. Upon completion of Challenge 2, you will be able to:

If you think you can't afford to train your employees, consider this: in a 1994 survey of American businesses, large and small, employers said that one-fifth of American workers are not fully proficient in their jobs (EQW Preview). If one-fifth of *your* employees are not "up-to-snuff," you are already paying the price of lower productivity, correcting employee mistakes, and employee turnover. A good training program can save you money in the long run.

FYI

- Develop and implement an orientation program for new employees.
- Assess the training needs of your employees.
- Write learning outcomes for any training program.
- Develop an instructional plan that will reach every type of learner.
- Design training programs that ensure job transfer.
- Evaluate your training programs for effectiveness.

What Is Employee Development?

> *"I hear and I forget.
> I see and I remember.
> I do and I understand."*
>
> —Confucius

Employee development is the process of providing employees with the insights, information and skills needed to make them productive in the organization. Employee development is a form of continuing education for your employees. It begins when you teach new hires about the business, and it continues as employees learn new things throughout their employment with the company. Orientation and training are the tools most commonly used for employee development. The employee development process is shown in Figure 2.1.

Key Words

Orientation introduces your new employees to the business and the staff, as well as practices and culture of your company. It is, in essence, the beginning of training. **Training** is the teaching and learning process that occurs in the workplace— it gives your employees the ongoing knowledge and skills they need to perform their jobs. You can use training to update existing skills, as well as to introduce your employees to any new information, technologies, skills, and procedures over time. Orientation may begin before the new hire even reports for work, and it often is difficult to tell where orientation ends and training begins. Employee development is a process of educating employees over time, and ideally, as needed throughout their employment with your company.

Does Training Make Sense?

Orientation and training programs take time and cost money, but benefits for the small business are compelling. Consider why people choose to work for small companies in the first place. Usually it is not because they have been enticed by a rich compensation and benefits package—small businesses often have a hard time matching the salaries and fringe benefits offered by larger companies. But many people prefer working for a small firm because they want a warm, friendly atmosphere. They may also be looking for a challenge, a bigger role and more responsibility in the business, a clearer understanding of how they fit in and how they can make a difference.

Figure 2.1: The Employee Development Process

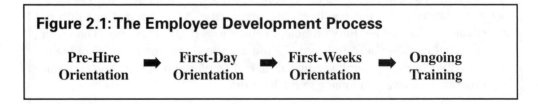

Pre-Hire Orientation → First-Day Orientation → First-Weeks Orientation → Ongoing Training

Orientation and training can enhance these motivations. By taking the time to orient your employees, you can develop in your business a warm, caring atmosphere that reinforces the employee's decision to take the job. And when you offer ongoing training for all of your employees, you provide them with the tools and skills they need to become productive and efficient. If you implement orientation and training in your company, you can expect the following benefits:

- your employees will know the proper methods and procedures for doing their jobs; meaning they will be more productive and less likely to make costly mistakes

- your employees will have a better understanding not only of their own jobs, but also of the business, its values and its goals

- your employees will be more likely to feel good about their jobs and your company, because they will be competent, and because you care enough to help them succeed

Orientation: The First Training

When new employees join your company, what they see and hear forms a first and lasting impression. How an individual employee feels on the first day at work in your company will help mold attitudes about productivity and the business. The thought and quality you put into the orientation sends a message about the thought and quality put into every other element of the business. With so much at stake, it makes sense for your business to provide new employees with thoughtful, informative orientations.

> *"You only have one chance to make a first impression."*

What Orientation Should Do

An orientation for new employees should do two important things for your small business:

- First, the orientation program should help the new employees feel welcome and happy about their decision to join your company. A good orientation provides a congenial introduction to the workplace and fellow employees, and it helps put new workers at ease by making them a part of the team.

- Second, orientation begins to teach your new employees what they need to know to be productive. Orientation should show the new employees how the business operates, acquaint them with business facilities and introduce their job responsibilities.

Your business can use a variety of activities and involve several people to achieve these goals, but that doesn't mean your orientation program has to be expensive or complicated. Most small businesses don't need fancy or formal orientation classes. What they do need, however, is a plan or some guidelines to ensure that every new employee receives a warm welcome and a general introduction to the business and the new job. Try to develop an orientation program that is simple, that fits smoothly into the routines of your company, and yet achieves the goals of making new people feel welcome as they are introduced to their jobs.

Ingredients of Effective Orientation

What should you tell your new employees? And how should you present that information? Most of the information provided in orientations falls into one of the following categories:

- Information that brings employees on board

- Information that helps employees understand the system

- Information that gives employees a sense of belonging

- History and philosophy of the company

- Business goals and objectives

- Information that acquaints employees with their responsibilities

Personal Workshop Preparation #7: My Personal Notes

Later in this Challenge, you will learn how to develop an orientation checklist—a tool that will help you design a comprehensive orientation program for your employees. As you read more about each of the ingredients of an effective orientation and in preparation for the 7 Step Personal Workshops that follow, begin to take some personal notes on how you might cover each category of information in your company's orientation. Don't worry if you forget some things at this point—these personal notes are just to get you started and will help you develop a thorough orientation checklist later.

Step 1: Information That Brings Employees on Board

Every company has specific administrative procedures that make new employees a formal part of the business. Your new employees will need to:

- Sign up for payroll and understand pay periods and pay days

- Understand benefit options and enroll in benefit programs, if applicable

---

Legal Notes

In addition to the IRS W-4 and INS Form I-9, the employee and/or employer may need to complete other legal documents. For example, if the new employee is under age 18, the employer must assure that the employee has a valid work permit for certain categories of work. Personnel laws vary from state to state. You should contact your area Small Business Development Center for information about requirements in your state, and rely on an attorney for legal advice regarding employment.

- Complete the IRS W-4 form and obtain tax information

- Complete the INS Form I-9 and provide documentation establishing identity and eligibility to work

- Receive, if appropriate, a company identification card, keys, etc.

THE PURPOSE OF THIS WORKSHOP IS TO MAKE NOTES ON THE SPECIFIC ADMINISTRATIVE PROCEDURE IN YOUR COMPANY THAT WILL NEED TO BE DESCRIBED TO NEW EMPLOYEES DURING "ORIENTATION."

Personal Workshop #7
Step 1: My Personal Notes

Step 1—Information That Brings Employees on Board

Jot down those administrative procedures which you feel new employees should complete during their orientation.

Payroll/Payroll Information:

Benefit Information:

Tax Information/Forms:

Insurance Information/Forms:

Company Identification card, keys, etc.:

Additional Information:

Step 2: Information That Helps Employees Understand the System

Orientation should introduce new employees to the company's physical layout, its operations, its people and processes. Start with a tour of your company. Show new employees how the company is physically set up and explain the logic behind its physical layout. Introduce new employees to their work space and describe how they will interact with other employees in other work spaces. Don't forget to include restrooms, lunch and break rooms, copy, mail or other work rooms, parking areas, telephones, fire exits and fire extinguishers in your tour.

During the tour, you should begin to introduce new employees to some of the business policies and procedures, safety rules, health requirements and evacuation procedures of the company. For example, if your business is a food service establishment, talk about your rules for hand washing and demonstrate the proper procedure when you tour the restroom or kitchen area.

Key Word

It is a good idea to reinforce the verbal information you provide during the tour with written policies, procedures, rules and regulations for employees. An **employee handbook** is a useful tool for communicating these policies and procedures, and new workers can keep it for future reference. Or you might choose to communicate policies and procedures only as needed in memos, in a newsletter, or through some other means. In either case, orientation needs to include a basic overview of the policies and procedures, and employees need to know where to go for help or clarification of those policies and procedures in the future.

Finally, during the tour and over the next several weeks, introduce your new employees to the significant people and processes which affect their jobs. Assist employees in setting up meetings with key people to learn more about how their jobs interact, how the system works and how they will work as a team. Talk about the culture of the company, teach new employees the "language" of the business, and share information about how things work in general, such as the telephone system, how workers decide when to go for lunch, the mail system, how to dispose of confidential documents, etc. Take time to acquaint new employees to the unique features of your business. Injecting humor into this orientation step is a good way to make these points memorable.

FYI

If your business does not have an employee handbook, you should consider developing one. Challenge 3, "Developing Personnel Policies," will help you identify and develop the important policies and procedures that should serve as your employees' operating guide.

THE PURPOSE OF THIS WORKSHOP IS TO JOT DOWN INFORMATION WHICH WILL HELP NEW EMPLOYEES BECOME ORIENTED TO YOUR COMPANY'S PHYSICAL LAYOUT, ITS OPERATIONS, ITS PEOPLE AND PROCESSES.

Personal Workshop #7
Step 2: My Personal Notes

Step 2—Information That Helps Employees Understand the System

Write down the information you need to provide new employees so that they will understand your company's systems and procedures:

List those areas which should be included in the company tour. (i.e.: restrooms, lunch and break rooms, mail rooms, parking, etc.)

List any business policies and procedures which you feel should be reviewed. (i.e.: customer service policies, telephone procedures, etc.)

Identify your company safety rules and evacuation procedures.

Identify your company safety rules and evacuation procedures.

Identify company health requirements.

List the people with whom your new employee should meet during the orientation process.

Basic overview of your company policies and procedures. (i.e.: your company handbook)

Step 3: Information that Gives Employees a Sense of Belonging

If you want your new employees to become productive members of the team, then the other people on the team need to make an effort to involve them and make them feel welcome. Don't overlook the things your small business can do to assure that new employees feel comfortable—especially in the early weeks of employment.

Ask your current employees for ideas on how to welcome newcomers; there are many creative possibilities. You could host an "open house" for a new employee, or spruce up the individual's work space with fresh paint or a plant. At the very least, other employees should be invited to introduce themselves and encouraged to include the new employee in lunch or break plans. The new employee's supervisor needs to make a special effort to introduce the person to other employees.

Ideas for Making an Employee's First Day Memorable

- Have an open house. Serve cookies or coffee. Invite everyone in the business to stop by to meet the new employee.

- Get the new employee set up for business. Make sure his or her desk is stocked with necessary supplies. Provide an appointment calendar, if needed. If you use them, have name plates and business cards ready to present.

- Put up a welcome sign for the new employee in a prominent place.

- Give the new employee a memento from your business such as a mug, a t-shirt, a pen or a pocket calculator inscribed with the business logo.

- Treat the new employee to lunch.

- Put together a new employee survival kit. It can contain off-beat items that, when explained, provide some insight into the company's culture. For example, if an employee has been hired into a customer service job where the customers are usually upset, the kit might include a band-aid for use when bruised by a customer, earplugs for when they have heard enough, and note cards saying "Yes, Sir" or "Yes, Ma'am," just in case they need them.

- Write a welcome letter to the new employee using all of your company's jargon. As he or she reads the letter, explain the jargon.

- Ask other employees in your company to identify a "unique" feature of the business when they stop by to introduce themselves. For example, one employee might tell about an eccentric customer. Another might identify the fact that Fridays are casual days. Another might mention the annual Christmas "pigout" when employees share holiday treats. By the end of the introductions, the new employee will have gathered a great deal of information about the company and its people.

The company might also implement a "mentor" or "buddy" program, where a veteran employee makes a special effort to get to know the new hire and help that person get involved. There are hundreds of possibilities—but remember the goal is to help the new employee become a productive team member, not to promote social gatherings. Try to involve veteran employees that you know will be excellent role models for the new person.

THE PURPOSE OF THIS WORKSHOP IS TO COME UP WITH IDEAS FOR THINGS YOU CAN DO TO MAKE A NEW EMPLOYEE FEEL WELCOME.

Personal Workshop #7
Step 3: My Personal Notes

Step 3—Information That Gives Employees a Sense of Belonging

Use the space below to brainstorm ideas that will help give new employees in your company a sense of belonging. Ideas might include: holding an open house, taking the new employee to lunch, providing the new employee with a company T-shirt or hat. The ideas are endless. Just use your imagination!

Step 4: History and Philosophy of the Company

This category of information is often overlooked, but it is a straightforward way to give your new employees a feeling for the business, as well as to build their loyalty to your company. Orientation should include a description of what the business is, how it started, what significant events influenced its growth, and how it compares to its competitors. A good orientation program will help your new employee understand the philosophy of the business and your management style. This information will, in turn, guide the worker's behavior.

A good introduction to the history and philosophy of the company will help your new employees understand the answers to these common questions:

- Who makes the decisions in this company?

- Who is responsible for quality in this company?

- How are customers treated?

- What is the management style of this company?

THE PURPOSE OF THIS WORKSHOP IS TO PREPARE A HISTORY AND/OR A PHILOSOPHY OF YOUR COMPANY WHICH WILL BE GIVEN TO A NEW EMPLOYEE.

Personal Workshop #7
Step 4: My Personal Notes

Step 4—History and Philosophy of the Company

History   Assume that you have only five minutes to explain to a complete stranger what your business is, how it got started, and how it has developed into what it is today. Use the space below to jot down key words and/or events you would include in your description for a new employee.

Philosophy   What is the philosophy of your company? In other words, what are the key values and beliefs that guide the way the company operates and the way the employees conduct business? What personal characteristics do you expect every successful employee in your company to possess? Jot down your ideas in the space below.

Now, how will you share the history and/or philosophy of your company with the new employee? Will you place this information in a company handbook? Will you share this information verbally? Will you write it in the form of a letter or a handout to be given to the new employee? Write your answer below.

Step 5: Business Goals and Objectives

In whatever you do, always keep the mission and vision of your small business in the forefront. Every small business should have a **mission statement** and a **vision statement**. Both statements should be included in your business plan and should guide all of your business decisions. A mission statement describes what your company does and why it exists. A vision statement describes what you want your company to become; giving a description of your ideal. Both statements should be brief, easy to understand, and communicated frequently to your employees.

Key Words

Your employees need to know where the company is headed and why. In addition to the mission and vision statements, share with your employees your business goals and objectives, as well as your plans for achieving those goals. Explain why the new employee is important to the success

> *"Even if you are on the right track, you will get run over if you just sit there."*
>
> —Will Rogers

of the organization. Try to answer any questions the new employee may have about what the company is trying to accomplish and how each worker fits into the plan.

If you use a team approach to planning in your business, consider involving the new employee in that process as soon as possible. Employees who are involved in planning tend to be more committed to carrying out those plans. In a small business, if every employee isn't moving in the same direction, there may be no movement at all.

THE PURPOSE OF THIS WORKSHOP IS TO IDENTIFY THE COMPANY GOALS AND OBJECTIVES WHICH WILL BE GIVEN TO NEW EMPLOYEES.

Personal Workshop #7
Step 5: My Personal Notes

Step 5—Business Goals and Objectives

Use your business plan and/or strategic plan to determine what your company's mission and vision statements should be.

What is the **mission** of your company?

What is the **vision** of your company?

Use your business plan and/or strategic plan as a guide to decide what every employee needs to know about the goals and objectives of your company.

What are the major goals of your company? What objectives will you use to meet each goal?

Goals   **Objectives**

How will you share your company's goals and objectives with the new employee? Will it be placed in a handbook or letter? Will it be shared verbally in a meeting? Write your ideas in the space below.

Step 6: Information that Acquaints Employees with Their Responsibilities

As well as introducing the new employee to the company as a whole, orientation should provide information about the job itself. In an early meeting with the new employee, review together the job description, the position responsibilities and the results you expect. Describe and demonstrate acceptable work behavior, and set a schedule for learning the job over some reasonable period of time. Throughout the orientation process, continue to teach the skills needed to do the

THE PURPOSE OF THIS WORKSHOP IS TO IDENTIFY NEW EMPLOYEE RESPONSIBILITIES.

Personal Workshop #7
Step 6: My Personal Notes

Step 6—Information that Acquaints Employees with their Responsibilities

Prepare for a new employee training period by answering the following questions.

What steps will the new employee take to learn the job?

Who will be responsible for training the new employee?

What is a reasonable schedule for completing the training?

job, and continue to be accessible to the new employee to answer questions and provide guidance. Finally, as you work together, assess the skills of your new employee—look for both strengths to build on and weaknesses where additional training may be needed.

If you have any doubts about what the individual's responsibilities are at this point, go back to Challenge 1. Conduct a job analysis of the position and develop a results-oriented job description for the new employee, if this has not already been done.

Step 7: Who to Involve in Orientation

A good orientation program involves many people. In a very small company, in fact, every employee is likely to be involved in one way or another.

Owner/Manager: Involving the owner/manager in orientation is one area where small businesses have a huge advantage over larger companies. Small business owner/managers tend to know all their employees personally, and this personal touch is something no large business can offer its new employees. If your business is very small, the owner/manager might meet individually with new employees to tell the "story" of the company and to discuss the company vision and philosophy. Maybe this can be done over breakfast or lunch. In a somewhat larger business, the owner/manager might speak to an orientation class or stop by to greet new employees at their work space sometime during their first week with the company.

Supervisors: The new employee's supervisor needs to take the lead role by arranging the orientation schedule and making certain other employees are involved. The supervisor is the first person a new employee should see on the first day of work. Their initial meetings will help set the tone for their future work relationship, and the supervisor serves as the primary role model for the new employee. The supervisor needs to be accessible to the new employee throughout the orientation period, serving both as a teacher and a coach.

It is the supervisor's job to tell new employees with whom they need to interact, what projects they will handle under what schedules, and what expectations they must meet. Supervisors also should tell new employees what special challenges they may face as they do their work, and help them develop strategies for facing those challenges.

Payroll and Administrative Personnel: Staff members who handle payroll or other personnel administrative matters may get involved in orientation by doing paperwork and providing information to help your new employees understand the system. These individuals typically enroll new employees on the payroll, sign them up for benefits, help them file appropriate tax and I-9 forms, inform them of certain company-wide policies and procedures, and offer other administrative assistance.

Other Employees: Why take other employees away from their work to participate in orientation? Because, more than anyone in the firm, co-workers can help relieve the tension and fears of starting a new job, since they are the people new employees will deal with day in and day out. Part of their job is to welcome new employees and help introduce them to the business. This might involve a veteran employee telling the new employee a little bit about his or her own job and how the two jobs are related. This type of assistance and positive interaction with the old employee will help the new employee get settled in more quickly. A smooth start benefits everyone in the company.

THE PURPOSE OF THIS WORKSHOP IS TO IDENTIFY WHO WILL BE INVOLVED IN THE NEW EMPLOYEE ORIENTATION.

Personal Workshop #7
Step 7: My Personal Notes

Step 7—Who to Involve in Orientation

List the people in your company who need to be involved in the orientation process for the new employee. Next to that person, indicate what his or her responsibilities will be.

	Contact People	Responsibilities
Owners/Managers		
Supervisors		
Payroll and Administrative Personnel		
Other Employees		

How to Implement an Orientation Program

With some initial planning, orientation can become a rather routine and painless process in your company. To plan an orientation program for your new employees, you must decide:

- what information to provide;

- who should deliver the information; and

- how and when the information should be shared.

When you plan the orientation program, recognize that you cannot cover everything on the first day. Effective orientation begins even before new employees join the company and provides information and support well past the first day on the job. In fact, depending on the job, orientation could continue for months. Early in this Challenge, you were introduced to the employee development process, which included three stages for orientation. Following are some guidelines for what to include in each stage.

Pre-Employment

Even before a new employee is selected, the selection process provides you with "teachable moments"—opportunities to give the future employee some background information about the company and its philosophy, and about the job, in particular. The interviewer also typically discusses pay, work hours, time off, benefits and other personnel issues with prospective employees. Conveying this information marks the start of the orientation process.

Once a job offer is made and the candidate accepts, you want to stay in touch until the new employee is on board. Perhaps you can send a confirmation letter and additional information about your company. Or, the new supervisor might send out pertinent internal correspondence or copies of the newsletter to keep the soon-to-be employee informed of company news. A personal telephone call by the owner is a wonderful touch that lets the prospective employee know that you are enthusiastic about having him or her join the company.

The First Day

A new employee is likely to arrive on the first day full of questions and feeling a little nervous. The supervisor should not only greet him or her, but go over the day's schedule and begin the orientation process. Trying to cram too much information into that first day is a mistake—your new employee can only retain so much and may go home feeling completely overwhelmed. In general, it is reasonable to try to accomplish the following five tasks on the first day:

- Make the employee's first day memorable with some type of welcoming activity.

- Complete essential paperwork and explain payroll and benefits procedures.

- Provide a tour of the office, store or plant.

- Introduce the employee to his or her work team and other important people.

- Review the employee's job description and requirements, and set up a schedule for learning the job in the coming weeks.

Always try to begin and end your new employee's first day on a positive note. Your goal is to send the new employee home with a sense of belonging and enthusiasm about facing tomorrow. If this is accomplished, then your first day of orientation has been a success.

The First Weeks

During the first several weeks, the supervisor should continue to work closely with the new employee. In this time, your employee will learn the ropes of the organization, as he or she learns how to do the tasks specifically associated with the new job. The supervisor and the new employee should continue their discussions about performance expectations. In fact, this is the ideal time for the employee and supervisor to set some performance goals and develop action plans for achieving those goals.

If the new employee needs any special skills training to do the job, such as learning a new computer program, it should be completed as soon as possible. Your goal in the first few weeks is to help the new employee become proficient and fully productive as quickly as possible.

Efforts to make the new employee feel like a part of the organization should continue throughout the first few weeks, or until the employee has formed some social contacts. Finally, create some publicity about the new employee and gradually introduce him or her to a wider group of people, perhaps through the company newsletter, via electronic mail, or in staff meetings.

Personal Workshop Preparation #8: Orientation Checklist

Use the Orientation Checklist form in the next Personal Workshop to plan your orientation process. Use your personal notes from Personal Workshop #7 to help you develop the checklist, but be sure to involve a group of people in this exercise, including the new employee's supervisor, other employees who might do the same or similar jobs, personnel staff, and the owner/manager. These people should provide different perspectives about what needs to be taught during orientation and how. Once you complete the orientation checklist, you will have a useful tool for planning this and future orientations.

In preparation for this Personal Workshop, take a look at how Candace and Tony Washington from PCB Corporation completed this workshop.

PCB Corporation/Candace and Tony Washington: We recently received a major contract that will increase our production by approximately one third over the next year. To meet this new demand, we hired 10 new assemblers, who will work one line during a second shift. Since this is the biggest group of new employees to join PCB since we started the company, we realized we needed to put some thought into how we were going to introduce them to the company and train them in their new jobs. We asked the shift supervisor and several of our more experienced assemblers to talk with us about what type of orientation and training they thought these new employees should get. As a group, we developed the Orientation Checklist below, and so now we have it all on paper—what we want to be sure each new employee learns about the company, who will teach it, and when.

THE PURPOSE OF THIS WORKSHOP IS TO IDENTIFY THE SPECIFIC INFORMATION YOU NEED TO INCLUDE IN AN ORIENTATION, WHO SHOULD PROVIDE THAT INFORMATION AND WHEN.

Personal Workshop #8
Orientation Checklist

Position: Assembler, 2nd Shift, PCB Corporation

Orientation Information	Who	When
I. Information that Brings Employees on Board:		
1. Payroll and benefits sign-up, I-9, W-4 forms	Admin. Asst.	1st day
2. Review benefit policies, absence tardiness procedures, breaks, etc.	Admin. Asst.	1st day
3. Introduce employee handbook	Admin. Asst.	1st day
4. Safety info/regulations	Shift Supervisor	1st day/week
5. Parking information	Admin. Asst.	1st day
II. Information About the System:		
1. Plant tour	Shift Supervisor	1st day
2. Safety procedures	Shift Supervisor	throughout 1st week
3. Review employee handbook	Shift Supervisor	throughout 1st week
4. Arrange visit to 1st shift	Shift Supervisor	1st week

III. Information that Gives a Sense of Belonging

1. Greet assemblers	Shift Supervisor	1st day
2. Introduce to admin. personnel and owner	Shift Supervisor	1st day & through-out week
3. Serve refreshments in break room during visit to 1st shift and invite 1st shift workers to meet 2nd shift workers	Admin. Asst.	1st week

IV. History and Philosophy of the Company:

1. Overview of company history	Interviewer	pre-employment
2. Review main points of history & philosophy	Shift Supervisor	1st week

V. Business Goals and Objectives:

1. Overview of mission and vision	Interviewer	pre-employment
2. Brief overview	Owner	1st day
3. Details	Shift Supervisor	1st week

VI. Information about Job Responsibilities:

1. Overview of responsibilities	Interviewer	pre-employment
2. Review job description	Shift Supervisor	1st day
3. Introduce work station	Shift Supervisor	1st day
4. On-the-job training	Assembler from 1st shift	1st week
5. Supervise start of line, ongoing training, coaching, etc.	Shift Supervisor	1st week & beyond

THE PURPOSE OF THIS WORKSHOP IS TO IDENTIFY THE SPECIFIC INFORMATION YOU NEED TO INCLUDE IN AN ORIENTATION, WHO SHOULD PROVIDE THAT INFORMATION AND WHEN.

Personal Workshop #8
Orientation Checklist

Position:

Orientation Information	Who	When
I. Information that Brings Employees on Board:		
II. Information About the System:		
III. Information that Gives a Sense of Belonging		
IV. History and Philosophy of the Company:		
V. Business Goals and Objectives:		
VI. Information about Job Responsibilities:		

Workshop Follow-Up

Use the checklist you have developed to schedule the specific orientation activities for your new employees. Keep it on file for future reference—the orientation checklist should continue to be a useful tool for planning future orientations, with minor adjustments.

PCB Corporation/Candace and Tony Washington: Once we had identified the information and people to involve in orientation using the checklist, it was fairly easy to plan a schedule for the first day. We paid some volunteer assemblers from the first shift to help train the new employees on the second shift during the first few days. After that, the shift supervisor was able to handle the ongoing orientation, as well as assess what additional special training any of the assemblers might need. Here is the orientation schedule we came up with for the 10 new assemblers.

Orientation Schedule

New Employee: Assemblers for Second Shift (4 P.M. - midnight)

Start Date: August 15
(note: Assemblers will start at 3 P.M. on first day)

Time	Activity	Person/Group
3 P.M.	Greet new employees	Shift supervisor
3:15–4 P.M.	Tour 1st shift in operation	Shift supervisor
4–4:30 P.M.	Welcome reception for both shifts	Admin. asst. and all
4:30–5:30 P.M.	New employee group meeting: welcome and discuss mission, vision, goals, etc.; complete paperwork	Admin. asst. and shift supervisor
5:30–6 P.M.	Discuss safety procedures	Shift supervisor
6–7:30 P.M.	Introduction to work stations	1st shift assemblers & shift supervisor
7:30–8 P.M.	Dinner break	
8–11:30 P.M.	Training at work station continues	1st shift assemblers and shift supervisor
11:30 P.M. til midnight	Group meeting: question/ answer session	Shift supervisor

---

Training Employees

Do you feel confident that all of your employees know everything they need to know to be competent and productive? And, what about tomorrow? Will they have the skills and knowledge needed to keep moving your company forward?

Training is any activity that teaches employees the skills or knowledge necessary to do a job. It is any form of work-related education, whether it is planned, as in a formal classroom setting, or whether it occurs incidentally as part of the daily work routine. If training is effective, it involves learning and the intellectual growth of your employees.

> *"We don't know a millionth of one percent about anything."*
>
> —Thomas Edison

Just as orientation gives employees the information they need to start a new job, training provides for their ongoing developmental needs. Training equips your employees with the tools and knowledge they will use to help the business grow. It also helps employees feel good about your company. Why? Because they will feel competent and they will know they work for a company interested in their professional development.

Why Should You Train Employees?

The three most common purposes of training are:

- to teach a technical skill
- to teach a process or procedure
- to teach professional and interpersonal skills

Technical Skills

> *"Education's purpose is to replace an empty mind with an open one."*
>
> —Malcolm Forbes

All businesses require a certain amount of technical expertise from employees. If a worker does not have some of the skills needed to effectively and efficiently do the job when hired, your business must provide the training needed to develop those skills. For example, a worker may need to learn how to operate equipment or machinery; a cash register, for instance, or a forklift or die machine. Or you may need to teach an employee how to operate a computer, a copy machine, the telephone system or other office equipment.

New employees may need training to adapt the skills they bring with them to your company's requirements. If your automotive repair shop, for example, services Buicks, you need to train that new employee whose only experience is in fixing Toyotas. Or, all of your employees, new or otherwise, might require technical training if you buy new, sophisticated automotive diagnostic equipment, or if you decide to change your repair processes in any significant way.

Training might involve learning a complex series of technical skills, or learning only one small part of the total process. For example, a claims examiner might need to learn the technical requirements of paying claims from start to finish, while a machinist would need to develop only the one technical skill required at his or her work station. While some employers try to hire people who already have the technical expertise needed, others opt to provide the training themselves. The approach you choose should depend upon your own training skills and resources.

Process or Procedure

Your business, like every business, has its own way of doing things. Over the years, you have set up systems for processing orders, collecting accounts receivable, writing reports, following up with customers, etc. Some of these processes and procedures are simple and easily learned. Others may require more extensive training. For example, your new employees might learn very quickly how to transfer people on the telephone, but they will need special and ongoing training to learn how to make an effective sales presentation to your clients. Training is typically required to bring a new employee on board and to help all employees deal with changes in any of these processes or procedures.

> *"When you are through changing, you are through!"*
>
> —Bruce Barton

Professional and Interpersonal Skills

Employees can improve their productivity by developing professional and interpersonal skills. Because no one works in a vacuum, interpersonal skills may be just as important as the other skills needed to do the job. Many business owners provide training to help their employees develop professional and interpersonal skills, because they believe it pays off through increased productivity and a more positive work environment. Professional or interpersonal skills training might be used to help your employees develop effective skills for communication, time management, selling, problem solving, supervisory management, or exceptional customer service, to name a few. Often such training is designed to develop more functional teams or to prepare employees for some significant change in the business; therefore the techniques used in the training process may be as important as the specific topic being covered.

> *"It's what you learn after you know it all that counts."*
>
> —John Wooden

When Should You Train?

Train when it is needed. Sounds obvious, doesn't it? But in fact, businesses often provide training when it is convenient or inexpensive, and not when it is truly necessary.

Here's an example. Let's say your business buys a new computer system that requires a one-day training program to learn to use. The vendor has offered to provide the training one day next week. To get the most for your money, you enroll your entire work force, even though some employees won't begin to use the system until next month. While this may seem to be a cost-effective decision at the time, most likely it will turn out to be a waste of time and money instead. Those employees who do not use the system right away will probably forget most of what they learn by the time they use it. They will either need to be retrained, or they will learn through trial-and-error, which might result in costly mistakes.

There are three situations when your business may need to train employees. The first is when a new employee joins the company. Most new employees require training on the company's equipment, processes, procedures and behavioral standards, all of which begins in the orientation process. Even if new employees bring excellent job skills to your company, they must still learn the nuances of your operation. Rarely will a new employee have all the skills needed upon arrival.

Your business will also need to provide training to veteran employees from time to time. If you upgrade your computer system, for example, training will help your employees learn the new technology. If you invest in new software, training may be required to teach everyone to use it. Every business changes procedures and policies in response to the needs of its customers, and many of those changes will create the need for some employee training.

Finally, you may need to offer training to fill a remedial need. Remedial needs occur when employees do not have the basic skills required to do the job. In some instances, especially when there is a tight job market, you may be forced to hire an employee that you know is lacking a necessary basic skill and will need training. Or, sometimes an employee who seems to have the required skills during the interview process comes up short on the job. In still other instances, the job requirements may change, and formerly qualified employees will need to develop new knowledge or skills. Although most businesses are willing to invest in some remedial training, it should be a planned and strategic choice. Your goal should be to invest in training that will move your business and employees forward, not to spend training money simply to bring people up to par.

> *"The human mind, once stretched by a new idea, never regains its original dimensions."*
>
> —Anonymous

In addition to such "as needed" training, you might offer your employees the opportunity to develop new skills and gain knowledge that could give them a promotional edge in your company in the future. Or you might cross-train employees on an ongoing basis, to teach them other jobs within the business. When employers promote continuous professional development, they instill in their employees the value of constant learning, and they build a more flexible and competent work force. Offering such training opportunities will also be considered an attractive "perk" by many employees.

If your business has a comprehensive training program, it means you have consciously thought about your training needs in all of the situations above. A comprehensive training program probably includes a thorough orientation and training plan for new employees, a list of training resources to meet any remedial

FYI

Although it may be more of a challenge logistically, you should always time training to coincide with employee needs. The payoff in immediate productivity far outweighs any cost or time savings from running fewer training sessions.

needs that might come up, and a system for assessing the training needs of all employees periodically and acquiring the necessary training to meet those needs. A comprehensive training program requires a commitment to the continuous improvement of your employees and your company.

Training Techniques for Small Business

When you hear the word training, perhaps you picture students sitting in a classroom as a teacher lectures to them. In fact, classroom training in a small business is probably the exception rather than the rule. Many employees involved in training never see the inside of a classroom. They learn on the job, through coaching and mentoring or through self-study. And, training conducted in a classroom is rarely lecture. Business training tends to be hands-on and interactive. There are many training techniques to choose from, and you should choose carefully, depending on the audience and the needs of the company.

On-the-Job Training

On-the-job training refers to learning that occurs when the employee is at work in the day-to-day job environment. This training may be formal or informal. In formal training, employees usually work with a trainer who follows some written procedures or training guidelines. When training is less formal, trainers usually work without written procedures or guidelines. They teach employees in their own way. In some on-the-job training, employees may not even have a trainer. They learn what they need to know by doing the job.

Key Word

"The work will teach you how to do it."

—Estonian Proverb

On-the-job training may be the best choice when materials or equipment used on the job cannot be transported to a classroom. This form of training is also a common choice when the subject is simple enough that it doesn't require formal classroom learning. On-the-job exposure is one of the most effective ways to learn, if you follow the basic steps below.

Steps for On-the-Job Training

1. Explain the process.
2. Demonstrate the process.
3. Allow the employee to ask questions and answer them.
4. Allow the employee to try it.
5. Give the employee feedback and the opportunity to practice as needed.

Step 1: Begin by explaining the job to the employee. This explanation should cover "the big picture"—why a particular job or process needs to be done, how it affects others in the business, and what happens if it isn't done correctly. Your goal is to make sure the employee understands the overall process before learning the specific steps to accomplish it.

Step 2: Demonstrate the process for the employee. If you are demonstrating a physical task, such as answering a telephone or running a fax or copy machine, the demonstration should be slow enough that the employee has a chance to register each step. Make certain that the demonstration accommodates the employee's physical perspective. If, for example, you face the employee while demonstrating the process, the employee may learn the process backwards. And, if the process is complex, you may want to demonstrate one step at a time, either starting with the first step or the last, depending upon the skill to be learned.

It can be extremely helpful for a new employee to learn the proper procedures for non-physical tasks as well. These tasks can also be introduced by demonstration. For example, you may want to demonstrate how to process telephone inquiries or how to handle an angry customer.

Step 3: When the demonstration is complete, encourage the employee to ask questions. Depending on the questions, you may need to repeat the demonstration and encourage additional questions during the process.

Step 4: The employee should now try to perform the task. Ask the trainee to explain what he or she is doing and why. This will help you determine whether the employee truly understands the process. If the employee is struggling or appears frustrated, offer your assistance or, if necessary, demonstrate the process again.

Step 5: Continue to watch the employee and give feedback until you are both satisfied that he or she is proficient in the job. Let your employee know when he or she is progressing and doing a good job, and allow time to practice until he or she feels confident enough to do the job without supervision. Teach the employee to check the quality of his or her work throughout the process, and then make the employee accountable for improving that quality over time.

When on-the-job training is complete and the employee has been using the new skills for a while, check back to see how he or she is doing. Have there been any difficulties with the process? Has the employee found ways to improve the process or the quality of output? Does he or she need any additional training or help?

FYI

Although it may seem counter-intuitive, it is sometimes easier to teach a complex skill by teaching it "backwards"—in other words, teaching the last step first and working your way to the first step. For example, in teaching a young child to tie a shoe, do everything for the child except the last step ("pull both loops tight"). Teach the child that final step, and once perfected, back up and teach the child the next-to-the-last step, followed by the last step ("pull this string through to make a loop, and then pull both loops tight"), and so on. This same technique may be effective for teaching certain complex skills in the workplace.

NEIGHBORHOOD MEDICAL CLINIC

Neighborhood Medical Clinic/Dr. Carole Stein: In keeping with my plans for expanding services, I just hired a new Physician's Assistant, Paul Allen, fresh out of school. While Paul has great credentials and obviously has received good professional training, I want to work closely with him over the next few weeks to be sure he correctly learns the systems that are important to the smooth operations of the clinic. For example, to teach him how we collect blood samples for lab work here, I decided to conduct some on-the-job training. I started by explaining the procedure to Paul in one of our early meetings. Then, as soon as some blood work was needed, I demonstrated the procedure for him, step-by-step, talking through each step as I did it. I showed him exactly how to label and prepare the specimen for shipment to the lab. Paul asked a few questions as we went along, but said he felt confident that he understood the process. When another patient required a blood test a short time later, I observed Paul as he correctly did the procedure. Afterwards, I made a small suggestion about labeling samples, I asked if he had any other questions, and then I gave him approval to do the procedure on his own in the future.

Self-Directed Learning and Programmed Instruction

Independent study, also called self-study learning, is a form of training that is often overlooked. Self-study, in which the employee directs his own training, can be useful when training needs are diverse. It allows employees to independently study the topics or learn the skills most relevant to their job situations without having to learn irrelevant material.

Self-study can be conducted in several ways. **Programmed instruction** refers to training materials designed specifically for self-directed learners. Employees can study a specific topic, complete activities or solve problems related to the topic, and then test their newfound knowledge and abilities. Programmed instruction might be offered through a variety of media, including video or audio tapes, computer discs or a computer network, printed manuals and workbooks, or some combination of these tools. In some cases, the employee may receive guidance from a trainer or teacher through the Internet on the computer or by telephone or mail.

Self-directed training can be custom-designed for a specific employee or employee group. For example, if you have an employee who is interested in learning more about leadership and supervision, but your company does not offer training in those topics, you might work with that employee to set some learning objectives and to design a self-study program that will meet those objectives. The employee might read some books and trade journals relevant to the topic, view some video tapes, or attend a conference. You might agree to give the employee some time off each week to study. At the end of the self-study period, the

Key Words

A word of advice: Training requires patience. Resist any impulse to jump in and do the job for your trainees. You must give employees time to think through the job, to practice, and to move forward at their own pace.

FYI

employee should present a report or a proposal which addresses a direct business need for your company based on the knowledge he or she picked up during self-study. The training the employee receives, then, will benefit your company and help prepare him or her for a leadership role in the future.

Although self-study can be effective, it has some disadvantages. Some employees may find it impersonal or boring. Because it is self-study, there is no one to encourage the employee to stick with it. Self-directed learning requires a great deal of personal discipline and can be difficult for employees who are not goal-oriented or who are unclear about the rewards to be gained from the effort. Your business can overcome some of these drawbacks by appointing a mentor or coach for the self-directed learner. Mentors and coaches can make programmed instruction more interesting by giving learners additional assignments. They can motivate and encourage their employees to keep a pace and set goals for their learning.

Neighborhood Medical Clinic/Dr. Carole Stein: I talked recently to a doctor from Georgia who had implemented many of the principles of TQM (Total Quality Management) into his practice and believed the changes were responsible for the phenomenal growth he had experienced over the past two years. I wanted to learn more about it, but most of the books I found were very theoretical or talked about quality improvement at Ford Motor Company—a little hard for me to relate to my small service business. And, as a doctor and a small business owner, I certainly didn't have time to run off to the local college to take a class. Instead, I purchased a "self-study course" on how to implement quality concepts in the small business. I was able to read the materials at my own pace, and I practiced applying some of the TQM tools to the clinic as I went along. The package of learning materials included an audio tape and a disc for my computer, which guided me through the process. It was great! I learned enough to know that I now want to bring in an outside trainer to work with everyone in the clinic to implement the "quality concept." And I know I never would have found the time to learn this stuff if I couldn't have done it on my own time and terms.

Coaching and Mentoring

Coaching and mentoring are similar to on-the-job training in that employees work closely with someone who observes their work behavior and offers feedback. The difference is in the focus of the training. Whereas on-the-job training

Key Words

FYI

When programmed instruction is combined with some level of contact with a teacher who is not physically present, it is called **distance learning** or **distance education**. In fact, the human resources management training you are currently receiving in this book is a form of programmed instruction designed to be delivered "at a distance." Distance education makes educational programs more accessible, since student learning is not "location-bound" or "time-bound"—that is, students don't have to be sitting in a particular classroom at a particular time and place in order to participate in a learning activity.

helps employees learn a specific skill or job task, coaching and mentoring tends to involve a longer time commitment and often is designed to help employees learn the "softer" skills, such as interpersonal, supervisory, or leadership skills. On-the-job training usually helps employees learn how to perform their current jobs. Coaching and mentoring can achieve that goal as well, but it is often used to prepare employees for new jobs. For example, coaching and mentoring are commonly used to prepare an employee for promotion to a leadership position within the company.

The relationship between an employee and a mentor is typically a long-term one, and it often develops naturally and informally, as a more experienced person takes someone less experienced "under his wing." Or, in some businesses, a more senior employee is assigned to serve as a coach or mentor to a less experienced person for a pre-determined period of time. In either case, the mentor/coach needs to be available to serve as a guide, a sounding board, a cheerleader, and a role model for his protegé.

Classroom Training

This formal training takes place away from the individual's usual work site. Typically, an instructor or facilitator guides the learning. Classroom training can be purchased as a "canned program" or designed to meet the training needs of your particular business. Sometimes vendors provide classroom training on a variety of skills. For example, many phone-service companies provide training on telephone courtesy and customer service. Well-designed classroom training can be a powerful way to teach a wide array of skills and knowledge, but like all types of training, it has both advantages and disadvantages.

Classroom training is an excellent way to teach a group of people the same skills or topics. Everyone gets the same information in the same way, and the participants may have an opportunity to interact or solve problems as a team. On the other hand, small businesses may find situations where classroom training is impractical. If training on equipment is required, for example, it simply may not be practical to use in a classroom setting. Or, perhaps your small business does not have enough employees to fill a classroom without shutting down its operations.

Even with these limitations, classroom training can benefit small businesses. Some classroom training works well with as few as four people, or you may want to approach another small business in your community about "sharing" the training, if you need a larger group. You may decide that it is actually worth the investment to hire a "temp" to cover the office or even close operations for a short

If your small business chooses to use programmed instruction, be aware that there are many products on the market on a multitude of topics. Some are good, and some are bad. Whenever possible, preview the materials to assure the content is relevant, accurate, and interesting before purchasing it for your company.

FYI

period to allow everyone to participate in the training. Or you may want to pay your employees to participate in the training during non-business hours.

Neighborhood Medical Clinic/Dr. Carole Stein: I located and interviewed a couple of area trainers who specialize in helping small businesses implement Total Quality Management (TQM). They were referred to me by the local Small Business Development Center. We hired one to work with us over the next year for an hour every other week. We set aside 7:30 - 8:30 A.M. every Friday for our TQM training—we simply didn't schedule any appointments for that time so all of us could work together as a team, and we let the answering service cover our calls. One week the trainer would come in and work with us "classroom style," the next week we would work on our own to put into practice what we had learned. We almost always had some techniques to practice on our own between meetings. The waiting area of the clinic became a makeshift classroom for our Friday meetings, and except for a few emergencies, things went very smoothly throughout the training.

Who Should Train in Your Small Business?

Assuming you have identified a need for training in your company, you now need to decide who will conduct it. A large business might turn to its training department, but most small businesses have no such animal. There are, however, several training resources to choose from.

Resources for Training

Internal Training Resources

- Managers and supervisors in the small business
- Employees with special skills and/or knowledge
- The small business owner

Outside Training Resources

- Professional training vendors
- Local universities, colleges, vocational or technical schools
- Public seminars and workshops
- Small Business Development Center programs
- Small business grants

Internal Training Resources

Your company has three key internal resources for training: its managers and supervisors; other employees who have special skills, knowledge and experiences; and the owner/manager. Do not overlook these key resources, since using them helps develop both the trainees and the individuals who conduct the training.

Supervisors and managers are a logical choice to train your employees. They have job expertise and valuable experiences to share. They are interested in seeing that employees succeed, since it reflects well on their own leadership ability. Finally, since their own employees are on the training roster, they are likely to make sure that the training transfers to the job. Managers and supervisors can be a valuable resource, no matter the type of training. And, by job description, they should constantly be involved in training and mentoring those employees who report directly to them.

> *"To teach is to learn twice."*
> —Joseph Joubert

Other employees in your business may also have the necessary job expertise to be trainers. They can assist with on-the-job training or serve as peer-mentors to other employees. When employees train other employees, a spirit of team work develops. Employee trainers are building their own leadership skills as well.

As with managers and supervisors, the small business owner should constantly be involved in developing the employees of the company. The owner is the "Head Coach" and should also be the "Head Cheerleader." As a small business owner, you have a wonderful advantage over a large business CEO—you can have access to and share your knowledge with everyone in your business, if you so choose.

Outside Training Resources

There are many outside organizations which provide training to small businesses. In some cases, training may be provided by a vendor who has sold your company a piece of equipment or machinery (such as a new copy machine), and who includes some on-site training as part of the contract. In other cases, you might purchase training in response to a particular need from one of several sources: colleges and universities, large public training firms, or independent trainer/consultants, to name a few.

Using outside training resources makes sense if your company is too busy to spare the personnel needed to design and deliver training to your employees. A major advantage of using external resources is that you usually get an expert

FYI

Just because you have many talented and knowledgeable people in your small business, do not assume those people have all the skills needed to effectively train other employees in a classroom setting. Effective teaching requires some knowledge of how people learn, careful planning, and presentation skills that will keep the attention of the audience. Ineffective teaching can be a waste of time and money. Training skills can be learned—completing this Challenge is a start. Another option for developing training/teaching skills is to attend a training methods course or a "Train the Trainer" workshop. To find out what is available in your area, contact any local community service or continuing education programs offered through colleges or technical schools, or check with your area Small Business Development Center, chamber of commerce, or a state agency which provides business support.

trainer who understands adult learning theory. An outside trainer can tailor a program to your needs, yet offer a new or broader perspective than someone from inside your organization.

A disadvantage of using external resources is that people outside your business cannot know it as well as your own employees. Your company can either spend the time and money to acquaint external trainers with your business and specific training needs, or you can settle for a generic training program. A second drawback is that outside training tends to disengage supervisors and managers from the training process. When a trainer is doing the job, supervisors may feel that they are "off the hook," that they are no longer responsible for the employees' development. To avoid this, use a combination of both internal and external resources for training in your business, as well as a variety of training methods, depending on the topic and the number of employees to be trained.

There are several outside training resources you should consider:

Professional Trainers and Consultants are in the business of training. Many have years of expertise in training design and delivery. Most have subject area specialties or, in some cases, industry-specific specialties, which allow them to set up and deliver training to your employees on short notice. Most professional trainers can also be a valuable resource in helping you determine what training is specifically needed. On the other hand, professional trainers and consultants can be expensive, depending on the services you want and how specialized the trainer is. Quality also can vary, since the training field has no licensing or testing standards.

Local Universities, Colleges, Vocational or Technical Schools also offer a variety of training and development programs that may meet the needs of your small business. Universities and colleges often have continuing education divisions which offer training for business. Vocational schools offer a range of technical programs. Some advantages of using higher education institutions for training is that their programs are diverse, some offer college credit, and those programs offered by public institutions may be quite affordable. On the down side, university and college programs tend to target larger organizations, so employees of a small business may not get as much out of them. Another potential pitfall is that some courses developed in a university setting may be more theory-oriented than

FYI

When shopping for an outside trainer, whether independent or through an educational institution, ask for references and information on previous work. Check around with your business colleagues, the chamber of commerce, or your area SBDC to find out who they would recommend as an effective trainer. Ask the prospective trainer if he or she can provide a "sample" on video or audio tape, or try to view prospective trainers and speakers at conferences. If you plan to hire someone for a significant amount of training, it is reasonable to ask the trainer to provide your management staff with a "preview" of what he or she would present if hired. All of these tactics should help you hire a quality trainer who will meet your company's needs.

practical. Finally, as with other outside vendors, the quality of programs varies greatly. Follow the same guidelines in selecting a training program through a college or university as you would if hiring an independent trainer.

Public Seminars and Workshops are also available in many communities. Watch for mail brochures or notices from local business and trade organizations, or check the business section of your newspaper for information about upcoming seminars. You will find programs offered on every topic, from accounting to zookeeper-safety techniques. Most workshops are reasonably priced; fees usually range from $49 to $149. Again, the quality of instruction varies. Sometimes instructors are so good that they rival the best professional consultants and university professors. Others are awful. It's hard to predict quality unless you can track down a colleague who has previously seen the trainer in action. But even a mediocre program might be worth its relatively low cost, especially if you ask employees who attend these seminars to pass on any new knowledge or relevant information to their co-workers after the training program.

Small Business Development Centers are another option for training programs in many states around the country. Face-to-face training programs typically cover a variety of topics, from financial planning to marketing management for small business. Instructors come from a pool of trainers, consultants, professors and business practitioners. In addition, the Wisconsin Small Business Development Center offers many programmed instruction modules for self-directed and distance learning. (You are looking at one of them now!) Training programs offered by SBDCs are relatively inexpensive and targeted specifically to small companies. Contact your area SBDC to find out what programs are available face-to-face.

Small Business Grants may be available from the federal government for some types of remedial training. Use of these training grants is restricted: the money must be spent to provide training on reading, math or the basic technical skills needed for employment. These grants cannot be used for non-basic training purposes such as management development. This grant money can only be accessed through vocational schools, colleges or other educational institutions.

Here's a tip to help you get the most from your training dollars. Whenever you send employees to outside training programs, require them to do two things when they return:

1. Share the knowledge or skills learned with their co-workers. This can be done by memo or by conducting a follow-up "in-house training session" to share the information.

2. Evaluate the quality of the program and the trainer. This information will be useful in deciding whether future training opportunities are worth the investment, and whether specific trainers are effective teachers. Again, this can be done by memo, or you might want to develop a brief evaluation form that asks the employee to rate both the skills of the trainer and the quality of the training program attended.

FYI

Contact your local college or technical school for additional information about these grants. Also, check to see if your state offers any training grants for small businesses.

Steps for Developing a Training System

By this point it should be clear that you should have no problem finding training resources for your small business. The challenge is to determine how to coordinate these resources to meet *your* company's training needs. Any training program you offer should be driven by the vision and goals of your small business; otherwise, the training will lack focus and direction. If necessary, update or review those goals before you begin to follow the steps for developing an effective training system.

1. Understand how adults learn.

2. Determine the training needs of your employees.

3. Develop a training plan and program.

4. Ensure job transfer.

5. Implement the training.

6. Evaluate the training.

Step 1: Understand How Adults Learn

In order to develop an effective training process for your business, you first need to know a little bit about how your employees learn. There is a large body of research dealing with learning styles in general, and another that looks specifically at how adults learn; further reading in these areas would be useful if you intend to develop and/or deliver training programs to your employees. In a nutshell, though, you should understand the following basics:

Key Word

Learning style refers to how individuals use their perceptual strengths to receive, process, and remember new information. Some people tend to be *auditory learners*, and they learn best by listening. Some are *visual learners*—they learn best when they see the words or a picture. *Kinesthetic learners* favor getting their whole bodies involved to get the most from a learning experience. And *tactile learners* prefer to have their hands involved some way in the learning activity. If you recognize that people have different learning styles, then you should understand that a classroom lecture might not be an effective way to teach something new to your employees. Good trainers recognize that they may need to deliver the same message in a number of different ways (lecture, demonstration, group activity, individual practice, etc.), to reach the majority of the people involved. If you go back and review the steps for on-the-job training, you will see that it offers something for each of the types of learners described above—that is why, if done correctly, on-the job training can be so effective.

With more than half of the adults in the United States involved in some form of learning each year, educators have been able to study the characteristics of adult learners. While, like younger students, their learning styles may vary, adults are different from younger students in their motivations to learn. In developing effective training programs, keep these special characteristics of adult learners in mind.

- Adult learners need to be respected.

- Adult learners are self-reliant and often self-directed.

- Adult learners are practical—they want to learn useful things, not frivolous things.

- Adult learners have accumulated a lifetime of knowledge.

- Adult learners don't like being told what to do.

- Adult learners have multiple responsibilities; therefore, they resent having their time wasted.

> *"We used to think of life as a two layer cake—learning at the bottom and living at the top. Living begins when learning ends. No longer. Now we have a marble cake, with learning and living interspersed throughout life."*
>
> —Carol Aslanian, Director of Adult Learning Service, The College Board

Training for your employees should be designed to build dignity, not destroy it. Your employees should be given opportunities to ask questions and to answer them, to share their knowledge, expertise, and personal experiences with the group. Design training programs that allow employees to develop their own opinions, come to their own conclusions, rather than simply telling them what to do and when. Finally, to appeal to employees' needs for practical knowledge, training should deliver information and skills that have immediate application. Trainers should include examples of actual problems and situations the employees may face. And they can accompany any conceptual information with practical suggestions for applying those concepts on the job.

Learning should be fun. A good trainer can keep the employees' attention if the task at hand is practical, interesting, fun, and fast-moving.

FYI

Most people have an idea of their preferred learning style. Obviously, simply reading this material is going to work best for a visual learner, but it may not be an effective way for people with other learning styles to pick up the major concepts. If you are not a visual learner, you may have to think of creative ways to appeal to your learning style preference. If you are an auditory learner, you might try reading aloud, having someone else read to you, or listening to audio tapes—these techniques might improve your understanding and retention of new material. Tactile learners are more likely to retain this material if they are busy highlighting the important points or taking notes. And kinesthetic learners may want to do their reading while pacing the floor or riding a stationary bike. The problem is, even if you know your learning style, you may not always have a choice in how your learning material is presented. So, be creative, since **you are the one who is ultimately responsible for your learning.**

Neighborhood Medical Clinic/Dr. Carole Stein: The trainer I hired to help us learn and implement the quality concept was great. She started off by giving us a test to help us understand our own learning styles, and we talked about what each of us could do to get the most out of the training sessions. Some time in each class session was devoted to learning the basic concepts of TQM, but every question we explored and every learning exercise we did as a team centered on our own clinic. As a result, we all learned a lot about everyone else's jobs and how all of our jobs interact—how our systems work. And, although we had some real skeptics in the beginning, everyone got pretty excited when they saw how the changes we were making were going to make their jobs easier and also make the clinic a friendlier place to work. Our TQM training was, in my opinion, a total success, only because the trainer made sure we took responsibility for our learning and for applying the information to our own work at the clinic.

Step 2: Determine the Training Needs of Your Employees

Assessing the training needs of your employees can be time-consuming, but it is worth every minute. Many businesses make the mistake of training without tying that training to the strategic goals of the company. The result is that employees may not gain the knowledge and skills they need to do their jobs, and they may resent the time spent on what they consider to be an irrelevant activity, a waste of their time.

Key Word

Doing a **training needs assessment** helps assure that the training you offer relates directly to the skills or knowledge your employees need. When you do a needs assessment, you are basically looking for gaps between what an employee needs to know or be able to do, and what he or she actually knows and is able to do. By eliminating these gaps through training, you will have a more productive work force.

To determine the training needs of your employees, take the following steps:

1. Conduct a job analysis for the position, describing the major responsibilities, tasks, and activities involved in doing the job.

2. List the skills and knowledge required to accomplish each task and activity.

(If necessary, go back to Challenge 1 of this series and review the sections on conducting a job analysis and writing job specifications.)

3. Assess the employee to identify possible gaps in skills and knowledge. This can be done through testing, observation, or performance review. Typically, both the employee and the supervisor will already have a good idea what the weaknesses are.

Sometimes the need for training is so obvious that you don't need to conduct a formal job analysis. For example, if you own a restaurant, and your community passes a law requiring all food service workers to complete 15 hours of training in food service sanitation procedures, then it is obvious that the employees of your restaurant will need to receive that training.

Personal Workshop Preparation #9:
Training Needs Assessment

In preparation for the next Personal Workshop, pull current copies of the job description and specifications for the position you wish to analyze. Also, enlist the help of the employee in the position and his or her supervisor to answer the questions as accurately as possible. To help you complete this workshop, follow these steps:

1. Review the job description and performance expectations for the position.

2. Identify the general categories of skills and/or knowledge required for the position and list these categories on the left side of the worksheet.

3. Identify the skills and/or knowledge *needed* by employees that seem to be lacking. Be sure to include employee names on the list.

Champy Athletic Products/Terry Rawl: I had some concerns about the performance of some of my sales representatives. Two of them have been with the company for less than one year, and neither one is performing as well as I had hoped. Two of my seasoned reps have also seen sales decline in the past year, which they blame on tougher competition and tighter school budgets. I decided some training for all of the reps would help us get back on track, but I wasn't exactly sure what each rep's training needs were. I decided to use the training needs analysis workshop to help me sort things out. First I reviewed the job description for sales representatives and my performance expectations for each person in the job, which varies somewhat by territory. I was able to identify three general categories of skills needed (sales, customer service, and administrative), and I went on to list on the left side of the workshop the specific skills or knowledge I believed any sales representative would need to be successful. Then I met personally with each sales representative to talk about their strengths and weaknesses, and we jointly tried to identify some areas where we thought training might be helpful. As we met, I noted on the right side of the form what the deficiencies were and which sales reps needed training in that skill. Afterwards, I put a star by those things I felt needed immediate attention. The other topics are important, but not as urgent, so we'll save those topics for later.

Training needs assessment is sometimes done for one employee in one job, and sometimes it is done for the entire company. There are many needs assessment instruments on the market, including some which are quite simple and inexpensive. Or, if you need professional help in conducting needs assessment, contact one of the outside training resources noted previously.

FYI

Before you begin this workshop, observe how Terry Rawl from Champy Athletic Products completed this form.

THE PURPOSE OF THIS WORKSHOP IS TO IDENTIFY THE TRAINING NEEDS OF AN EMPLOYEE OR GROUP OF EMPLOYEES IN YOUR COMPANY.

Personal Workshop #9
Training Needs Assessment

Position: Sales Representative

Staff: Joe, Sam, Sara, Mary, Gordy, Jamie

List below the knowledge and skills required to successfully meet performance expectations.	List the knowledge and skills that the employee needs but seems to be lacking.	Indicate the name of the employee(s) needing training.
Skills/Knowledge Required	**Skills/Knowledge Needed**	**Employee Name**
Sales Skills: • Knowledge of territory	Developing networks, identifying new clients, knowing competition	All
• Ability to develop new clients	How to get first meeting, cold calls, qualifying, determining decision-makers	Mary, Gordy, Jamie
• Ability to deliver effective sales presentations	Components of effective sales presentations, using visual aids	Mary, Gordy, Jamie
• Ability to close the sale	Promoting action by customer; overcoming objections; answering questions; building trust	Sam, Mary, Gordy, Jamie

Skills/Knowledge Required	Skills/Knowledge Needed	Employee Name
Customer Service Skills:		
• knowledge of customers and their needs	Identifying decision-makers; asking the right questions to determine needs	All
• understanding of features and benefits of product lines	Reviewing new product line	All
• effective systems for client contact	Developing effective contact and follow-up systems	Mary
Administrative Skills:		
• ability to process orders	Correctly describing products to avoid errors later	Sam, Gordy, Jamie
• appropriate handling of expense reports	Developing system for timely submission	Sam

THE PURPOSE OF THIS WORKSHOP IS TO IDENTIFY THE TRAINING NEEDS OF AN EMPLOYEE OR GROUP OF EMPLOYEES IN YOUR COMPANY.

Personal Workshop #9
Training Needs Assessment

Position:

Staff:

List below the knowledge and skills required to successfully meet performance expectations.

List the knowledge and skills that the employee needs but seems to be lacking.

Indicate the name of the employee(s) needing training.

Skills/Knowledge Required	Skills/Knowledge Needed	Employee Name
Sales Skills:		

Skills/Knowledge Required	Skills/Knowledge Needed	Employee Name
Service Skills:		
Administrative Skills:		

Workshop Follow-Up

 This exercise has helped you identify any deficiencies in skills or knowledge that your employees have. Now go back and put a star by the most critical deficiencies—those that, if addressed and resolved, would most significantly improve the employee's performance and your business. Use this information to decide what training is most urgently needed.

You can do this exercise for any single employee or for your company in general. For example, if you determine that excellent customer service skills are critical for everyone in your business, place this skill on your worksheet as an area which you feel should be required in your business. Continue by identifying those employees who are deficient in the area of customer service. From this information, you can then build a customer service training program.

Step 3: Develop a Training Plan and Program

Now that you have determined your training needs, your next decision is whether to design and conduct the training in-house or buy it from an outside vendor or supplier. As you consider your options, remember the third, and perhaps top choice: combining internal and external resources for a comprehensive training program. The key is to choose the resources that best suit your training needs.

If you choose to use an outside training vendor, invite two or three to meet with you to learn about your company and to discuss your training needs. Try to learn as much as you can about the trainers by asking them about their training experience and philosophy. Pay attention to the questions each trainer asks about your company, and try to get a sense of how each individual might relate to your employees. Ask those trainers you feel most comfortable with to submit a proposal describing what content and activities they would include in the training, how they would conduct the needed training, how they would evaluate the success of the training program, and what these services would cost your company. This information, along with any referrals you may have received, should allow you to hire a competent trainer to develop and conduct the training.

Identify the Learning Outcomes

Whether you use an inside or outside trainer, start by writing down the purpose of the training, and then identify the **learning outcomes** you want for each area of training. In other words, what specifically should the employee who has gone through this training know or be like as a result of the experience? What new skills should the employee have—what should the employee be able to do as a result of the training? The more specific and measurable you can make these learning outcomes, the better you can design the right training to accomplish them.

Key Word

Personal Workshop Preparation #10: Identify Learning Outcomes

To practice writing learning outcomes, pick a particular training need that you identified in Workshop #9. Using your performance expectations as a guide, think about what you want this training to accomplish. In other words, what do you want the employee to know, or be able to do as a result of this training? Use the following worksheet to help you prepare the learning outcomes for a designated training session. Your outcomes will be determined by the response you give the questions in this exercise.

Champy Athletic Products/Terry Rawl: I decided I had enough information from the needs assessment to put together a long-term plan for training the sales representatives. Here's what I came up with:

1. Immediate on-the-job sales training for each of the new sales reps and for one of the low-performing reps. I will conduct this training,

spending two days each month in the field with each representative for a period of six months.

2. Classroom training for all reps to introduce them to the features of the new product lines. This training will be conducted by the manufacturer's representatives, and will take place as soon as I can get it scheduled.

3. One-on-one training for the other low-performing sales representative to teach her skills in setting up systems for making customer contacts and follow-up. I will ask Joe, my top rep, to do this training; he has a slick system, and it shouldn't take more than one day to teach it to Mary.

4. Bi-annual classroom training for all reps on effective sales techniques and customer service. I will teach some of these and some of the reps may also teach. I probably will bring in some outside trainers, depending on the topic.

5. Coaching for all reps, as needed. I simply have to build time into my schedule to check in regularly with all the reps.

My next step was to begin to schedule and plan the training activities. For each topic, I wrote a sentence describing the purpose of the training. Then I listed the things I want the reps to be able to do after the training (the learning outcomes). Whether I do the training or someone else does, this information will help us design a program that will get results—and that's what we're after.

As a preview of the next workshop, observe how Terry Rawl completed the exercise. Note the outcomes Terry wants from the training on Systems for Customer Follow-up.

THE PURPOSE OF THIS WORKSHOP IS TO SPECIFY THE OUTCOMES YOU DESIRE FROM THE TRAINING EXPERIENCE.

Personal Workshop #10
Identify Learning Outcomes

Training Topic: Systems for Effective Customer Follow-up

Purpose or Training Goal: The purpose of this training is to help sales representatives improve customer service by implementing a dependable system for regular follow-up after the initial call.

What do you want the employee to know as a result of this training?

Learning Outcome:

1. The sales representative will be able to describe the benefits of an effective follow-up system.

What do you want the employee to be able to do as a result of this training?

Learning Outcome:

1. The sales representative will be able to design and implement an effective personal system for follow-up with clients.

2. The sales representative will be able to evaluate his or her system by measuring its impact on total sales and clients served.

What do you want the employee to be like or feel like as a result of this training?

Learning Outcome:

1. The sales representative will feel more organized and have better control over accounts.

THE PURPOSE OF THIS WORKSHOP IS TO SPECIFY THE OUTCOMES YOU DESIRE FROM THE TRAINING EXPERIENCE.

Personal Workshop #10
Identify Learning Outcomes

Training Topic:

Purpose or Training Goal:

What do you want the employee to know as a result of this training?
Learning Outcome:

What do you want the employee to be able to do as a result of this training?
Learning Outcome:

What do you want the employee to be like or feel like as a result of this training?
Learning Outcome:

Workshop Follow-Up

✔ Use the learning outcomes you have identified to help you decide exactly what the training should include. If you are hiring an outside trainer, ask him or her to review your desired outcomes up front and to tell you how the training will be designed to ensure that.

Design an Instructional Plan

Now that you are clear on the purpose of your training and the outcomes you want, you must decide exactly what information to include in the training and how to deliver it. If you are trying to help a single employee learn a specific task requiring worksite equipment, then on-the-job training might be an excellent choice. If you have several employees who need training to develop supervisory skills, however, selecting training content will be a much more difficult task. You will need to make decisions about whether to spend training time on developing their communication skills, conflict management skills, work scheduling skills, or any of a number of other skills that are critical to the success of first line supervisors.

You might choose to combine several training techniques to develop an integrated program that will meet all of your learning objectives. For example, perhaps the supervisory training will take place primarily in the classroom over a one-year period, but each participant will be expected to do some self-directed learning as well. In addition, everyone will participate in a series of video conferences on leadership, and they will work closely with a coach/mentor throughout the training period.

Key Word

The **instructional plan**, or **lesson plan**, is a detailed explanation of what will be taught. Instructional plans are useful because they help you think through every step of the teaching process. They also provide guidance to anyone else who might teach the same materials in the future. Lesson plans are important both for group classes and for one-on-one training which is likely to be delegated to other employees in the future.

Keep your lesson plan simple. It should include the purpose of the training, the learning outcomes, the activities the trainer will use, the materials needed for the training, and estimated times for each discussion and activity. Some plans outline

FYI

> Sometimes you may find that your original training program must be altered to meet the needs of the audience. For example, if you arrive at the training session and learn that your employees are lacking some basic knowledge needed to learn a task, you may have to take a step backwards and give them that basic knowledge first. A good trainer, of course, should know something about the audience before developing the instructional plan. But, a good trainer also learns to go with the flow in case of surprises, and yet makes every attempt to satisfy the learning outcomes by the end of the training session.

what the trainer should say and do. By the time a lesson plan is completed, you should have a clear picture of the structure and content of the training.

Personal Workshop Preparation #11: Design an Instructional Plan

Use the format shown in Personal Workshop #11 on p. 95 to design an instructional plan for a simple training program for your business. Remember to set learning outcomes for the training and then build the activities and information to be delivered from those outcomes.

In the next Personal Workshop, you will find the instructional plan Terry Rawl from Champy Athletics created for teaching a sales rep how to set up a system for customer follow-up.

Your Instructional Strategy: The "Five E's"

No matter how you deliver your training program or what the topic is, try to prepare it with an instructional plan in mind. Dr. Richard O. Schafer has developed an instructional plan, called the "Five E's," which can guide you as you prepare your program. This instructional strategy will help you design a program that will meet the needs and learning styles of all of your participants. This plan is also designed to encourage participants to transfer their new knowledge and skills to their work environment.

- *Engage your participants.* Engagement requires using tactics which create interest and curiosity, raise questions in the learners' minds, and help learners bring prior knowledge into play.

- *Explore the possibilities.* Exploration develops "inquiring minds" while promoting interactions among the learners. Exploration activities are investigatory, problem-solving, question-generating, hypothesizing and idea-generating.

- *Explain the concepts.* Explanation encourages learners to listen to the ideas of others, provides for critical analysis, asking questions and explaining or justifying positions. Explanations should draw analogies from previous learning, challenge critical thinking skills and encourage accurate observations.

- *Extend new knowledge and skills.* Extension integrates new skills, transfers elements previously learned and suggests new questions and information. Extension requires analysis of evidence, checking for understanding of peers, and suggests alternative explanations.

- *Evaluate the learning.* Evaluation requires a demonstration of understanding of knowledge or learning and encourages future investigations by asking and answering open-ended questions. Evidence is observed or presented by change in behavior or application of skills.

(Richard O. Schafer, Ph.D., 1995.)

Personal Workshop #11
Design an Instructional Plan

Training Topic: Systems for Effective Customer Follow-up

Purpose or Training Goal: The purpose of this training is to help sales representatives improve customer service by implementing a dependable system for follow-up after the initial call.

Learning Outcomes:

1. The sales representative will be able to describe the benefits of an effective follow-up system.

2. The sales representative will be able to design and implement an effective personal system for follow-up with clients.

3. The sales representative will be able to evaluate his or her system by measuring its impact on total sales and clients served.

4. The sales representative will feel more organized and have better control over accounts.

Materials: One-page descriptions of systems in use by other sales representatives; a list of possible resources for identifying effective follow-up systems.

Approximate length of training session: 1 day

Equipment: Flip chart with paper or white board; writing materials.

Process and content:

1. Introduce topic and talk about what the employee hopes to accomplish through the training. (30 min.)

2. Identify together the benefits of customer follow-up. Display the list of benefits. (30 min.)

3. Explain what an effective customer follow-up system should do and brainstorm together to identify the characteristics of an effective and efficient system. (60 min.)

4. Hand out the system descriptions submitted by other sales reps, and ask the trainees to spend about an hour reviewing them. The trainees should make notes about what they like and don't like in each system. (60 min.)

BREAK FOR LUNCH

5. Ask trainees to identify the parts of each system that they like and why. Display the list of good characteristics from this exercise. (30 min.)

6. Discuss which parts of these systems might work best for individual trainees. Ask trainees to describe other ideas they have for developing effective and efficient systems of their own. Identify ways in which follow-up systems can be evaluated, based on changes in sales, customers served, customer satisfaction, etc. (60 min.)

7. Talk about other resources employees might use to get more information. (15 min.)

8. Set goals and a timetable with the employees for developing and implementing their own system for follow-up. (30 min.)

9. Decide together how each employee should evaluate the success of his or her sys-

---

THE PURPOSE OF THIS WORKSHOP IS TO DESIGN AN INSTRUCTIONAL PLAN FOR TRAINING.

Personal Workshop #11
Design an Instructional Plan

Training Topic:

Purpose or Training Goal:

Learning Outcomes:

Materials:

Approximate length of training session:

Equipment:

Process and content:

Workshop Follow-Up

Refer back to the discussion on learning styles and the description of the "Five E's" in this Challenge on p. 93. Have you designed an instructional plan that offers something for every type of learner? Will the training program you have described engage the participants, explore the possibilities, explain the concepts, extend new knowledge and skills, and evaluate the learning? Are you confident that the learning outcomes will be met? If you aren't sure, think about how you might change your instructional plan to assure the training will accomplish what it needs to accomplish.

Step 4: Ensure Job Transfer

One of the greatest challenges of training is to find ways to ensure that employees will apply what they have learned on the job. Often employees fail to apply what they have learned to their "real world," because they don't know how it is applicable. Including job-specific exercises in your training, as well as allowing the trainees to take time to write down or discuss *how* they will apply their new knowledge, increases the odds that the training ensure **job transfer**.

Key Word

Also key to this transfer of knowledge is involving the trainees' supervisors. Managers and supervisors should be involved in training whenever possible. But at the very least, the trainer should contact supervisors before the training and supply them with an overview of what will happen in the training. Supervisors need to know what they can do to support their employees both before and after the training. Trainers should provide specific examples. For example, supervisors can talk to their employees before the training and give them a few tips on how to handle themselves in the training. After the training, a supervisor might ask an employee to teach him or her one of the skills learned. Or the supervisor and employee can actually develop a plan or goals for implementing the new skills and knowledge over some period of time. The best way to ensure transfer is to make as many connections as possible between the training and the job.

Personal Workshop Preparation #12:
Plan for Job Transfer

Take a few moments to think about the instructional plan you have developed and your learning outcomes. Since job transfer is the ultimate goal of training, you will want to make sure that this takes place. To guide you in your plan for job transfer, answer the questions in the next workshop. You may want to enlist the help of employees and supervisors, if possible.

Before you begin this exercise, take a look at how Terry Rawl from Champy Athletics completed this workshop.

THE PURPOSE OF THIS WORKSHOP IS TO IDENTIFY SPECIFIC WAYS TO ENSURE THE TRANSFER OF LEARNING TO THE JOB.

Personal Workshop #12
Plan for Job Transfer

Topic of the Training Session: Systems for Effective Customer Follow-Up

1. What are some examples of real problems these employees are experiencing on the job that relate to the topic of this training?

- Sales reps forget to follow-up or wait too long to follow-up.
- Sales reps have no system for tracking their success with a regular follow-up schedule.

2. What are some ways that achieving the learning outcomes will help the employees solve their problems?

- They will have a system which helps them keep track of customer follow-up, so they can provide better service to all customers.
- They will be able to track their success with customer follow-up.

3. What are some ways you can demonstrate these benefits to the employees?

- Involve the employees in the development of a list of benefits of customer follow-up.
- Let other sales reps describe how follow-up systems have helped them increase business and provide better customer service.

4. What activities can you build into the training to help employees understand how this new information transfers to their jobs?

- Involve trainees in discussion about how the various systems might work to solve their problems.
- Have trainees set goals and a timetable for developing and implementing their own system.
- Schedule follow-up time with each sales rep to see how their system is working.

5. How can you get supervisors involved in the training process?

- Supervisors will meet with sales reps as soon as systems are set up; and then on a quarterly basis to assess how the system is working, results of follow-up, etc.

THE PURPOSE OF THIS WORKSHOP IS TO IDENTIFY SPECIFIC WAYS TO ENSURE THE TRANSFER OF LEARNING TO THE JOB.

Personal Workshop #12
Plan for Job Transfer

Topic of the Training Session:

1. What are some examples of real problems these employees are experiencing on the job that relate to the topic of this training?

2. What are some ways that achieving the learning outcomes will help the employees solve their problems?

3. What are some ways you can demonstrate these benefits to the employees?

4. What activities can you build into the training to help employees understand how this new information transfers to their jobs?

5. How can you get supervisors involved in the training process?

Workshop Follow-Up

✓ Go back and review the learning outcomes for the training session you have planned. Do they address the problems you have identified in this workshop? Have you built an instructional plan that will involve the employees and the supervisors as you have described? If not, use the information that you have been given to further refine your instructional plan to ensure job transfer. When you feel confident that your plan is complete and will give your employees the knowledge and skills needed to achieve the learning outcomes, you are ready to implement the training.

Step 5: Implement the Training

The day of the training is here. Trainers should arrive early and make sure everything in the training area is the way they want it to be. If they will be using equipment, they should test it to make sure it works properly. As employees arrive, trainers should introduce themselves and try to make the participants feel comfortable. It helps to build rapport even before the training session begins.

Every training session, whether skills training for a single person or knowledge-based training for a large group, has three basic parts: an opening, the learning session, and a closing. A description of each phase of training follows, along with some tips for succeeding in each stage.

The *opening* is used to get your session off the ground. An effective opening should accomplish three things:

- It should focus your audience on the training, pulling them in mentally and breaking their preoccupation with other things. Don't start talking before people are ready to listen—an effective opener gets them ready and makes them curious about what's next.

- It should involve the audience in some way and facilitate networking. Formal introductions often aren't necessary, but people in the audience need to begin to feel comfortable with each other and with the trainer. When tension goes up, retention goes down. An effective opening helps the audience feel relaxed, comfortable with each other, and involved in what's going on. Getting the participants engaged at this time sets the tone for their continued involvement throughout the training session.

- It should introduce the training topic and be relevant to the content of the program. There are several techniques for accomplishing this, for example, telling a story, asking a challenging question, using a quotation or significant statement and asking for feedback.

- In addition, an opening should help the trainer establish credibility with the audience, not only through an introduction or biographical summary, but through the use of body language, the use of facts to back up what he or she is saying, and by creating a receptive, non-threatening learning environment. Time spent on the opening could range from 5 to 20 minutes, depending on the length of the total training session.

The *learning session* itself might be brief—as little as 15 minutes, depending on what is to be learned—or it might consist of a number of sessions, each one to two days long, over several months. One key to effective training is, of course, content. Always prepare more material than you can use. How much you actually use will depend upon the group's needs. And be sure that the material will allow the employees to achieve the learning objectives.

Just as important as the training content is the presentation. The trainer should always be fully prepared and should direct the learning using effective communication techniques, since even the best content will be lost on an audience that is asleep or cannot connect in some way with the trainer/facilitator.

The following is a list of tips for a trainer.

- *Focus on the audience*. Know something about the trainees, make them feel important and vital to the training experience, and be prepared to answer that age-old question, "What's in it for me?" Connect with your audience through eye contact and by using your enthusiasm to draw them in.

- *Use a variety of training techniques* to keep the trainees' interest and to appeal to their different learning styles. Supplement what you are teaching with examples to help the employees connect the knowledge with their real work situation. Use facts and statistics to reinforce what you tell them. Use participatory exercises, ask questions, stimulate curiosity, and put people in situations where they can discover their own effectiveness or ineffectiveness. Use humor, visual aids, demonstrations, and your enthusiasm to keep the attention of the audience. Change the pace at least every 20 minutes to keep people interested and involved.

- *Encourage questions and answer them effectively*. First, listen for both the content (what is asked) and the intent (what is meant) of the question. Then repeat the question and ask for clarification to be sure you understand what was asked. Finally, answer the question, without being judgmental and without making the employee who asked feel stupid for asking. Always try to answer questions when asked; but if you must put off an answer, make a note and come back to it later.

- *Use audio-visual equipment and attractive visual aids* to enhance the learning and the presentation. Always be sure to set up and test AV equipment before the training to be sure it is ready to go. Provide handouts or workbooks or other materials for trainees to use throughout the training process. These supplemental

One opening technique that always ties the topic to the program is to ask participants to share their experiences of the "best or worst" for the training topic. For example, if the topic is leadership, they might share with the group the characteristics of the best boss they ever had and the worst boss they ever had. These lists of characteristics can then be tied to the leadership topic by the trainer and serve as the basis for continued discussion.

FYI

materials should be designed to be attractive and informative, and they should include space for trainees to take notes, write ideas or answer questions. After the training, these printed materials and the trainee's own notes can serve as a valuable resource back in the workplace.

- *Have fun!* Using natural humor in training (not bad jokes), helps keep your audience relaxed and helps you develop rapport.

- *Finally, avoid the "deadly sins" of trainers*: starting late, being poorly prepared or disorganized, having unclear learning objectives, getting hopelessly behind schedule, improperly handling questions, not involving participants, and boring them to death.

The *closing* should tie things together for the training participants and allow for action planning—how each participant will put the new skills or knowledge to use on the job. Closing activities might include a brief summary or recap of the major points or skills learned, discussion or time for personal reflection on the training activities by participants, the development of an "action list" by individuals or the group, a call for action, a story, a quote or a relevant anecdote. An effective closing might also allow for celebration among the participants—a chance to feel good about what was accomplished and what will be accomplished because of the new skills and knowledge learned.

> *"Adults are babies with big bodies."*
> —Robert Pike's 1st Law of Training

Step 6: Evaluate the Training

No training is complete until it has been evaluated. You need to know whether your employees liked the training and if they learned what they were supposed to learn. Both factors are important. If your employees didn't like the training, chances are they didn't learn much either. On the other hand, it's not enough for employees simply to enjoy the training; have their skills improved? Have they gained new knowledge or information that makes them more effective on the job? Are they doing something now that they weren't doing before the training? When a company can establish a link between training and job performance, it can be sure the program was successful.

> *"Questions are the creative acts of intelligence."*
> —Frank Kingdom

There are many ways to evaluate the effectiveness of training. Typically, classroom training sessions end with a written evaluation form, which provides feedback about the quality of the trainer and the training activities. But since people typically retain only a small percentage of what is taught in the classroom, these evaluations may be of limited use in determining how well the employees will be able to transfer their new skills or knowledge to their jobs. A follow-up in a month or two might better reveal whether employees have been able to put what they learned to work. Non-classroom training can be evaluated, in many cases, by observing the employee doing the task in the workplace. Finally, supervisors and employees may simply want to talk about how the new skills have been implemented in each employee's job, as well as set goals for future implementation.

The following is a list of tips for evaluating training effectiveness.

- Ask participants to complete a written evaluation form at the end of the training session.

- Start the session by asking participants what they want to learn. End the session by reviewing that list and what they have learned.

- Continually ask questions which allow participants to demonstrate that they understand the concepts and how they apply to their jobs.

- Do "mini-quizzes" after each new skill or concept is taught to be sure all participants have learned it.

- Review the learning outcomes and let participants demonstrate their expertise for each one.

- Ask participants to take 5 to 10 minutes at the end of the training session to write down how and when they will apply what they have learned to their jobs.

- Identify measurable factors that might change as a result of the training, such as sales, customer complaints, productivity, etc. Compare those factors before and after training to see if they have changed.

- Observe the employee at work, using the new skills or knowledge learned.

- Compare employee performance before and after training.

- Ask participants to write down what part of the training will be most useful and what will be least useful when they return to their jobs.

- Give participants a work assignment that will require they use their new skills and knowledge. Upon completion of the assignment, meet with each employee to review his or her work, identify weaknesses, and reinforce learning.

Champy Athletic Products/Terry Rawl: Both Mary and I were interested in knowing whether the customer follow-up system she designed during training would help her increase sales and improve the level of customer service in her territory. I personally was interested in whether the training program itself was informative and useful to her. We agreed that she would give me a report describing the follow-up system she developed and keep me advised of its implementation. She also described for me what parts of the training session she found most useful, and where I needed to change things. We decided she would track sales, the number of customers served, and the number and type of customer complaints received over the next two years and use this information as a means of measuring the effectiveness of the training. We are both really interested in whether her new system means money in the pocket for both of us!!

When Training is not the Answer

If you understand the value of training, there is no limit to how far you can develop your employees. At the same time, you must realize that training is not the answer to every problem your business faces. Some businesses wrongly identify a business problem as a training issue. If you use training to try to solve those problems, your efforts will likely fail.

Hiring People with the Wrong Skills

Many jobs require a minimum level of skill or expertise. If the people hired to fill jobs do not have the minimum requirements, the company has a recruiting problem, not a training need. Training may correct the skills deficit, but it only treats a symptom, not the root of the problem. The company needs to examine why unqualified employees are hired and correct its recruiting practices. You can learn more about recruiting and hiring the right people in Challenge 1 of this guide, "Hiring the Right Employees."

Attitude is not a Training Issue

Most of the time, training cannot improve a bad attitude. If your employees' attitudes affect their job performance, the business needs to determine what's behind their outlook. If bad attitudes are related to the business climate—stress from either too much work or not enough, for example—the company needs to tackle that issue before its employees' attitudes will improve. Sending people to training to improve their outlook when the real problem is organizational may end up making bad attitudes worse.

Training Cannot Correct all Performance Problems

Sometimes an employee will not improve his or her performance, no matter what type of training you provide. Here are two examples of this situation:

- An employee attends training to learn how to operate a complex computer system. He barely makes it through the training and now, a few short months after the training, he is unable to handle the complexities of the system. It is unlikely that another round of training will improve his capability to handle this job. Sometimes an employee is just not suited for a job, and no amount of training will change that.

> *"Don't try to teach a pig to dance ... they can't dance and it just irritates the pig!"*
> —Anonymous

- The second example is of a manager who avoids the job of coaching and disciplining an employee. The worker has been through a training session on problem solving with the customer. But she has a hot temper and whenever she deals with an angry customer, she blows up. Instead of talking to her about this behavior, her supervisor enrolls her in another training program. This is a discipline issue, not a training problem. Disciplining employees is discussed in Challenge 4, "Managing for Peak Performance."

You Have Completed Challenge 2

Orientation and training are two forms of continuing education available to small business owner/managers for developing productive employees. Owners who understand the value of a comprehensive training program know that they can go a long way toward building a positive employee outlook and strong employee skills. By completing this Challenge, you have developed the skills needed to design a comprehensive training system for your employees, starting with a thorough orientation for new employees and continuing with needs assessment and the development and delivery of high quality training programs for all employees on an ongoing basis.

You Leave Challenge 2 with the Following

Information: This Challenge has been designed to give you the basic information needed to develop an effective and comprehensive education/training system for the employees in your small business. You have been informed of the characteristics of adult learners and their different learning styles. Several key words have been identified to help you understand the field of training better. You now know what goes into a training session—both in planning and in presentation—and you have been given many tips to help you make your sessions as relevant and as interesting as possible.

Tools: The Personal Workshops in Challenge 2 have helped you develop several tools that will be useful in implementing a comprehensive training program in your small business. For example, the **Orientation Checklist** you developed should make planning future orientations much easier. The **Steps for On-the-job Training** can guide you through that process in the future, as well the **Steps for Developing an Effective Training System.** The **Training Needs Assessment** workshop should be repeated whenever you anticipate a need for training, but you are having difficulty understanding exactly what new skills and knowledge your employees require. And, the Personal Workshop, **Identify Learning Outcomes**, should become a critical part of your training process, since learning outcomes help keep the training topics focused and job related. In addition, the **"Five E's"** will prove an invaluable tool for designing instructional plans which result in effective learning through training. Finally, you have been given a set of tools to help you evaluate your training programs and the impact those programs have on your employees and the success of your business.

Learning: This Challenge has taken you through the steps for designing and implementing an orientation program that will make new employees of your small business as knowledgeable and productive as possible. You have also learned how to assess the training needs of your employees, how to write learning outcomes to guide the development of the training programs, and how to design programs that will reach all types of adult learners and give them the skills and knowledge needed to become more productive employees. Finally, you have learned how to evaluate training programs to be sure the skills and knowledge learned are applicable to the job.

Networking: Throughout this Challenge, you are encouraged to involve other people in the orientation and training process. Your current employees can be an invaluable source of information and ideas, and they are critical to the development of an outstanding orientation program. Likewise, no one understands the training needs of employees better than the employees themselves. Be sure to involve them in the development of a comprehensive training system for your small business. Several other outside resources for training help are provided in this Challenge, and you are given some tips for selecting and evaluating those resources.

There is a wealth of information available in your library about training and employee development. But remember that actually doing some training, from start to finish, following the guidelines in this Challenge, will be the best way to increase your knowledge and skills in employee development. Good luck!

Challenge 2 Self-Assessment

After completing this Challenge you should be able to design and implement a comprehensive employee development system for your small business, which includes orientation and high quality training programs. Check your understanding of the concepts and the training process presented by using the following checklist. If needed, go back and review the process where you feel you need more practice.

**Pages
49 - 69**

Developing and Implementing an Orientation Program for New Employees

( ) I have developed an orientation checklist to guide the orientation planning process.

( ) I have enlisted the help of other employees for orientation.

( ) I have developed and am prepared to implement an orientation program that contains all the ingredients of effective orientation.

**Pages
70 - 88**

Assessing the Training Needs of Your Employees

( ) I know that training should be done "when it is needed," and I am able to determine when it is needed in my small business.

( ) I can use the job description and my performance expectations to identify the skills and knowledge needed by an employee to do a particular job.

( ) My employees and I can work together to identify any deficiencies in skills and knowledge.

Writing Learning Outcomes for any Training Program

( ) I can identify a primary purpose or goal for each training session needed.

( ) I am able to specify what I want employees to be able to **know** or **do** as a result of the training.

Pages 89 - 92

Develop an Instructional Plan that Will Reach Every Type of Learner

( ) I can use the learning outcomes as a guide for developing an instructional plan that specifies what the training will include and how it will be presented.

( ) I can apply the various training techniques, including on-the-job training, self-directed learning, coaching and mentoring, and classroom training.

( ) I understand that different people have different learning styles, and I know how to check my instructional plan to ensure it offers something for every type of learner.

( ) I can develop an instructional plan which appeals to adult learners and allows them to share their accumulated knowledge and skills.

Pages 92 - 97

Design Training Programs that Ensure Job Transfer

( ) I have knowledge of the specific problems my employees are experiencing on the job which relate to the training topic, and I have developed an instructional plan which addresses those problems.

( ) I am prepared to demonstrate to employees how training will benefit them in their work.

( ) I have involved supervisors in the training process through needs assessment, planning, implementation, and/or evaluation.

( ) I know several techniques for involving employees in the training process.

Pages 97 - 102

Evaluate Your Training Programs for Effectiveness

( ) I understand that the ultimate test for effective training is whether the employees can apply new skills and knowledge to their jobs.

( ) I can identify several techniques for evaluating training effectiveness.

( ) I can use the learning outcomes as the basis for evaluating the effectiveness of the training.

Pages 102 - 104

Record anything from Challenge 2, your Personal Workshops, or your personal reflections that you want to remember.

Take Another Look

Review the results of your self-assessment for Challenge 2. If you feel you need more work in some area, go back into the text and challenge yourself again. Developing a comprehensive training program is not an overnight task, so don't be discouraged if you aren't totally clear on exactly what training makes sense for your business at this time. Continue to use the information in Challenge 2 to guide your training and employee development activities as the need arises.

Challenge 3
Developing Personnel Policies

"Wisdom lies in masterful administration of the unforeseen."

—Robert Bridges

As a small business owner, can you imagine ever going to court against one of your employees? It's not a pleasant thought, is it? And yet many small business owners may be at risk, having let their personnel policies simply evolve over time with little consideration of legal implications or how those policies might affect future operations. For example, perhaps you just came up with what seemed to be a reasonable maternity leave policy the first time you had a pregnant employee. You later find out that what seemed reasonable to you did not comply with state or federal Family and Medical Leave laws, and that you owe that employee a substantial sum of money.

Or, perhaps an employee makes a sexual harassment charge against one of your managers. Since you have told all of your managers not to sexually harass anyone, you assume you are off the hook. But you learn in court that you are just as guilty as if you had verbally condoned such behavior, because you do not have a formal, written policy prohibiting sexual harassment and outlining a procedure for handling any complaints. You need to develop reasonable and legal personnel policies for your small business, and you need to be sure those policies are communicated clearly to each of your employees.

The purpose of Challenge 3 is to help you develop written personnel policies and a means for effectively communicating them: an **Employee Handbook** or **Personnel Manual.** The case studies in this Challenge provide examples of written personnel policies, and the Personal Workshops will give you an opportunity to develop policies for your own small business. If you are starting from scratch, you are strongly encouraged to involve your employees in the development of personnel policies and an employee handbook that is a clear, concise and valuable tool for both employer and employees.

Key Word

Upon completion of Challenge 3, you will be able to:

• Establish a system for developing and regularly revising personnel policies

- Outline the types of policies needed in your small business

- Develop personnel policies and an employee handbook which do not threaten employment-at-will status

- Develop means for effectively communicating personnel policies to all employees

- Minimize the risk of litigation in personnel issues

Why Your Company Needs Written Policies

Organizations develop standard personnel policies at different times and in different ways. Some policies may be developed for managers' use only, while others are intended for employees at all levels. Some are communicated individually to employees in memos, during orientation or training sessions, or on an as-needed basis. As your business grows, however, so does the need to formalize company policies and to communicate them to all employees in a handbook or personnel manual.

Many circumstances could lead to the development of written policies. The following are some examples of those situations:

- As a business owner/manager, you decide employees need a description of company benefits and the eligibility restrictions for those benefits.

- Following an unfortunate incident, you establish rules for the fair and consistent treatment of employees.

- Your company develops a policy to assure compliance with a new law and to inform your employees of special requirements that may affect how they do their jobs.

- Your business creates a standard document to inform employees of the proper procedure for requesting employee assistance.

Some managers may be reluctant to put policies in writing because they fear loss of flexibility in managing employees. The opposite tends to be true. At the very least, inconsistent treatment of employees can trigger dissatisfaction. And worse, employee dissatisfaction could lead to an increase in discrimination claims, a reduction in productivity, union organizing and other potential problems. If you

FYI

In a recent case against a prominent national department store, a 55-year-old salesman claimed age discrimination after he was fired from his position for falsifying his time card when he was 30 minutes late. He had been employed at the store for 30 years and had an otherwise good work record. The court ruled in favor of the store, since younger employees who had committed similar violations had in fact been discharged in the past, and there was no evidence that the reason for firing was a pretext to get rid of an aging worker. In this case, consistent enforcement of a policy was key to the case outcome.

have a personnel policy in effect, get it on the books; and then enforce it consistently. The selective enforcement of any rule is ammunition for a lawsuit if an employee against whom the rule is enforced is fired or otherwise disciplined. As an owner/manager of a growing small business, you simply cannot afford to make up the rules as you go along.

Possible Pitfalls of Employee Handbooks

Employment-at-Will Doctrine

Contractual relationships between employees and employers have generated a great deal of press in the last few years. One concern is that written policies and employee handbooks can erode the **employment-at-will** status of employees by suggesting an "implied contract" between employer and employee.

Key Word

Employment-at-will refers to the historical "right" of employers to legally terminate an employment relationship "at will"—in other words, at any time with or without notice and with or without cause. Employees, likewise, can leave employment without notice or cause. This doctrine applies to employees who are not covered by a collective bargaining contract or civil service rules, and who were not hired under a written employment agreement.

Legal Notes

Some written policies are required by federal or state law. Formal policies on many topics are not required by law, but could reduce your company's liability in a legal dispute. Here are some examples of ways that written policies can help employers:

- Employers can minimize their liability in sexual harassment claims if they have a written policy prohibiting sexual harassment in the workplace and outlining procedures to address such complaints.

- Depending on the size of the business, family and medical leave policies could be regulated by state or federal laws. Such laws provide a specified amount of unpaid leave to employees who may need transition time for the birth or adoption of a child or who may need to attend to their own medical needs or those of a family member. Written policies regarding family and medical leave should be included in the employee handbook. Some laws require the employer to post notices of these policies in conspicuous places; compliance by the employer could limit an employee's claim to family or medical leave.

- Federal, state and local statutes in many jurisdictions require a written policy on equal employment opportunity. Posted notice of that policy and its inclusion in a handbook may reduce your company's liability if a discrimination claim is ever filed.

These are only a few examples of how written policies can be helpful or required. Because laws change constantly, you should consult with an attorney to stay informed of regulations set by federal, state and municipal statutes.

When judges review employee-employer relationships in a court case, they look over written and oral policies and correspondence to determine if any assurances were given to the employee that led him or her to believe that he or she had a contract or that was guaranteed long-term or permanent employment. Here are some examples of such "implied" promises:

- Use of words like "permanent employees" may lead workers to believe that they have a job for life. An alternative is the term, "regular employees." Use of the words "salary" or "annual compensation" may lead workers to believe they are guaranteed a one-year contract. Alternatives are "compensation" or "wages."

- Reference to "probationary employees" may imply that once workers complete their probation, they achieve a protected status and cannot be terminated.

- Disciplinary procedures can be an issue when policies that outline disciplinary steps require that supervisors "must" follow those steps. Employees may infer from those policies that they cannot be terminated unless their supervisors follow those steps exactly.

- Performance appraisal policies which state that "as long as the employee maintains an acceptable level of performance, they have a job" may be considered as contractual.

These examples demonstrate how important it is to carefully write and review your company's policies. These concerns should not scare you away from preparing written policies or an employee handbook, but they do emphasize the need to

---

Legal Notes

Since the inception of the "Employment-at-Will Doctrine" (Tennessee Supreme Court, 1884), several state and federal laws have set limits on an employer's right to dismiss employees. Here are some examples:

- Discriminatory dismissal against protected groups is prohibited by both federal and state laws (based on race, age, religion, sex, disability, national origin, marital status, etc.).

- Employees acting within "public policy" are protected, prohibiting, for example, dismissal of an employee who refuses to do something illegal for the company or who has reported wrongdoing by the company.

- The "implied contract" exception, where an employer has, in effect, promised continued employment through conduct or words.

Some states now prohibit terminating any employee without "just cause." Check with an attorney to find out if you live in an "at will" state and to learn what limitations you have in dismissing employees. Also, have an attorney review your employee handbook and personnel policies to be sure the language used does not in any way imply a contractual relationship with the employee.

proceed cautiously and to hire an attorney to review your handbook before it is distributed to employees.

Keeping Handbooks and Policies Up-to-Date

After you put the time and effort into writing and distributing personnel policies for your small business, it is worth the additional effort to keep them up-to-date. You will undoubtedly need to change policies over time—but if you never get around to updating the employee handbook or otherwise informing your employees, how can you expect them to comply? It isn't reasonable or necessary to revise your entire handbook every time you make a policy change—but you must establish a system to assure all employees are informed of any changes between revisions.

A System for Policy Development and Revision

Whether or not you currently have written personnel policies, you need to establish a system for writing, reviewing and communicating those policies to your employees on a regular basis. A model of such a system, and a description of the steps you can take to develop your own system, is shown in Figure 3.1.

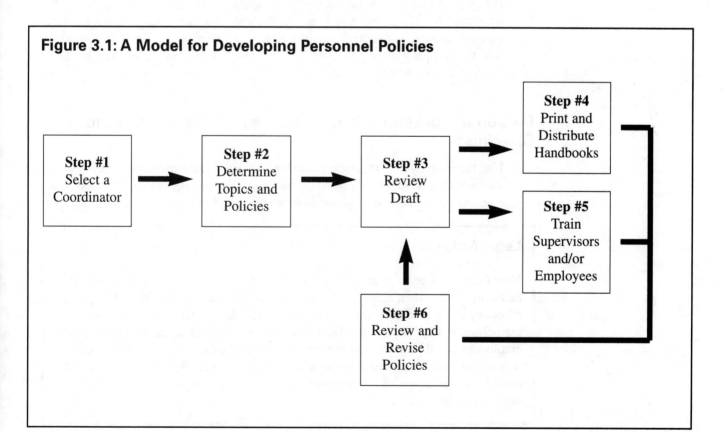

Figure 3.1: A Model for Developing Personnel Policies

Step #1 Select a Coordinator

Step #2 Determine Topics and Policies

Step #3 Review Draft

Step #4 Print and Distribute Handbooks

Step #5 Train Supervisors and/or Employees

Step #6 Review and Revise Policies

Step 1: Select a Coordinator

Developing written policies and a handbook may seem like a straightforward task, but the process can be complex and time-consuming. Appoint one person in your company to coordinate the project. Ideal candidates include human resources specialists and managers who have the authority to make policy recommendations. The job of the Handbook Coordinator should be:

- To coordinate each step of the process and keep it on schedule.

- To pull together the "right" people to draft the policies, for example, if the policy has to do with benefits eligibility and enrollment, the "right" people might include the owner, the human resources manager, and the staff person who handles benefits paperwork.

- To understand the possible legal constraints of employee policies and the implications of those policies for both employer and employees. This suggests that the coordinator should work with an attorney, at some point, to review the policies for possible legal ramifications.

- To edit the writing and arrange the contents so the handbook is functional and can be easily revised.

Step 2: Determine Topics and Policies

Policy issues vary from one company to another. Some policies may be totally irrelevant for some organizations but critical to others. As a small business owner/manager, you should consider what your employees need to know about how the company does business, and then develop a list of topics that should be covered in your employee handbook.

Personal Workshop Preparation #13: Employee Handbook Checklist

Use the Employee Handbook Checklist that follows to identify those topics or issues which need written policies and that you feel should be included in an employee handbook for your small business. In some cases a written policy may

---

Legal Notes

Your failure to inform your employees of any change in policy or procedure could be a critical error if an employee files a claim or grievance that relates to the updated policy or its administration. Employees could argue that they did not know of the revised policy or that they did not receive notice of changes. Failure to notify employees could destroy your credibility and case, in the event of litigation. The fact is that your employee handbook and personnel policies might some day be considered "evidence" in a courtroom; be sure they support your position, not destroy it.

already exist. In others, you may not currently have a formal policy but need to write one. Later in this Challenge, you will have an opportunity to write some policies for your company. In this workshop, however, your goal is to simply identify which policies to include in your employee handbook.

THE PURPOSE OF THIS WORKSHOP IS TO IDENTIFY ISSUES OR TOPICS WHICH NEED TO HAVE WRITTEN POLICIES AND NEED TO BE INCLUDED IN YOUR EMPLOYEE HANDBOOK.

Personal Workshop #13
Employee Handbook Checklist

Place a check in the box of each topic or issue below which needs to be covered in your employee handbook. Add other topics as needed.

I. Introduction

❑ Welcome statement
❑ "At-will" statement
❑ Right to amend
❑ Company history
❑ Company philosophy
❑ Mission and vision statements
❑ How to use the employee handbook
❑ _____
❑ _____

II. General Employment/Management Policies

❑ Employee classifications
❑ Length of service
❑ EEO statement
❑ Sexual harassment
❑ Hiring policies: hiring of relatives
❑ Promotion policies
❑ Physical examinations
❑ Accommodation for disabilities and compliance with ADA
❑ Immigration issues
❑ Probation
❑ Orientation and training
❑ Non-compete policy/ trade secrets
❑ Confidentiality
❑ Outside employment
❑ Personal appearance/dress code
❑ Gifts and gratuities

- ❏ Solicitations and distributions
- ❏ Personnel records (access and privacy)
- ❏ Smoking
- ❏ Alcoholism and drug abuse
- ❏ Travel policies
- ❏ Personal property
- ❏ Telephone usage
- ❏ Parking
- ❏ Keys and identification cards
- ❏ Bulletin boards
- ❏ Open door policy
- ❏ _____
- ❏ _____

III. Policies about Work Schedules

- ❏ Regular work hours and schedule setting
- ❏ Breaks
- ❏ Attendance policy
- ❏ Weather
- ❏ _____
- ❏ _____

IV. Compensation and Benefits Policies

- ❏ Compensation/wages/salaries
- ❏ Overtime pay and compensatory ("comp") time
- ❏ "On-call" employee pay
- ❏ Garnishment
- ❏ Legally-required benefits (workers' compensation insurance, Unemployment insurance, FICA)
- ❏ Leave policies
  - ❏ Holidays
  - ❏ Vacation
  - ❏ Sick leave and personal leave
  - ❏ Jury duty
  - ❏ Funeral/bereavement leave
  - ❏ Military duty
  - ❏ Leave of absence
- ❏ Health and life insurance
- ❏ Short- or long-term disability insurance
- ❏ Retirement benefits and annuity options
- ❏ Educational assistance programs
- ❏ _____
- ❏ _____

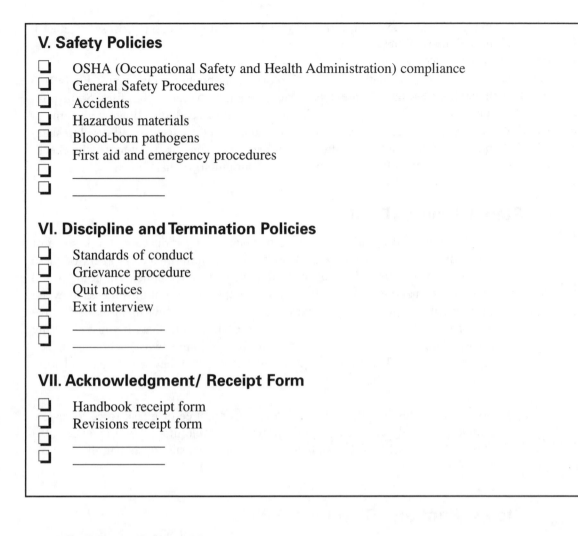

V. Safety Policies

❑ OSHA (Occupational Safety and Health Administration) compliance
❑ General Safety Procedures
❑ Accidents
❑ Hazardous materials
❑ Blood-born pathogens
❑ First aid and emergency procedures
❑ _____
❑ _____

VI. Discipline and Termination Policies

❑ Standards of conduct
❑ Grievance procedure
❑ Quit notices
❑ Exit interview
❑ _____
❑ _____

VII. Acknowledgment/ Receipt Form

❑ Handbook receipt form
❑ Revisions receipt form
❑ _____
❑ _____

Workshop Follow-Up

✔ If your employee handbook checklist seems extensive, keep in mind that not all policies are equally important. Go back over your checklist and put a star by those policies that you feel are critical to include. As you begin to develop your handbook, write these critical policies first. You can develop and add the less-important policies and procedures over time.

Now that you know what to include in your employee handbook, you can begin to write the actual policies. In some cases, an owner/manager will independently decide what the policies and procedures will be for the small business. But in

Many companies will involve employees in the policy department process by forming a policy review committee. Such committees usually serve in an advisory capacity only, offering suggestions on policy content and implementation. If you choose to form a policy review committee, its role and limits of influence need to be clarified up front.

FYI

many cases, it makes more sense to involve employees in the process, whether it be writing or reviewing policies.

If you do not currently have an employee handbook, you will most likely find many policies stated in previous correspondence, so search your files. Some policies may exist, but only in your head. Or you may need to sit down with some of your employees, management or non-management, to discuss and develop statements of policy and procedure for your business. You may want to use the checklist you just completed as an outline for your employee handbook.

Step 3: Review Draft

Once a draft of company policy or procedure has been developed, ask some of your supervisors and managers to review it. As the primary enforcers of these policies, supervisors and managers need to understand the policies thoroughly and feel some ownership for them. If these key people are part of the process, they are more likely to support the policies and less likely to view them as ineffective and/or unnecessary. And instead of using the old excuse that "it's just company policy," informed supervisors will be able to explain the "why" behind each policy to employees. This should improve the chances that they will accept and comply with the new policy.

Some companies form an employee review committee or a task force to review policies. Not only can such a group provide valuable input, but employees also may bring up policy issues that owners, managers and supervisors might not have considered.

Step 4: Print and Distribute Policies

Here are some helpful suggestions for producing an employee handbook and effectively communicating the policies to your employees:

- Consider a looseleaf binder format which allows for the easy insertion of new policies and replacement of updates. A binder also can include copies of benefit booklets or summary plan descriptions in pockets or inserted behind policies. Binders give employees a convenient place to keep everything.

- Make sure to date each page. That way employees can be sure they have the most recent copy of every policy.

FYI

Don't re-invent the wheel! A great resource for writing personnel policies for your business are the employee handbooks and personnel policies from other organizations. Reviewing these handbooks will help you decide what to include in your own manual and what to omit; and you may pick up some good ideas for your own personnel policies. Contact a couple of your business associates and ask to borrow their employee handbooks for a few days.

- Distribute copies to all employees, even those on leave of absence or working away from the central business location.

- Require all employees to complete a form that acknowledges that they received a copy of the handbook and understand that they are responsible for reading its contents. This form can be placed at the front or back of the manual. It should be signed by the employee, detached and given to the Handbook Coordinator. Each revision to the handbook should also include an acknowledgment form to complete and return. Signed forms should be kept in personnel files.

- Hold a meeting for all employees to distribute and review the contents of the employee handbook. This helps ensure that employees learn how to use the handbook and that they have been introduced to the personnel policies in it. It also gives employees a chance to ask clarifying questions about policies, and to sign and turn in their acknowledgment forms.

Step 5: Train Supervisors

When you issue personnel policies or a handbook, be sure that supervisors understand the policies. Consider holding a training session for employees in supervisory positions to talk about the policies and to help prepare them to answer any questions that may come up from employees about a particular policy. A good supervisor should be able to answer these questions:

- What is the intent of the policy, program or benefit? Why was it created or changed?

- What are details of the program, or who should employees call to get more detail?

- Who administers the policy and how do they do it? Must the employees complete special forms or other paperwork?

- What authority or flexibility do supervisors have to make exceptions or changes to the policy?

- What are the ramifications if the policy is not followed?

Training supervisors is critical to the success of programs and policies. Employees expect their supervisors to understand company policies, and supervisors cannot communicate effectively until they have all the information they need.

There are some computer programs on the market that guide you through the development of personnel policies and an employee handbook. These programs offer sample policies which can be "customized" for your business with the push of a button. Some programs also have language scanners to make certain you avoid potentially controversial words. Programs are available for both Windows and Macintosh.

Step 6: Revise Policies

Revising policies and updating handbooks on a regular basis is essential. A company may need to add benefits or policies, change unclear language or revise a policy because of changes in federal, state or local laws. While changes and updates should be done as needed, the Handbook Coordinator should also read through the entire handbook (probably once a year is enough), to look for any policy or language which needs to be updated.

Owner/managers must carefully consider the ramifications of adding restrictions to existing policies. Limiting benefits or initiating other restrictions may be necessary for any number of reasons, but it is likely to be tough on morale. Employers should give their workers adequate notice about any restrictions. If a company decides to scale back vacation benefits, for instance, it might make those changes effective for the next calendar year.

Once again, it is very important that all changes in policy are communicated to employees. At minimum, a company can post policy changes on bulletin boards and then keep the bulletin board notices in a file. These notices must be dated and kept up for a period of time to give all employees the opportunity to see them. A more effective method of communication is to give each employee a copy of the revised policy and mail copies to workers on a leave of absence or away from the business for another reason.

Periodically, businesses should issue a new employee manual that incorporates all policy changes. At the very least, the manual should be dated; some companies include a publication date on every page so there is no question that employees have the most recent edition. Dating pages may seem like a minor detail, but it could be important if your company ever faces a policy-related court case.

Legal Note

Reasonable notice of policy changes is more than a considerate practice; judges consider it when reviewing employee claims.

FYI

In some cases, you may want to conduct training for all employees, not just supervisors, regarding a particular policy or procedure. For example, recent regulations for controlling blood-born pathogens require employers to follow certain safety procedures and to train certain employees in those procedures. Or, if you change your company's policy regarding how to treat a dissatisfied customer, you may want to conduct training to teach all employees who come in contact with customers the new skills required. For more information on developing and conducting training programs for your employees, go back to Challenge 2.

Writing Policies

If you do not currently have an employee handbook, start by using the checklist you developed in the first workshop of this Challenge as an outline for your own manual. The discussion that follows will go in the order of the checklist, but feel free to rearrange your own employee handbook to fit the needs of your company. Remember that your goal is to develop a manual that is useful to both your employees and to you—easy to read and easy to revise.

If you already have a handbook, then keep it at your side as you work through this section of Challenge 3. In either case, don't be overwhelmed by the task before you. Just complete those sections that apply to your business, and take it one policy at a time. In some cases, you may need to pull information from other resources such as memos or letters, or gather ideas and policies from other people in your organization. And in some cases, you may need some time to think about what you want a policy to be—that's okay. Remember that what you write may have both legal and operational implications, so do not settle on a policy until you have considered all of the possible outcomes if it is implemented, and until you have had it checked for clarity and legality.

A Note about the Personal Workshops that Follow

While it is not possible to include sample policies for each of the following topics listed on the employee handbook checklist, samples are provided for some of the more common types of policies. The sample policies that are included are provided for instructional purposes only and should not be considered as legal advice. Keep in mind that other employees in your company can be very helpful in writing policies and procedures. Work with your Handbook Coordinator to decide who should be involved in writing policies on each of the topics you have selected.

I. The Employee Handbook Introduction

The introduction of a policy manual should briefly tell your employees about the company and its business philosophy. The introduction can help set the tone for business operations. It should also spell out the intent of the handbook.

> *"The only way to eat an elephant is one bite at a time."*
> —Anonymous

At a minimum, include in your introduction a welcome statement, an "at will" statement, your right to amend, and how the handbook should be used in your company. Other items you might want to include are the company history, philosophy, mission, vision, an organizational chart, a list of officers, or anything else you think would be useful to give employees an overview of your company.

Personal Workshop Preparation #14: Writing the Introduction

Review your employee handbook checklist and note the items you want to include in your introduction. Pull any materials from your files or other resources you might need to write the introduction to your handbook. If possible, look at examples of introductions in other handbooks.

PCB Corporation/Candace and Tony Washington: It is our philosophy that our customers need to be the top priority of each of our employees, and our employees are the next most important priority for us. We wanted to express that philosophy to our employees in the introduction of the handbook. We really want them to feel welcome when they join PCB. Following is what we came up with for an introduction to our handbook.

THE PURPOSE OF THIS WORKSHOP IS TO WRITE AN INTRODUCTORY SECTION FOR YOUR EMPLOYEE HANDBOOK.

Personal Workshop #14
Writing the Introduction

Part I: Check off the items you need or want to include in your introduction.

Always include	Optional items to include
_X_ welcome statement	___ company history
_X_ "at will" statement	_x_ philosophy
_X_ right to amend policies	_X_ mission and/or vision
_X_ how the handbook should be used	___ organizational chart
___ list of officers	
___ other: _____	

Part II: Write an introductory statement for your company here:

PCB Corporation

Introduction

Welcome to PCB Corporation! As an employee of this company, you become part of a team dedicated to giving its customers the best quality circuit boards and the best service possible. Every employee at PCB has the unique opportunity to enhance our image and spread goodwill among our customers and our community. This makes your job one of the most important in the company—and PCB wants to do whatever it can to help you succeed and grow in your position.

This is your handbook. It is meant to be an informative guide to the policies and benefits of our company. By acquainting yourself with this information, you will have a better understanding of our operations and management style—what you may expect from us and what we expect of you. If you don't understand something, please ask. We want you to feel comfortable as a member of the PCB team. You are now a part of an organization that has prospered through the wholehearted efforts of every employee.

In addition to this handbook, you will be trained in your job by your supervisor and other members of the PCB team. The policies in this handbook are subject to revision by the company at any time. Business conditions can change, and therefore these policies may also change at the discretion of the company. You will be promptly notified in writing of any policy changes. The contents of this book (as a whole or in any part), in no way imply an employment contract or guaranteed employment.

FYI

You may choose to write your own policies for your handbook. However, a series of policy templates have been created to help you in your policy writing process. These templates are located in Appendix I of this book.

Personal Workshop #14
Writing the Introduction

Part I: Check off the items you need or want to include in your introduction.

Always include	**Optional items to include**
___ welcome statement	___ company history
___ "at will" statement	___ philosophy
___ right to amend policies	___ mission and/or vision
___ how the handbook should be used	___ organizational chart
___ list of officers	
___ other: _____	

Part II: Write an introductory statement for your company here:

Workshop Follow-Up

Review what you have written. Have you included all the items you wanted to include in your introduction? Does the introduction you wrote have enough information to give employees a sense of what your company is all about? Have you included those critical statements that may protect your "at-will" status and your right to revise policies? Is it easy to read? Finally, does it have the tone you want? Now ask a few other people to read it and make suggestions for improvements. But be selective about what you add—employees won't read it if it gets too long. Keep it simple, friendly, and functional.

II. General Employment Policies

This is a catch-all category for policies that do not fit nicely into another category, but are important and apply to *all* employees. General employment policies include information about employee classifications and hiring procedures, how employees should behave on the job, and company procedures which affect every day work life, such as parking policies, smoking policies and dress codes.

Employee Classifications

Most businesses have more than one type of employee (full-time or part-time, management or non-management, etc.). Certain benefits or policies of the company might apply to one type of employee but not to another. Your employee handbook should clearly define the types, or classifications, of employees you have and the eligibility for benefits of each type. In most companies, part-time, temporary or on-call employees do not receive full benefits.

Personal Workshop Preparation #15: Employee Classifications

In this workshop, you will identify the different employee classifications for your company and write a brief description of each classification. The description should include, at a minimum, information about the working conditions of the classification (hours, pay procedures, etc.) and benefits eligibility. You may also want to reinforce your "at will" status by including a brief statement under each classification description. While this may seem redundant, it will help assure that there is no misunderstanding about your right to dismiss employees with or without cause, no matter what their employment classification.

If you have different expectations or benefits for management and non-management employees in each classification, then you may need to write separate descriptions for them. If necessary, review your organizational chart or company job descriptions to be sure you have a complete classification system.

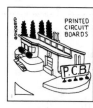

PCB Corporation/Candace and Tony Washington: Most of the people who work on the line during first and second shifts are considered regular full-time employees. We also have two part-timers in the office during regular work hours (first shift). Since our production goes up and down with orders, we hire a number of temporary assemblers. Some of these people also work "on-call"—that way we know we can always keep the line moving, even if one of our regular employees is out for some reason. Using Personal Workshop #15, we were able to identify our employee classifications and write descriptions for each.

THE PURPOSE OF THIS WORKSHOP IS TO DEFINE EMPLOYEE CLASSIFICATIONS.

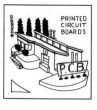

Personal Workshop #15
Employee Classifications

Part I: Identify the different types of employee classifications you have in your company.

X regular full-time   X temporary part-time
X regular part-time   X on-call
X temporary full-time   ___ other: _____

Part II: Write a description for each classification which includes information about:
• working conditions (such as hours, how paid, etc.)
• benefits eligibility
• the employer's "at will" status
Note: If this information is different for non-management and management, write separate descriptions for each.

Regular Full-Time	Non-Management	Management
	Full-time employees are expected to work the normal established work week (40 hours per week). These employees are eligible for full company benefits as defined under the requirements of each specific benefit. Employment is terminable at will, by either the employee or the employer.	Full-time management employees are expected to work a minimum of 40 hours per week. Double shifts, evening or weekend work may occasionally be required to meet production schedules. Management employees are eligible for full company benefits as defined under the requirements of each specific benefit. Employment is terminable at will, by either the employee or the employer.

Regular Part-Time	Non-Management	Management
	Part-time employees usually work less than the normal established work week. Part-time employees are quoted an hourly rate of pay. Time cards are submitted each week reporting the number of hours worked. Part-time employees are eligible for some benefit programs as defined by the requirement of each specific benefit. Vacation, holidays, and sick leave are pro-rated based on the number of hours worked during the week and days normally scheduled to work during the week. Employment is terminable at will, by either the employee or the employer.	n/a
Temporary		
	Temporary employees are hired for a defined period of time with the understanding that employment is temporary and for a set period of time. Temporary employees are quoted an hourly rate of pay. Time cards are submitted each week reporting the number of hours worked. Temporary employees are not eligible for any employee benefits. Employment is terminable at will, by either the employee or the employer.	n/a

On-Call	Non-Management	Management
	On-call employees are hired on a day-to-day, on-call basis. On-call employees are quoted an hourly rate of pay. Time cards are submitted each week reporting the number of hours worked. On-call employees are not eligible for any employee benefits. Employment is terminable at will by either the employee or the employer.	n/a
Other		
	n/a	n/a

THE PURPOSE OF THIS WORKSHOP IS TO DEFINE EMPLOYEE CLASSIFICATIONS.

Personal Workshop #15
Employee Classifications

Part I: Identify the different types of employee classifications you have in your company.

___ regular full-time   ___ temporary part-time

___ regular part-time   ___ on-call

___ temporary full-time   ___ other: _____

Part II: Write a description for each classification which includes information about:
• working conditions (such as hours, how paid, etc.)
• benefits eligibility
• the employer's "at will" status

Note: If this information is different for non-management and management, write separate descriptions for each.

Regular Full-Time	Non-Management	Management
Regular Part-Time		
Temporary		
On-Call		
Other		

Workshop Follow-Up

If a classification system is new for your company, review each position in the company to determine each employee's classification. Include the classification on the position description, and be sure all employees understand their status at the time of hire.

Length of Service

In some companies, an employee's length of service might influence eligibility for certain benefits, promotion, or lay off. If this is the case in your company, you should develop a policy which defines how an employee's length of service is calculated and how it may be ended.

If any of your employees belong to a union, length of service will be an important issue in the collective bargaining process. Unions almost universally support seniority and length of service as the main criterion for promotion and lay off. As an employer, you may want to avoid such an agreement in order to protect your right to make personnel decisions using criteria other than length of service, such as employee performance.

PCB Corporation/Candace and Tony Washington: PCB is a nonunion company, but length of service can be important, since our production level fluctuates with our orders.

Length of Service

Length of service is defined as the length of time you have been continuously employed with the PCB Corporation. Your length of service will be based on your most recent hire date. When skill and ability levels are equal, length of service will be considered with respect to promotions, training opportunities and vacation priorities.

Length of service will be ended by these events:

❑ Voluntary resignation

❑ Termination for any reason

❑ Failure to report for work without notification for three consecutive days

❑ Lay-off in excess of your length of service or six months, whichever is less

---

Equal Employment Opportunity (EEO)

In these litigious times, employers must take care to make decisions and adopt policies that are non-discriminatory. All of your managers and supervisors are agents of the company and their actions are subject to scrutiny. Be careful to communicate clearly and in writing that discriminatory behavior will not be tolerated. The EEO policy should be included in employee guidelines and posted on bulletin boards. The statement should also be printed on job application forms. An abbreviated statement may be used for employment advertisements, such as "Pegasus Computer Systems is an EEO employer."

A written sexual harassment policy is a necessity for every business. Sexual harassment is prohibited by federal law, as well as by many state and local laws. It can be incorporated into the company's EEO policy, or it may be a separate policy.

Pegasus Computer Systems/Jean Watson: With the help of our attorney, here is the EEO statement we developed for Pegasus.

Equal Employment Opportunity (EEO)

Pegasus Computer Systems is committed to equal employment opportunity. We practice this policy through all phases of our operation, including hiring, salary increases, promotion, training opportunities, and job assignments. Pegasus complies with all applicable state, federal and local laws governing nondiscrimination in employment. This means that every employee has the same opportunity for advancement, regardless of race, color, creed, national origin, sex, age, or disability. If you feel you are not being treated equally as an employee, we encourage you to talk with your supervisor or another member of management.

Sexual Harassment

Sexual harassment has become an important issue for businesses over the past ten years. Sexual harassment is expressly prohibited by Title VII of the Civil Rights Act of 1964, as well as by many state and local laws. **A written sexual harassment policy is a necessity for every business.**

Employees of either sex can be victims of sexual harassment. Sexual harassment includes unwelcome sexual advances, unwelcome physical contact of a sexual nature, or unwelcome verbal or physical conduct of a sexual nature. Unwelcome

Key Word

Legal Notes

Title VII of the Civil Rights Act of 1964 makes it illegal to discriminate in employment on the basis of race, religion, ethnic origin, color or sex. Other significant federal laws prohibit discrimination on the basis of age or disability. Individual states also have a variety of laws prohibiting discrimination on these or other bases, such as sexual preference, marital status, etc.

verbal or physical conduct includes, but is not limited to the deliberate, repeated making of unsolicited gestures or comments, or the deliberate, repeated display of offensive sexually graphic materials which is not necessary for business purposes, not to mention the more overt request for sexual favors in exchange for continued employment or advancement.

As an employer, you may be held liable for acts of sexual harassment in your company regardless of whether you were aware of its occurrence. Your employment policy, therefore, needs to include four things:

- a definition of sexual harassment;

- a clear statement that sexual harassment is prohibited and will not be tolerated;

- specific procedures for employees to follow to report sexual harassment; and

- a statement that engaging in sexual harassment will result in discipline, up to and including discharge.

Personal Workshop Preparation #16: Sexual Harassment

You may want to talk to an attorney before writing your own sexual harassment policy, or you could contact the Equal Employment Opportunity Commission (EEOC) to request their guidelines on sexual harassment. It would also be helpful to look at the policies of other companies—the definition of sexual harassment tends to be pretty standard. In describing a procedure for reporting harassment, it is important to give the victim some options. If your procedure states that the victim must report the harassment to his or her supervisor, but the supervisor is the harasser, your system falls apart, and you may be liable.

Following is the sexual harassment policy that Pegasus Computer Systems developed.

Legal Notes

Recent developments in the law indicate that improper conduct may go beyond sexual conduct. Given these changes, your business may want to broaden its policy to prohibit other kinds of harassment, such as harassment based on race, religion, ethnicity, etc. Companies also should establish internal procedures for investigating complaints. These procedures should outline how to maintain records and confidentiality. The procedures you establish, if consistently followed, can help protect your company in the event of a harassment charge against an employee.

THE PURPOSE OF THIS WORKSHOP IS TO DEVELOP A POLICY PROHIBITING SEXUAL HARASSMENT IN THE WORKPLACE.

Personal Workshop #16
Sexual Harassment

Sexual harassment by or of employees of Pegasus Computer Systems will not be tolerated. Such conduct may result in disciplinary actions up to and including termination of employment. Unwelcome sexual advances, requests for sexual favors, and other verbal or physical conduct of a sexual nature constitute sexual harassment when:

- Submission to such conduct is made either explicitly or implicitly a term or condition of employment.

- Submission to or rejection of such conduct is used as the basis for employment decisions.

- Such conduct has the purpose or effect of unreasonably interfering with an individual's work performance.

- Such conduct creates an intimidating, hostile or offensive working environment.

If you encounter such conduct from supervisors, other employees, or clients, you should contact any of the following as you think appropriate:

- Your supervisor or department manager

- Any other manager

- The owner

Complaints will be investigated in a confidential manner. Please do not assume that management is aware of an activity prohibited by this policy. It is your responsibility to bring your complaints and concerns to management's attention so that they can be addressed.

Pegasus wants employees to know that they can work in a secure environment and be treated with dignity. Insulting, degrading, or exploitative treatment of any employee will not be tolerated.

THE PURPOSE OF THIS WORKSHOP IS TO DEVELOP A POLICY PROHIBITING SEXUAL HARASSMENT IN THE WORKPLACE.

Personal Workshop #16
Sexual Harassment

Use this template to write a sexual harassment policy for your company, or develop your own policy.

Sexual Harassment by or of employees of _____ will not be tolerated. Such conduct may result in disciplinary actions up to and including termination of employment. Unwelcome sexual advances, requests for sexual favors, and other verbal or physical conduct of a sexual nature constitute sexual harassment when:

- Submission to such conduct is made either explicitly or implicitly a term or condition of employment.

- Submission to or rejection of such conduct is used as the basis for employment decisions.

- Such conduct has the purpose or effect of unreasonably interfering with an individual's work performance.

- Such conduct creates an intimidating, hostile or offensive working environment.

If you encounter such conduct from supervisors, other employees, or clients, you should contact any of the following as you think appropriate:

- _____

- _____

- _____

Complaints will be investigated in a confidential manner. Please do not assume that management is aware of an activity prohibited by this policy. It is your responsibility to bring your complaints and concerns to management's attention so that they can be addressed.

_____ wants employees to know that they can work in a secure environment and be treated with dignity. Insulting, degrading, or exploitative treatment of any employee will not be tolerated.

Sexual Harassment

Workshop Follow-Up

✔ It is extremely important that sexual harassment be treated seriously by each and every employee of your company. Sexual innuendo or worse is never a laughing matter in the workplace. Your failure to promptly respond to any employee's complaint of harassment, male or female, could seriously jeopardize your defense if the case goes to court, no matter what your written policy. Training of all personnel may be appropriate on this issue.

Hiring Policies: Hiring of Relatives

Companies hold varied views about hiring the relatives of employees. Some have had good experiences with related employees; others base their policy against hiring relatives on bad experiences. Some businesses, such as banks, restrict hiring relatives for security reasons. Defining hiring parameters in a written policy can head off the possibility of future conflicts in your company.

Champy Athletic Products/Terry Rawl: I had to establish a policy about hiring relatives after we had a bad experience hiring the brother of one of our sales reps. Actually, the guy was qualified and did quite well, but one of the other sales reps was upset when we didn't hire his brother when another position opened up. I wrote the following policy to clarify the issue; and I added a policy on spouses, because I could anticipate that issue becoming a problem in the future.

Hiring of Relatives

Champy Athletic Products allows the employment of relatives of employees under these guidelines:

- The relative must be qualified for the position and compete as any other job applicant.

- Individuals are not permitted to directly supervise their own spouses.

Legal Notes

If you choose to limit the hiring of relatives, remember that you cannot discriminate on the basis of marital status. A company may be accused of discrimination if it refuses to hire the spouse of an employee. It may not even be able to stipulate that husband and wife work in separate departments, but it can state that employees may not supervise their spouses.

Promotion Policies

Promotion policies specify the criteria used for promotion decisions in the company, such as performance, length of service, or seniority. A promotion policy should also reiterate that promotional decisions are made without regard to age, sex, religion, race, national origin, color, marital status, or disability.

Physical Examinations

Some organizations require periodic physical exams for their employees. They may be used in these situations:

• *Pre-employment exams*. The Americans with Disabilities Act of 1990 (ADA) prohibits physical exams prior to a job offer. A company must offer an applicant a job before requesting an exam. If the exam indicates the applicant cannot perform the primary functions of the job, the company must try to accommodate the individual. A company can rescind its job offer only if reasonable accommodations cannot be made. Doctors performing these exams need to understand the duties of the job so they can offer an accurate assessment.

• *Periodic physical exams*. Some companies conduct periodic exams for individuals or employee groups based on the nature of their work. For example, periodic and unannounced drug testing may be legal and appropriate for employees who hold positions that put others at risk, such as day care bus drivers.

• *Audiometric testing*. If noise levels in the workplace are a problem, hearing tests may be prudent. The first step is to conduct a noise level survey. Then employees should be given base line tests on which to base future exams. In companies where noise is a fact of life, exit exams may be required to protect the company against future claims of hearing loss.

• *Other tests*. Some organizations, as a service to their employees, periodically offer cholesterol, glaucoma, blood pressure or other health tests. Employee participation in such exams is voluntary.

If you have a policy requiring physical exams for employees, you should state that fact in your employee handbook. Be extremely careful, though, that your policy and the process you set up do not violate the rights of your employees.

FYI

Before you develop policies for your company's compliance with ADA, you are encouraged to study the requirements of the act in more detail. One good resource is the article, "A Small Business Owner's Guide to the Americans with Disabilities Act," in the *Small Business Forum,* Winter 1992/93. For a reprint of this article, call the University of Wisconsin Small Business Development Center at (608) 263-7843. You are also encouraged to check with an attorney regarding your responsibilities as an employer, and to be sure your policy statement and compliance plan are legal.

Accommodation for Disabilities and Compliance with ADA

The Americans with Disabilities Act of 1990 (ADA) went into effect for employers with 15 or more employees in 1994. The purpose of the act is to prevent discrimination against disabled individuals by providing equal access to employment opportunities. Eligible employers should include a statement of compliance in their handbook.

 Neighborhood Medical Clinic/Dr. Carole Stein: I looked at several sample ADA policy statements from other employers. Some of them were quite detailed and included definitions of disabilities and accommodation. The policy we developed for Neighborhood Medical Clinic is pretty simple and straightforward. Because of that, we believe it is important to train our employees regarding ADA compliance, and we are proud of the fact that each of our employees participates in a session on how to communicate with and accommodate people with disabilities, whether they are our patients or fellow employees. Here is our ADA policy statement.

> ### ADA Policy
>
> Neighborhood Medical Clinic does not discriminate or condone discrimination on the basis of disability, as defined in the Americans with Disabilities Act (ADA). We make every effort to reasonably accommodate qualified disabled persons so they can perform the essential functions of the job.

Immigration Issues

Some companies will include a policy statement regarding their compliance with the Immigration Reform and Control Act of 1986 (IRCA) and the documentation required by employees when they start work.

Probation

If your company requires a probationary period for all new employees, describe the terms and conditions of probation in your employee handbook. Be careful to specify that once any probationary period has passed, an employee is not guaranteed permanent employment. In other words, reinforce your "at will" status by noting that, "both during and after probation, employment is terminable at will by either the employee or the employer."

Orientation and Training

If employees are required to participate in orientation or training, or if there are any limits to participation, those policies should be noted. For example, a small business might say, "Employees may attend two outside training sessions each year. All outside training needs to be job-related and must be approved by the employee's supervisor."

Non-Compete Policy and Trade Secrets

Some small businesses require certain employees to sign a non-compete agreement at the time of hire. Non-compete policies are written to protect trade secrets, to prevent conflicts of interest or stealing customers, and to prevent an employee from accepting employment just to learn the trade, and then leaving to directly compete with the company.

Confidentiality

Confidentiality is more of a concern for some businesses than others. Your company's operations will dictate the need for a written policy on this subject.

Personnel matters should never be discussed with outsiders or even beyond the people who need to know within the company. Likewise, information about upcoming business deals, price changes, product development, or even the general financial condition of the company could be devastating if leaked to the wrong people. In general, the business that goes on in any business should not be discussed freely by employees with outsiders. A simple statement regarding confidentiality is a good idea for most businesses.

 **PCB Corporation/Candace and Tony Washington:** The following is the statement regarding confidentiality for our business.

> ### Confidentiality
>
> All matters relating to our business are considered confidential and should not be discussed with anyone outside the business. Misuse or abuse of confidential information is subject to disciplinary action and can result in termination of employment.

Outside Employment

Typically, what an employee does on his "own time" is not a concern of the company. Occasionally, though, an employee may have a second job which creates a conflict of interest or interferes with performance at your company. If that is a concern, you should address it in your employee handbook.

 **Pegasus Computer Systems/Jean Watson:** Last year we had a case where one of our sales reps was doing some independent computer consulting. Because she was using our client lists to generate leads, we felt there was a definite conflict of interest, and we had to ask her to stop or leave her employment with us. As a result of that incident, we developed a policy regarding outside employment.

Outside Employment

Pegasus Computer Systems does not object if you hold an outside job as long as it does not interfere with your position at our company. We reserve the right to ask you to leave your second job if we believe it is interfering with your work performance or if we believe it presents a conflict of interest.

Personal Appearance or Dress Code

The nature of each business determines its need for a dress code. Even if your company nurtures a more casual environment than others in its field, you may still need to define what is appropriate attire for employees.

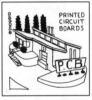

PCB Corporation/Candace and Tony Washington: We decided to incorporate a personal appearance policy for two reasons. First, there are some real safety hazards when machine operators wear loose clothing or dangly jewelry. Second, we want our employees to feel pride in their workplace and in their workmanship. Building that pride is tough when people show up for work wearing dirty jeans and T-shirts with provocative themes. We developed the following policy on personal appearance:

Personal Appearance

Emphasis at PCB Corporation is to maintain a neat, clean appearance. We expect employees to exercise good sense in determining what to wear to work. Appropriate attire depends on the employee's job within these guidelines:

• Clothing must not constitute a safety hazard.

• All employees should practice common sense rules of neatness, good taste and comfort. Provocative clothing is not allowed.

In cases where good taste is not demonstrated, supervisors have the responsibility to point out what is considered inappropriate attire for PCB Corporation.

Gifts and Gratuities

At times, vendors and suppliers, friends of the company or regular customers may bring in gifts at holiday time or as a special thank you. Such gifts typically may include flowers or food items. But in some cases, a gift may seem so expensive or extravagant that an employee feels uncomfortable about accepting it. A written policy can spell out under which circumstances a company will accept or decline a gift.

Champy Athletic Products/Terry Rawl: A few years ago, one of our sales reps was offered a rather extravagant gift—a cruise for two—from a clothing manufacturer that we represent. Although the manufacturer didn't come right out and ask for any favoritism, we had the feeling that was the intent. Since Champy represents several clothing manufacturers, some of them competing, we decided to develop a policy on receiving gifts and gratuities. I think the sales reps actually appreciate the policy—it helps them stay neutral and better represent each of our manufacturers.

Gifts and Gratuities

To eliminate any perception of impropriety, it is the policy of Champy Athletic Products to prohibit any employee from receiving personal gifts from vendors, suppliers or other individuals associated with or doing business with the company without permission from a member of management. Holiday gifts in the form of food items are acceptable if shared with other staff members.

Solicitations and Distributions

A written policy can help control solicitations by employees and materials that are distributed in the workplace. Companies who choose to adopt such a policy must make sure it is enforced consistently.

PCB Corporation/Candace and Tony Washington: For a while last year, it seemed like everybody was bringing in items to sell to other employees—candy bars for school playgrounds, Avon products, and raffle tickets for their service clubs. Most people limited their solicitations to break and lunch periods, but it still got to be a bit much for the employees. It seemed like you couldn't walk into the break room without being hit up for something. We wrote the following policy to end the practice of solicitations at PCB:

Policy on Solicitations

Non-work activities (including solicitations, distribution of written materials, requests for money, collections and ticket sales), are not allowed on company property during regular work hours. Non-work-related literature may not be distributed in the workplace at any time.

Personnel Records

All companies maintain some sort of personnel files on employees. The information in these files is confidential, and in most states employees have the legal right to see these files. Companies may find it helpful to create a procedure for employees who wish to see their own files.

Personal Workshop Preparation #17: Personnel Records

Don't wait for an employee to request a file to develop a policy regarding access. The law specifies that employees can have access, and any unnecessary delays could later cause you problems if a formal complaint is made against your company. Your policy on personnel records should state four things:

- what the personnel record contains;

- your policy regarding confidentiality and security of records;

- the procedure for employee access to the file; and

- the procedure for changing information in the file.

PCB Corporation/Candace and Tony Washington: Following the advice of our attorney, we developed a policy regarding our personnel records. We did so because we realized we had been rather lax in our handling of these important records in the past. Now we are much more careful about what we put into the file and what information is given out. We used the Personal Workshop to develop the policy on the following page.

Personal Notes

_____

_____

_____

_____

FYI

Companies must maintain the confidentiality of all medical records. Medical records need to be kept separate from personnel files, and access to these records must be monitored carefully. Only individuals with a "need to know" should have access to them.

Personal Workshop #17
Personnel Records

Instructions: Write a policy regarding the handling of your personnel records which covers each of the following points:

- what the personnel record contains;

- your policy regarding confidentiality and security of records;

- the procedure for employee access to the file; and

- the procedure for changing information in the file.

PCB Corporation maintains personnel files on each employee. Your personnel file contains documentation regarding all aspects of your tenure with the company. All material in the file is strictly confidential. Access to the file is restricted to those management employees who have a "direct need to know." The only information that will be released in the event of an employer's reference request is your name, dates of employment, and job title. Other employment data or credit information will be released only with your written approval.

The company allows you to view your personnel file upon written request. File access will be allowed during normal business hours and only in the presence of an authorized representative.

It is your responsibility to make sure that all your employment records are kept current. Any change in name, address, etc., should be reported to your supervisor who will assist you in reporting the change to Human Resources. Any change in marital or dependency status or in beneficiary should also be reported so that necessary changes in deductions or benefit plans can be made.

THE PURPOSE OF THIS WORKSHOP IS TO DEVELOP A POLICY REGARDING PERSONNEL FILES.

Personal Workshop #17
Personnel Records

Instructions: Write a policy regarding the handling of your personnel records which covers each of the following points:

- what the personnel record contains;

- your policy regarding confidentiality and security of records;

- the procedure for employee access to the file; and

- the procedure for changing information in the file.

Workshop Follow-Up

 It is very important that you follow your policies on personnel records consistently. Office personnel should be trained regarding the process for viewing records and the release of information to outside parties.

Smoking

More and more organizations are adopting policies which limit smoking on the job. Some companies have no choice—state, federal or local laws dictate their smoking policy. Whatever policy you decide to adopt, you must communicate those rules to employees. They need to know if smoking is allowed and where. Smoke-free companies should also notify applicants of their policy at the time of hire.

Neighborhood Medical Clinic/Dr. Carole Stein: Being a health care facility, we naturally want our employees to support healthful lifestyles. That is why we decided to adopt a strict non-smoking policy. The following is our clinic's policy regarding smoking.

Smoking Policy

Neighborhood Medical Clinic is committed to health and wellness and believes a non-smoking policy will enhance your health and the quality of your work life. With this in mind, smoking will not be permitted on clinic property. All visitors, vendors, and other guests in the facility are asked to comply with the non-smoking policy. Violations of the smoking policy by employees will be handled in the same manner that violations of any company policy are handled up to and including termination.

Alcoholism and Drug Abuse

Due to the increased awareness of drugs (including alcohol) in the workplace, the federal government encourages companies to have written policies to address these issues and to establish their status as a "Drug Free Work Place."

You may want to include in your policy a statement regarding the company's right to search an employee's desk, locker, or work area if you have good reason to believe the employee has drugs or alcohol in his or her possession. Check with an

---

Legal Notes

Some companies have implemented drug testing programs. Because drug testing has legal ramifications, companies are advised to work with a clinic or doctor to set up a program and an attorney to establish proper communication about the program. Testing might be done before employment, after an accident, only with reasonable cause, regularly, or randomly. Advance notification of a drug testing program can help alleviate privacy concerns.

attorney first to find out under what circumstances, if any, you may conduct such a search—typically employers *cannot* search an employee.

Champy Athletics Products/Terry Rawl: The following is our policy statement regarding alcoholism and drug abuse.

Alcoholism and Drug Abuse

Champy Athletic Products recognizes alcoholism and drug abuse as illnesses that may be successfully treated. Our concern with misuse of alcohol or drugs is directed toward the effect on the employee's job performance and behavior, and there is no intention of intruding on the employee's private life. It is important to note that alcoholism or drug abuse may appear in combination with many other kinds of problems. Drug abuse can involve medications such as tranquilizers as well as the more commonly thought of "hard drugs." The following guidelines shall apply to alcoholism and drug abuse:

1. While the principal focus of company policy is on job performance and behavior, it should be clear that any use of alcohol or any illegal possession, use, purchase, or sale of drugs while on duty as an employee or on company premises, is misconduct which may justify immediate dismissal regardless of job performance. Appropriate authorities may be notified in drug cases.

2. A diagnosis of alcoholism or drug dependency for an employee who shows a desire and willingness for treatment will be handled the same way as any other illness. Any employee requiring hospitalization for treatment will be covered within the scope of our present hospital and medical insurance.

3. If the employee's work performance continues to suffer and the employee refuses any outside help, the employee will be subject to termination.

Travel Policies

Companies which require travel by some employees need to specify those policies. Policies might include the procedure for getting approval to travel, approved means of travel (company vehicle, personal vehicle, air travel, etc.), limits on travel expenses (such as per diem allowances, meal and accommodation allowances, travel class, etc.), and procedures for receiving expense reimbursements for travel.

Personal Property

Employees bring personal property to the workplace, including desk items, books, jewelry, purses and wallets. The purpose of this policy is to alert employees to their responsibility in caring for their own personal items.

Pegasus Computer Systems/Jean Watson: We fortunately haven't had a lot of problems with personal property, but occasionally someone will carelessly leave a purse or other item in public sight or sitting on their desk. We wrote the following policy to remind employees that they are responsible for the security of their own things.

Personal Property

Pegasus Computer Systems does not assume responsibility for your personal property. Personal items and property of value should not be left in the building. If you find it necessary to leave valuables in the office, lock them up and take the key with you. Valuables should not be left unattended at your work station at any time.

Telephone Use

Every company should have a policy about answering telephones, since this is an important and frequent form of customer contact. Some companies may also need a policy on personal telephone use.

Personal Workshop Preparation: #18: Telephone Use

Decide first whether you want everyone to answer the telephone in the same way, or whether you will allow some flexibility, as long as certain information is covered and a friendly voice is used. Other issues to cover in your policy are message taking and whether personal or long distance calls are allowed, and if so, the proper procedures for making them.

Neighborhood Medical Clinic/Dr. Carole Stein: We conduct training on telephone techniques, because we believe it is critically important to our success. After all, no matter how good the doctor is, the patient may not come in if he or she is treated rudely on the telephone. We wrote a policy which supports what the employees learn in the training session.

Personal Notes

_____

_____

_____

Personal Workshop #18
Telephone Use

NEIGHBORHOOD
MEDICAL CLINIC

Write a policy regarding telephone use in your company.

When answering the telephone, identify the Neighborhood Medical Clinic and yourself. If answering someone else's phone, always offer to help or take a message. Remember to obtain the caller's name, place of business, if applicable, phone number, and the date and time of the call. If you plan to be away from your phone, let someone know when you expect to return.

It is good business practice to restrict personal phone calls during regular business hours to emergencies only. If it is necessary to make a personal call, please do so during your lunch or coffee breaks; any personal long distance calls should be put on your personal calling card. All personal calls should be kept as brief as possible.

Personal Workshop #18
Telephone Use

Write a policy regarding telephone use in your company.

Workshop Follow-Up

A telephone policy is a good thing to have, but it will never replace a good training session on proper telephone technique. Be sure your policy and training cover the basics of answering the phone and taking messages. These skills are critical to customer service and the success of any business.

Parking

Parking policies might specify where employees may park, restrictions on parking, costs of parking (if applicable), etc. In some cases, free parking may be listed as an employee benefit.

Keys and Identification Cards

Policies sometimes describe who is eligible to carry company keys and the checkout procedure for keys. Some companies require employees to carry or display an ID card. The employee policy might specify how those cards are to be issued or used.

Bulletin Boards

Many companies use bulletin boards to display required government posters, but they are also a convenient place to post information about company events, programs, policies and job openings. A bulletin board policy tells who is authorized to post notices on the company bulletin board, and what types of notices are allowed. If notices are restricted to company business only, your company needs to state that policy and enforce it.

PCB Corporation/Candace and Tony Washington: It is important that we control space on the bulletin boards, since it is one of our primary ways of communicating with our employees. Also, we are required by law to display certain items, and if those items get covered up by personal notices, we could be in trouble. Here is our bulletin board policy.

Bulletin Boards

Information of general interest to all employees appears on the bulletin boards located in the break room and outside the main office door. You may have personal material posted on the bulletin boards after it has been submitted and approved by the Office Manager. All notices will be dated and removed after one month.

FYI

Bulletin boards should be placed in conspicuous places where employees have ample access. More than one bulletin board may be necessary; or you might want to have one bulletin board for required government posters and company information and a second for employees to put up personal notices.

Open Door Policy

An open door policy can encourage employees to come to management with complaints, problems and questions. Employees may feel uncomfortable doing so unless company policy ensures that they will face no negative ramifications. Establishing such a policy may resolve problems internally and head off an employee's decision to seek outside help to resolve a problem.

Champy Athletic Products/Terry Rawl: We are a pretty close-knit group, and so I want employees to know they can take up any concerns they might have with management. On the other hand, we don't want to encourage people to go over their supervisors' heads with every little complaint. I developed the following Open Door Policy to make this point to the employees.

Open Door Policy

We have an open door policy which encourages any employee to discuss work-related problems with management. You are encouraged to take any issues you wish to discuss to your immediate supervisor first. Your supervisor will treat your complaint or problem with respect. If your supervisor cannot resolve the problem or if you feel uncomfortable discussing the issue with your supervisor, you should request a meeting with another member of management on an appointment basis. These individuals will try to work out a satisfactory resolution to the problem, or will direct you to someone else who can help.

Follow-Up on General Employment Policies

You have just written several policies that fit into the category of **General Employment Policies**. At this point, you may want to forward your drafted policies for this section to a review committee for their input. Or, if you prefer, wait until you have drafted policies for each section of the employee handbook before you begin the policy review process.

III. Policies about Work Schedules

This section of your handbook should clarify policies regarding work scheduling. This category of policies should be particularly helpful to new employees.

To allow yourself maximum flexibility, you may want to add this line to your work schedules policy: "Production or work demands may lead the company to vary work hours."

FYI

Regular Work Hours and Schedule Setting

If your company has varying work schedules and different shifts, it is helpful to define those hours in a written policy. Also, many retail establishments set schedules on a weekly, bi-weekly, or monthly basis. The procedure for setting schedules and/or for changing them should be described in your handbook.

Personal Workshop Preparation #19: Regular Work Hours

Your policy should describe the hours of operation for the business and the usual work hours for the employees. If there is a special procedure or pecking order for setting work schedules, be sure to include that information in your policy.

Pegasus Computer Systems/Jean Watson: We have different work schedules for our sales associates and service technicians, which are set by the sales manager and service manager respectively. Our policy on work hours tries to describe the process for the employees.

THE PURPOSE OF THIS WORKSHOP IS TO DRAFT A POLICY REGARDING REGULAR WORK HOURS AND/OR SCHEDULE SETTING FOR YOUR BUSINESS.

Personal Workshop #19
Regular Work Hours

Draft a policy regarding regular work hours and schedule setting below.

Pegasus Computer Systems is open from 8 a.m.–9 p.m., Monday through Saturday, and noon–6 p.m. on Sundays. Work schedules for sales associates will be set by the sales manager on a bi-weekly basis and in consideration of advanced approval for vacations or other personal time off. Sales associates will normally work no more than 40 hours per week. Service Technicians will normally work 8 a.m.–5 p.m., Monday - Friday, but will rotate Saturday and on-call emergency evening and weekend repair service. The service manager coordinates schedules for all service technicians.

Management reserves the right to change work schedules as needed to meet customer demand.

THE PURPOSE OF THIS WORKSHOP IS TO DRAFT A POLICY REGARDING REGULAR WORK HOURS AND/OR SCHEDULE SETTING FOR YOUR BUSINESS.

Personal Workshop #19
Regular Work Hours

Draft a policy regarding regular work hours and schedule setting below.

Breaks

Some employers have the mistaken impression that they are required by law to provide rest breaks for employees, but such laws vary from state to state. Breaks are required by law for minors everywhere, however, and companies employing young people should check the appropriate statutes. Most companies encourage breaks for all of their employees, since a "refreshed" employee tends to be more alert and productive.

 Pegasus Computer Systems/Jean Watson: As with any retail business, it isn't always possible to get away to take a break. We encourage our employees to take breaks, though, and we try to be flexible about scheduling breaks—that way our employees tend to be more flexible about missing breaks, and everybody benefits. The following is the policy we adopted regarding breaks.

> ### Breaks
> Breaks and lunch periods need to be coordinated with your supervisor to ensure adequate coverage for your department. Break times may change as our needs change. We encourage all employees to observe these break times. Extended breaks are not allowed, and breaks cannot be banked to be used for time off.

Attendance Policy

Attendance policies and the company's philosophy on absenteeism and tardiness are common topics in employee manuals. Be careful in setting any attendance policy—once a company establishes an attendance policy, it is difficult to allow exceptions. If you want to allow your supervisors discretion in dealing with employees, you need to keep your attendance policy loose.

Some companies find it sufficient to state that employees are expected to fulfill their work schedules and that excessive absenteeism will result in disciplinary action. This philosophy allows companies to treat each case individually, but employers should develop a consistent approach to dealing with tardiness and absenteeism. Companies should train supervisors on consistent and acceptable approaches to dealing with excessively late and/or absent employees.

Other provisions you may want to include in an attendance policy include the following:

Legal Note

Whatever attendance policy a company chooses, it cannot include absences regulated by state and federal laws providing for family and medical leaves. Days off allowed by these laws are protected, and employers cannot discipline workers who take them.

Doctor's return to work verification: Companies may require a doctor's return to work verification when an employee has been away from work for several days due to illness. Here is an example:

If you are absent due to illness for more than three days, we may require a doctor's return to work verification. This verification is to establish that you are physically able to return to work.

This provision accomplishes two purposes. It confirms that employees are able to return to work, and it may discourage them from staying off the job when they are able to work.

Advance notice: An employer should inform workers of their responsibility to notify the company of an absence, as in this sample policy:

All absences which are not prearranged must be reported prior to your starting time. You are required to speak personally to your supervisor about the absence, if possible. Employees who fail to report for work for three consecutive work days without notice have voluntarily ended their employment.

Some companies set absolute standards for attendance. In other words, disciplinary action will follow if an employee fails to meet the set standards. Your policy might specify, for example, that employees will be terminated if they are absent 10 or more days in a calendar year, or that employees will receive a written warning if they are tardy twice in one month.

Some policies differentiate between excused and unexcused absences. Such policies require that someone judge whether an absence is excused or not, a practice which may be subject to inconsistencies in the way different departments and/or supervisors deal with their employees. If you decide to establish this type of policy, you should train your supervisors to ensure that they enforce rules consistently and follow through on discipline when an employee violates the standard.

Personal Workshop Preparation #20: Attendance Policy

Whatever attendance policy you establish will need to be followed consistently. It is not okay to apply the policy one way for one employee and another way for another employee, even if that second employee is an otherwise stellar employee.

FYI

In recent years, a "no-fault" approach to absenteeism has become increasingly popular. The philosophy behind this policy is that employees are adults and will not miss work without a good reason. Employees are simply allowed a certain number of absences each year (excepting pre-approved vacation leave or disability leave), and no one judges the validity of those absences or decides whether they are excused or unexcused. Every absence or tardiness is tallied, and after a set number, the employee faces disciplinary action.

Unless absenteeism is a major problem in your company, try to keep your policy as simple and flexible as possible.

Neighborhood Medical Clinic/Dr. Carole Stein: Our goal is always to get our employees to think about how their work behavior will affect our customers and the other employees. We tried to express that when we wrote an attendance policy for the clinic. We also wanted to keep it flexible. Here is what we decided on:

THE PURPOSE OF THIS WORKSHOP IS TO DRAFT AN ATTENDANCE POLICY.

Personal Workshop #20
Attendance Policy

Draft an attendance policy for your business in the space below.

> When you are absent, it means extra work for someone else, and in turn when others are absent, it means more work for you. You should be interested in and responsible for holding absenteeism to an absolute minimum. When you know you are going to be absent from work, or unavoidably late, it is your responsibility to notify your supervisor before or as soon as the clinic opens. If you cannot notify your supervisor, you are expected to have your family or a friend call for you. Failure to do so may result in dismissal. Failure to notify or report for two consecutive workdays shall be deemed to be a voluntary termination.
>
> Absence and tardiness become a part of your work record and are reviewed before promotions and salary increases are considered. Absences that are not approved by your supervisor can result in disciplinary action up to and including termination.

THE PURPOSE OF THIS WORKSHOP IS TO DRAFT AN ATTENDANCE POLICY.

Personal Workshop #20
Attendance Policy

Draft an attendance policy for your business in the space below.

Workshop Follow-Up

If you later discover that people are taking advantage of the flexibility you have tried to preserve in your attendance policy, you may have to tighten it. Only do this, though, if the problem cannot be handled on a case-by-case basis. The tighter your policy, the more difficult it is for supervisors and employees to follow it.

Perfect Attendance Recognition Policies

Some companies find it helpful to reward employees for perfect attendance. This is a more common practice in companies that experience high levels of absenteeism and turnover. Employees who complete a set period of perfect attendance may be presented with dinner certificates, tickets to a sporting event, time off or some other reward.

Weather

Company policy should spell out if absences caused by bad weather or other emergencies will count on attendance records.

Pegasus Computer Systems/Jean Watson: It seemed funny that, no matter how bad the weather, some people were always at work on time, and some people never seemed to be able to get there. We developed the following policy to clarify the procedures related to inclement weather.

Inclement Weather

It is your responsibility to report to work whenever the store is open for a normal workday. In order to be fair to everyone, we will be unable to pay those who fail to report because of weather conditions. Vacation time may be used for any missed time, provided you have the approval of your supervisor.

Follow-Up on Work Scheduling Policies

You have just drafted policies related to work scheduling. These policies can now be combined into a section for your employee manual entitled **Work Schedules.** They are now ready for the review process.

IV. Compensation and Benefits Policies

You need to inform employees about compensation policies and benefit programs offered by your company. Employees want to know when and how they will be paid, whether they qualify for benefits and what those programs entail.

Compensation and Wages

Among the first things new employees want to know is how much they will earn and when they will be paid. Policies about compensation and wages should clarify those issues.

Legal Notes

The Federal Fair Labor Standards Act regulates minimum wage. In addition, many states have laws requiring minimum wages or otherwise regulating how employees are to be paid. If you are not familiar with the laws regulating compensation in your state, contact your attorney. Remember that you must be careful about using the word "salary" in your employee handbook. Even though you may pay some employees on an annual salary basis, you do not want to include anything in your handbook that might be interpreted as a promise of continued or permanent employment.

Personal Workshop Preparation #21: Compensation/Wages

When you write your policy regarding compensation and wages, be sure to include these things:

- information about pay periods and paydays;

- special instructions for getting on the payroll or recording hours worked;

- information about deductions from the paycheck; and

- information about how pay rates or salaries are determined.

In some cases, a company will attach a chart which shows pay rates for certain job classifications and/or length of service.

PCB Corporation/Candace and Tony Washington: We didn't think our pay policies were complicated, until we started to write it all down for the employee handbook. We are hoping that the policy we developed will cut down on the questions from our employees.

Personal Notes

_____

_____

_____

_____

Legal Notes

Your policies regarding overtime pay and compensatory time are regulated by the Federal Fair Labor Standards Act and various state statutes. Typically, employers are not required to pay overtime unless an employee exceeds 40 hours per week; and some establishments are exempt from overtime. Also, certain employees (typically management and professional staff) are classified as "exempt" from overtime pay. In other words, exempt employees are expected to put in as much time as it takes to do the job on whatever their regular salary is — no overtime pay. Check with your attorney for specifics.

Personal Workshop #21
Compensation/Wages

Draft a policy regarding compensation and wages in the space below. Be sure to include in your policy, if applicable:

- information about pay periods and paydays;

- special instructions for getting on the payroll or recording hours worked;

- information about deductions from the paycheck; and

- information about how pay rates or salaries are determined.

Payday is every other Friday. For full-time employees, your check will reflect payment of regular hours through Friday of the current two-week period. However, since each payroll is prepared several days in advance, any exceptions to a normal pay period, such as overtime or leave without pay that is submitted on an individual time card, may be reflected on a later paycheck. If payday falls on a holiday, you will receive your pay prior to the holiday. You may receive your paycheck or have your pay deposited directly to a checking or savings account.

Time cards for part-time and on-call employees are due each non-payday Friday by 5 p.m. and must reflect the hours worked in the prior two weeks. Your check will be issued one week later on the regular payday.

Certain deductions from your pay are required by law, such as federal and state income taxes, Social Security taxes, and any local taxes, if applicable. Other payroll deductions may be authorized by you and may include such items as government savings bonds or contributions to the United Way. Your paycheck stub will reflect all information about your pay and deductions including current and year-to-date figures. If you have any questions concerning your paycheck, see your supervisor or stop by the main office.

Your rate of pay is determined by the job you are doing, the market rate for similar work and your performance. Your rate of pay will also be reviewed annually. Based on company performance and your individual performance, your rate of pay may be adjusted.

THE PURPOSE OF THIS WORKSHOP IS TO WRITE A POLICY REGARDING EMPLOYEE COMPENSATION.

Personal Workshop #21
Compensation/Wages

Draft a policy regarding compensation and wages in the space below. Be sure to include in your policy, if applicable:

- information about pay periods and paydays;

- special instructions for getting on the payroll or recording hours worked;

- information about deductions from the paycheck; and

- information about how pay rates or salaries are determined.

FYI

In addition to the policies printed in your employee handbook, a one-page summary of company benefits is an excellent tool, not only for recruiting, but also as a quick reference for current employees. The benefit summary should briefly describe each benefit, as well as employee eligibility requirements and premiums. If employees need more specific information, they should be encouraged to consult plan documents.

Overtime Pay and Compensatory ("Comp") Time

To avoid overtime pay, be sure to write a policy that controls who can approve overtime work. And, if it is possible for your business to require employees to use "comp" time in lieu of paying overtime, this might be a more economical option.

In addition, companies need to decide how to pay employees if they work on a holiday or a Sunday. Some companies pay at 1-1/2 times the base rate. Others pay twice the base rate on Sundays and three times the base rate on holidays. In the case of floating holidays, some companies give employees the option to choose another day off; therefore, they are paid base rate for the day they work.

Some organizations consider holidays and vacations as time worked. If a holiday falls during the week and the employee works four hours on Saturday, the employee will receive 40 hours at his/her base rate and four hours at time and a half. If a holiday is not considered as time worked for overtime purposes, the four hours would be paid at the base rate of pay.

Pegasus Computer Systems/Jean Watson: Being in the retail business, it is almost impossible to avoid overtime at certain times of the year. However, whenever possible, we give our employees compensatory time instead of overtime pay. Our exempt employees (management) are expected to put in as many hours as it takes to get their job done without overtime pay. We included that information in our policy to avoid any misunderstandings.

Overtime Pay and "Comp" Time

If you are eligible for overtime, you will be paid straight time for any hours you work under 40 hours a week. You will be paid time-and-a-half for the time you work over 40 hours. Whenever possible, employees are encouraged to take compensatory time off for hours worked beyond their normal schedule. "Comp" time must be taken within one week of the overtime worked.

If you are considered "nonexempt," you must receive prior approval to work overtime. If you are considered "exempt" under the Federal Wage and Hour Law, these policies of overtime pay and compensatory time do not apply. If there is any question as to your exempt or nonexempt status, please contact your supervisor.

FYI

When you describe benefit highlights in your employee handbook, be sure to include a disclaimer referring workers to their plan documents for more details. Here is an example of such a disclaimer: "The material provided in this handbook is only for your information. Benefits are described in summary form and are governed by the various plan documents and policies. The company reserves the right to change or revise any of the described benefits at any time with or without advance notice."

On-Call Employee Pay

Some organizations may need to call in off-duty employees to handle unexpected problems. Companies who do so should outline pay provisions for those situations. Some companies pay employees a minimum of four hours for call-ins even though the employee may work less than that. Others pay employees a minimum amount of time if they report to work and then are sent home because of a company emergency, adverse weather or other circumstance.

Garnishment

Sometimes all or a portion of an employee's wages must be automatically deducted from his or her pay due to a court order. This is called garnishment.

A brief statement regarding wage garnishment may be appropriate for your handbook.

Champy Athletic Products/Terry Rawl: This is another of those policies we developed out of necessity—one of our employees had his wages garnished for back child support. To protect the company, we put together the following policy.

> ### Garnishments
>
> You will be notified immediately upon the receipt of a wage assignment or garnishment. You are expected to relieve the company from its obligation immediately by obtaining a release of any wage assignments or garnishments.

Legally Required Benefits

These benefits are required by law:

- Social security (FICA)
- Workers compensation
- Unemployment compensation

Some organizations include information about these benefits in their handbooks, and others choose not to because, as legal requirements, they are not actually

---

FYI

In addition to including information about benefits in the employee handbook, some companies also distribute an annual benefit statement that details the costs of employee benefit plans paid by both the employee and the company. Employees rarely realize the total cost of the benefit package. Even though they may expect the company to provide these benefits, your employees may better appreciate their value if they know how much they cost. If rising insurance costs force the company to raise employees' premiums, workers can at least see that the company is sharing the financial burden. That knowledge may reduce complaints about premium increases.

company benefits. However, employees need to know that their employers finance these programs. Some companies make that point by including workers compensation in their safety policy and unemployment compensation in their general termination policy.

Employer-Offered Benefits

Organizations offer a wide variety of benefit choices and options. The benefits your company chooses to offer will depend upon its size, its financial resources, competition and industry standards, and the standards of your locale. For companies that must compete for employees and have a hard time recruiting, a selection of popular benefits can increase the success rate of recruiting and retaining employees. However, most small businesses cannot afford to offer a wide variety of benefit options.

Leave

Your company must determine its policies regarding vacations, sick leave, and other reasons for company-provided time off. Your policy statements should also clarify who is eligible for these benefits.

Holidays

Holiday schedules are dictated by law, local custom, clients' and owners' preferences and other factors.

Personal Workshop Preparation #22: Paid Holidays

The holiday schedule and whether or not those holidays are paid depends upon the industry standard as well as law and local custom. To find out what is standard for your type of business in your area, check with some business colleagues. As you write your policy, consider how holidays which fall on weekends will be handled, as well.

Neighborhood Medical Clinic/Dr. Carole Stein: As well as the usual information about holidays, we needed to include in our policy how people would be paid if they were required to work on a holiday. Our clients don't limit their illnesses and accidents to non-holidays, nor can we limit our services. Using the Personal Workshop that follows, we developed a holiday policy for the clinic.

THE PURPOSE OF THIS WORKSHOP IS TO WRITE A POLICY REGARDING PAID HOLIDAYS.

Personal Workshop #22
Paid Holidays

NEIGHBORHOOD
MEDICAL CLINIC

Write a policy below which lists holidays observed, whether they are paid or not, and any special information regarding eligibility or holiday pay.

Neighborhood Medical Clinic observes seven scheduled paid holidays each year as follows:

New Year's Day . . . . January 1
Memorial Day. . . . . Last Monday of May
Independence Day . . . . July 4
Labor Day. . . . . First Monday of September
Thanksgiving and the Friday following: Christmas Day
Holidays falling on Saturday will be observed on Friday.
Holidays falling on Sunday will be observed on Monday.

If employees are required to work on a holiday, they will be paid their regular rate plus holiday pay. Part-time employees are eligible for pro-rated holiday pay provided the holiday falls on a day when they would normally work.

THE PURPOSE OF THIS WORKSHOP IS TO WRITE A POLICY REGARDING PAID HOLIDAYS.

Personal Workshop #22
Paid Holidays

Write a policy below which lists holidays observed, whether they are paid or not, and any special information regarding eligibility or holiday pay.

Vacation

Your vacation policy should describe who is eligible for vacation and when it may be taken. Eligibility and extent of paid vacation benefits are often based on the employee's classification and length of employment. Vacation policies might also specify any restrictions for banking vacation leave, or any limits on taking vacation leave. For example, some companies do not allow any employee to be gone on vacation for more than two consecutive weeks; or a company might require all employees to take vacation at the same time—a company-wide vacation shut-down.

Personal Workshop Preparation #23: Vacation

If you offer paid vacation as a benefit, you will want to be sure that your written policy includes any restrictions on eligibility. If you have different vacation benefits for management and non-management, you should write two separate policies to avoid any misunderstandings about eligibility or limitations.

Champy Athletic Products/Terry Rawl: Our vacation policy seems a little complicated, but we sat down before we wrote it and listed all of the questions we regularly get about vacations, and then tried to address those questions in our policy. Here's what we came up with:

THE PURPOSE OF THIS WORKSHOP IS TO WRITE A VACATION POLICY FOR YOUR COMPANY.

Personal Workshop #23
Vacation

Write a vacation policy below which describes eligibility and any special limitations for taking vacation.

All regular full-time employees will receive vacation with pay based on their length of service with the company as follows:

Length of Employment	Vacation Earned
1–5 years	10 days
6–14 years	15 days
15 years and over	20 days

Employees accumulate 1/12 of their annual vacation each month. Vacation leave must be earned before it can be taken. New employees are eligible for vacation after six months of full-time employment. Vacation leave must be scheduled with your supervisor to ensure the smooth operation of your department. When a company-observed holiday falls within a vacation period, it does not count as a day of vacation. Up to five days of vacation may be carried over from one year into the next year. All remaining unused days each year will be forfeited. Any unused vacation at date of termination, retirement, or permanent disability will be paid upon such occurrence.

Part-time and temporary employees are not eligible for paid vacation. If a temporary or part-time employee changes to continuous full-time status, the effective date of the change is used to compute the vacation benefit.

THE PURPOSE OF THIS WORKSHOP IS TO WRITE A VACATION POLICY FOR YOUR COMPANY.

Personal Workshop #23

Vacation

Write a vacation policy below which describes eligibility and any special limitations for taking vacation.

Sick Leave and Personal Leave

Companies handle sick days in different ways. In organizations with no defined program, employees are not paid if they are absent, unless they are covered by a disability plan that starts after they have been off work for a period of time. Companies establishing a sick leave policy typically require the employee to call in if ill. In some cases, employees must accrue sick leave before they receive the benefit; in others, companies just allow a certain number of days per year which can be taken whenever needed. Some employers require a doctor's verification for absences of more than a few days.

It is becoming more common for employers to allow employees to use sick leave to care for a sick family member. If you wish to allow for such personal leave, your policy should spell out any limits.

Personal Workshop Preparation #24: Sick Leave

If you offer paid sick leave as a benefit, you will want to describe employee eligibility for that benefit and any limitations on using the leave. Also, if employees are allowed to use sick leave for circumstances other than personal illness, describe those circumstances in your policy.

Champy Athletic Products/Terry Rawl: We have never had trouble with our people abusing sick leave, since they are in sales and know that their success depends on them being in the field. Also, since our sales reps do so much of their work at home anyway, it wasn't necessary to have a personal leave policy. If a sales rep has to stay home with a sick child, they just make phone calls and do paperwork from home—no problem.

Legal Notes

Leave of Absence policies must comply with state and federal Family and Medical Leave laws, which state that a leave must be granted for a birth or adoption of a child or for serious personal or family illness. In general, these laws cover employees who have been employed for at least 12 months. Employers with 25 or more employees need to have a policy statement to cover birth and/or adoption, serious illness of parent, child and spouse, and personal serious illness. Businesses which employ 50 or more may have additional requirements. Federal and state laws differ; employees must apply the most generous provision of each law. In addition, under state or federal law in certain circumstances, an employee can substitute paid or unpaid leave of any other type provided by the employer. Check with an attorney to be sure your Leave of Absence policy complies with federal and state laws.

THE PURPOSE OF THIS WORKSHOP IS TO WRITE A SICK LEAVE POLICY FOR YOUR COMPANY.

Personal Workshop #24
Sick Leave

Use the space below to draft a sick leave policy for your company.

Full-time employees accumulate one sick day per full month of employment for a maximum of 12 days per year. You must have completed three months of continuous, full-time service to be eligible to use your sick leave. Unused sick leave can be carried into future years and accumulated to a maximum of 70 days. You may convert any unused vacation if your sick day accumulation is exhausted.

THE PURPOSE OF THIS WORKSHOP IS TO WRITE A SICK LEAVE POLICY FOR YOUR COMPANY.

Personal Workshop #24
Sick Leave

Use the space below to draft a sick leave policy for your company.

In addition to traditional family members, a company may be asked to consider funeral time and pay for live-in companions and other people significant to employees. You may want to address those relationships in your policy; or leave it to the discretion of the supervisor.

FYI

Jury Duty

The law requires employers to grant leave to employees for jury duty. Since jurors are paid, company policies vary on paying employees for this time off. In some cases the company will make up the difference between the regular rate of pay and jury duty pay for a specified period of time. In other cases, the company continues to issue regular pay checks to the employee, and the employee is required to release to the company the jury fees paid.

Pegasus Computer Systems/Jean Watson: I decided to write a fairly generous policy for jury duty. I personally think it is a very important obligation, and I don't want our employees to feel they are being punished if they are called on to serve. On average, jury duty pay has only cost us about a week's wages per year.

Jury Duty

Full-time employees who are called for jury duty during regular work hours will be granted time off, provided proper verification of the days of service is furnished by the Clerk of Courts. The company will make up the difference between the regular rate of pay and the jury duty pay for up to 30 days per year. You are expected to report for work if a reasonable amount of time remains in the regular workday. After 30 days, employees may take an unpaid leave of absence until their jury duty obligation is fulfilled. Verification of jury duty pay must be submitted to the payroll department before employees will receive reimbursement.

Funeral/Bereavement Leave

Funeral leave is a common employee benefit. Policies vary on matters of when and for whom bereavement leave is paid. Some policies are specific, while others are general and leave the decision up to management.

Neighborhood Medical Clinic/Dr. Carole Stein: I checked around town to see what sort of bereavement leave other clinics offered. The policy on the following page was developed after looking at several samples.

FYI

An alternative to offering separate leave policies for vacation, illness, and/or personal time off is to have a single policy for paid time off. In essence, this benefit allows employees a set number of days off each year to be used as needed by the employee, whether for illness, vacation, or to go to a family event. The advantage of this policy is employee choice and privacy. It also simplifies record-keeping for the employer. Except when used for day-to-day illness, paid time off needs to be approved in advance by management, to assure the smooth running of the company.

> ### Funeral/Bereavement Leave
>
> When a death occurs in your family, notify your supervisor or manager to request time off. If you are a full-time employee and a death occurs in your immediate family (father, mother, brother, sister, child, spouse, father-in-law, mother-in-law), time off with pay will be permitted at the discretion of the manager. This is generally limited to no more than from the day of death through the day of the funeral. In the event circumstances require additional time off, use of vacation days or general leave of absence should be requested.
>
> For close relatives (grandparents, uncles, aunts, grandchildren, etc.), or co-workers, the clinic generally allows time off to attend the funeral only. Part-time employees are not paid for time off as a result of a funeral.

Military Duty

Although an employer must give an employee time off for military duty, the employee must apply for the leave under requirements set forth by federal and state law. The employer must decide if the leave will be paid or unpaid. Some employers make up the difference between pay and military pay for a specified period of time. Employers cannot ask employees to use up their vacation pay for military duty leave.

PCB Corporation/Candace and Tony Washington: We have a couple of employees who are in the Army Reserve, and so are not always available for weekend work and are gone for a bit each summer. We wrote the following policy to address military leave.

> ### Military Leave
>
> Properly authorized military leave grants time off from work without pay for the purpose of performing required military duty. Employees entering the service or reporting for training duty are to advise their supervisor of entry or reporting dates and provide a copy of written military orders. Employees who fail to properly notify PCB Corporation as noted above may lose the protection of the Veteran's Re-employment Act.

Legal Notes

Federal law provides for veteran's re-employment rights. The statute defines three major categories of military service: Active Duty; Initial Active Duty Training; and Training Duty. Each category has separate rights and restrictions. The nature of the orders under which the duty is performed determines which category of rights and eligibility requirements apply. Consult an attorney for specifics.

Leave of Absence

Employees may need time off for personal reasons, such as personal or family illness or special hardship. Companies establishing a leave of absence policy need to consider these issues:

1. What will be the maximum allowable leave of absence?

2. Will the company continue benefits during leave, and for how long? Will the employee or the employer pay benefit premiums during the leave?

3. How will the company handle work restrictions when the employee is able to return to work?

PCB Corporation/Candace and Tony Washington: Because of the size of our company, we usually receive at least one request for a leave of absence every year. This policy, while complicated, has really worked well to protect both the employee's rights and PCB's.

Leave of Absence

A general leave of absence is defined as authorized time off from work without pay for a specified period which exceeds five consecutive workdays but does not exceed three months duration. Employees who take an approved leave of absence will not lose their employment status. Employees must have completed at least 12 months of continuous full-time service to request a leave.

Employee requests for leave are to be submitted in writing to your supervisor and should include the beginning date of the leave, the return to work date, and the specific reason for the leave. The following criteria will be considered by management in deciding whether or not to grant leave: return to work after the leave; work performance and attendance record; ability of remaining staff to cover duties during the leave; and the total length of the requested leave.

The company will pay its portion of all insurance and retirement expenses which occur during an approved leave period. The employee must pay or authorize payment for all deductions for which the employee is responsible. Failure to pay deductions will result in cancellation of the benefits for nonpayment of premium. Employees on approved leave of absence will continue to accrue vacation and sick leave, but these benefits can be used only after the employee returns to work on a continuous, full-time basis. Any office or holiday closing occurring during a leave is considered as part of the leave time and is not compensable. Any change in salary will not become effective for an employee on leave until the employee returns to work on a continuous, full-time basis.

Employees who are granted leaves are to contact their supervisor at least two weeks prior to the return to work date and confirm their return as scheduled. Failure to confirm and/or return to work on the approved return to work date could result in termination of employment. You may return to work earlier than the approved return to work date with the approval of your supervisor, and in the case of medical leave, a release to return to work from the attending physician. Such a release must detail any or all work restrictions. The company will try to accommodate these restrictions, but cannot guarantee a job if the employee is unable to perform the essential functions of the job.

If you are unable to return to work as scheduled because of a disability, you must notify your supervisor and submit written proof of disability from the attending physician. Failure to notify your supervisor, submit written proof of disability, or promptly return to work may result in denial of benefits and/or termination of employment.

Failure to return to work at the end of the leave of absence will be considered a voluntary resignation. PCB Corporation will attempt to place an employee returning from leave in the same or equivalent job, but does not guarantee return to the same job as held before commencement of the leave.

Health and Life Insurance

Although insurance companies and benefit plan administrators are required to provide employees with a summary plan description and/or a plan document, these documents are not always user-friendly. For this reason, you may want to provide an overview of these benefits in your employee handbook. Benefit descriptions in employee handbooks should only cover benefit highlights and leave the details for plan documents.

Short- or Long-term Disability Benefits

As with insurance benefits, any description of disability benefits in your employee handbook should direct employees to the plan documents for details.

Retirement Plans and Annuity Options

If your small business offers a retirement plan or annuity options for employees, those policies and employee eligibility should be described in your handbook.

Leave of absence policies also apply to workers compensation leaves. In other words, if you have a defined maximum leave, this applies to workers' compensation. If employees exceed this leave, they are taken off the payroll. However, the company must consider re-employment when the employee is ready to return to work. If the employee can do the job, the employer must hire him or her back. Failure to do so may result in a penalty under the "failure to return to work" provision of the workers' compensation law. If the employee is unable to do his or her former job or another job in the company, the company is under no obligation to rehire him or her. Companies should carefully investigate and document this process because it most likely will be critically reviewed in a workers' compensation hearing.

FYI

Educational Assistance Programs

Some employers offer educational assistance programs to encourage employees to further their education and advance their careers. If you decide to provide time off for study or full or partial tuition reimbursement, your policy statement should describe any limitations. For example, you may want to require that the course or program be job or work related. And, you may want to require a passing grade for tuition reimbursement.

Follow-Up to Compensation and Benefits Policies

Have you created policies for all the items you checked on the checklist relating to compensation and benefits? These policies can now be combined into a section of your employee handbook and are ready for the review process.

V. Safety Policies

You will be given the opportunity to develop policies regarding safety in this section of Challenge 3. Depending on the type of business you own, this section in your handbook could be detailed and complex, or it could be rather simple.

Prudent companies devise written safety policies to define their philosophy and commitment to providing a safe work environment. These policies should outline procedures to follow and should be designed to limit an organization's liability. Many safety procedures are defined by law—be sure that you understand your legal requirements and use them as the basis for writing policies regarding safety.

OSHA Compliance

A general statement about your company's desire to ensure the safety of its employees and to comply with the standards of the Occupational Safety and Health Administration (OSHA) may be appropriate. Include in your policy statement an invitation to employees to notify management of any concerns they have regarding their safety in the workplace.

General Safety Procedures

The policies you establish will vary depending on your business and working conditions. General safety procedures for a manufacturing facility should be distinctly different than those for a business office, for example. In both cases, employees

FYI

Companies cannot treat pregnancy leave differently than other medical leave requests. Pregnancy is legally considered a medical disability if the employee has medical verification. Companies should ask for the same medical certification as for any other medical leave of absence. And if your company provides short-term disability benefits, those benefits may also apply to pregnant employees.

should be made aware of safety procedures and their responsibilities in carrying out safe work practices.

 **PCB Corporation/Candace and Tony Washington:** Safety is a critical issue for any manufacturer. In addition to the policy on safety, our safety officer holds regular training sessions for employees. We keep this safety policy on our company bulletin boards, and we have implemented a suggestion program for making operations safer.

Safety Procedures

PCB is committed to providing every employee with a safe working environment. We make every effort to comply with relevant federal and state occupational health and safety laws. **It is the obligation of each employee to observe all safety regulations and to use safe practices at all times.** Here are some general safety rules:

- Think before taking any chances. Our company is only as safe as the people who work in it.

- Be alert. Inattention is a major cause of accidents.

- Walk a safe route at all times and do not take shortcuts. Follow marked aisles and do not run.

- Remember that practical jokes can hurt people. Running, wrestling, scuffling, sparring, throwing objects and horseplay will not be tolerated.

- Be sure that hand trucks are correctly loaded and used properly. Never ride on forklifts or hand trucks as a passenger. Watch where and how you drive lift trucks and use the horn.

- Do not tamper with fire extinguishers. Report immediately the use of any fire extinguisher to your supervisor. Find out where fire extinguishers are located.

- Do not smoke. Smoking is only permitted in a few designated areas. Discard your smoking materials only in containers provided for this purpose.

- Keep your work area clean at all times. Neatness makes a company safe.

- Do not touch or talk to a person who is working on a machine. If necessary, wait until the machine is turned off.

- Do not bypass or remove any safety guards. These precautions are on machinery for our safety and are often required by law.

- Always wear required protective headgear, eyewear, or earplugs.

- Turn off the machine when you are cleaning it or making any adjustments.

- Report all injuries. If an injury occurs, immediately notify your supervisor or another member of management.

- Watch what your wear. Jewelry, neckties and other dangling items must not be worn in the plant; they can easily catch in the machines and are likely to cause serious accidents. You must have long hair tied back in a net or on top of your head. High heels, open toed shoes, open heeled shoes, loose clothing, halter tops and shorts of any kind are not allowed.

Champy Athletic Products/Terry Rawl: Our greatest safety concern is with our sales reps out in the field. However, we don't have much control over that. For the main office, we implemented the following safety policy.

Safety Procedures

Champy Athletic Products always considers the safety of its employees as a prime concern. It is our expectation that all employees will respect the safety of others and work in a safe manner. If an injury or illness occurs on the job, you should proceed as follows:

- Report all injuries to management.

- If you need medical attention, you must receive authorization from management to leave the premises.

Accidents

You may want to spell out the procedure for reporting accidents in the workplace. It is critical that even the smallest accidents be immediately reported to management. In the event a workplace injury leads to a workers' compensation claim later, documentation of the accident becomes critical.

PCB Corporation/Candace and Tony Washington: It is critically important that all accidents be reported immediately. Our supervisors are trained to determine what medical treatment, if any, needs to be administered. The paperwork that follows any accident, no matter how minor, is important to protect both the worker and the company in the event of a workers' compensation claim.

Accidents

As an employee in a company dedicated to accident and fire prevention, you should be safety cautious at all times. Follow safety rules, use safe equipment, and report any unsafe conditions. If you should suffer an accident during working hours, notify your supervisor immediately and obtain any necessary first aid. If the accident or injury is severe, professional help should be obtained immediately.

Supervisors should complete a First Report of Injury form on all accidents or injuries that occur at the work place and forward it to Human Resources.

FYI

The insurance company which underwrites your liability insurance is just as interested in safety in your company as you are. Ask your agent for a complimentary inspection of the workplace. He or she should be able to arrange for noise or air quality testing and help you identify other potential occupational hazards in your company.

Hazardous Materials

Hazardous materials must be stored, handled and disposed of carefully and legally. Your policies should specify the proper handling of all hazardous materials in the workplace, and employees should be trained in those procedures.

Blood-Born Pathogens

If any of your employees are likely to come into contact with blood in the workplace, they may be required to follow certain procedures and participate in training to prevent the spread of blood-born diseases. Your employee handbook should identify the positions required to participate in that training.

First Aid and Emergency Procedures

Every company should have a policy regarding first aid and emergency procedures. Fire prevention and emergency procedure should always be covered. Natural disaster emergency procedures for flood, tornado, or earthquake will vary by geographic area.

Personal Workshop Preparation #25: First Aid and Emergencies

Your policy should inform employees about where they will find emergency procedures posted and emergency and first-aid equipment stored. There isn't much point in detailing your emergency procedures in the handbook—after all, in the event of earthquake or fire, employees are not going to take time to find and read their handbooks. Instead, emergency procedures need to be posted prominently in your place of business.

 Pegasus Computer Systems/Jean Watson: We wanted our employees to know that it is their responsibility to learn about our emergency procedures. Once each year, we cover the procedures in a staff meeting. Here is the policy we developed using the Personal Workshop:

If any of your employees work under a union contract, discipline and termination policies, as well as grievance procedures, will undoubtedly be spelled out in that document.

FYI

Personal Workshop #25
First Aid and Emergencies

Draft a policy regarding first aid and emergencies in the space below.

Emergency procedures for fire and tornado are posted on the company bulletin board. It is each employee's responsibility to review those procedures and emergency exits and to be prepared to evacuate in the event of such a disaster. Emergency telephone numbers for fire and police are to be displayed on all telephones in the building. Fire extinguishers are located in the service department and in the break room. A first aid kit is located in the main office.

Personal Workshop #25
First Aid and Emergencies

Draft a policy regarding first aid and emergencies in the space below.

Follow-Up to Safety Policies

The safety policies you write could mean the difference between a safe work environment and a dangerous one. A dangerous work environment can put your workers out of commission and put you out of business. Be sure that your work environment is safe and the policies you have written are consistent with OSHA and/or state guidelines. Unlike many other types of policies, safety procedures may not be negotiable. Still, they should be reviewed by employees for clarity.

VI. Discipline and Termination Policies

Whenever you hire a new employee, you anticipate a rewarding and productive experience for both parties. Unfortunately this is not always the case. Sometimes an organization must communicate to an employee which actions must be corrected and what will happen if an unacceptable action or behavior continues. Even when an employee leaves your company under better circumstances, such as retirement, certain procedures may need to be followed to assure a smooth departure. This section describes policies related to discipline and termination.

Standards of Conduct

Some companies include a general statement regarding appropriate standards of conduct in their employee handbook. Such policies typically include a list of actions or behaviors that are prohibited and subject to disciplinary actions. In some cases, the various steps of disciplinary action leading to termination are specifically described. You must decide if you want a policy regarding standards of conduct to be relatively rigid, or whether you want to allow your supervisors some discretion in making decisions about disciplinary actions.

PCB Corporation/Candace and Tony Washington: When you have a manufacturing company this size, it is important that all employees understand what is and isn't acceptable behavior. Unacceptable behavior can be disruptive and dangerous to employees. We thought long and hard about our policy on standards of conduct. We didn't want to list specific disciplinary actions for infractions, although we understand that we need to be consistent with any discipline if the circumstances are basically the same. Here is our new policy.

Your right to terminate employees, and how you do it, is limited by various federal and state laws. One good resource to help you understand when and how to fire employees is the article, "Firing 101: Before, During and After" by Milton Bordwin in the *Small Business Forum*, Winter 1994-1995. For a reprint of this article, call the Wisconsin Small Business Development Center at (608) 263-7843.

Standards of Conduct

PCB Corporation is confident that all employees will conduct themselves in a businesslike and professional manner. No written list of company rules can be complete or substitute for the good judgment and cooperation of employees. However, for the protection of employees and the company, we have established rules and regulations. Some of these rules are outlined below. These rules do not limit the company's right to impose discipline for other conduct detrimental to the interests of the company, its customers and other employees.

The actions listed here will result in disciplinary action. This list is not all-inclusive. The severity of the disciplinary action will be assessed on an individual basis; it may, but need not include warning, suspension and termination. Management reserves the right to determine disciplinary action for each violation. Termination may occur without previous warning.

These actions or behaviors are prohibited:

- Insubordination, or deliberate refusal to perform a job or follow your supervisor's instructions.

- Theft of company or other personal property.

- Defacing or destroying company property.

- Threat of violence to another employee.

- Intoxication, use, sale or possession of alcoholic beverages or illegal drugs on company property or time.

- Punching or completing another's time card or record.

- Leaving company premises during work time without authorization or notice.

- Disorderly conduct on company time or premises.

- Gambling on company property or time.

- Excessive spoilage or scrapping of materials.

- Appearing to be asleep during working hours.

- Violation of safety rules.

- Use of abusive or foul language.

- Excessive absenteeism/tardiness.

- Unsatisfactory job performance, including but not limited to: poor quality, poor quantity and/or poor attitude.

- Solicitation, including distribution of any unauthorized materials in any form, for any purpose, on company work time.

- Sexual harassment, or unwelcome sexual advances including unwelcome verbal or physical conduct of a sexual nature.

- Falsifications, deletions or omissions from company records, including employment applications, personnel forms, and attendance forms.

Complaints and Grievances

A written policy will help employees understand the proper procedure for airing any complaints for grievances in your business.

Personal Workshop Preparation #26: Complaints and Grievances

If your business is very small, it may not be necessary to have a policy on complaints and grievances. Once you employ several people, however, it may be wise to advise your employees on the proper procedures for airing complaints and grievances. As was the case in sexual harassment, you want to develop a policy which encourages employees to go first to their supervisors, but which gives them other options in the event the supervisor is part of the problem.

Pegasus Computer Systems/Jean Watson: We are very interested in hearing the concerns of our employees. We tried to express that fact when we wrote our policy on complaints and grievances.

THE PURPOSE OF THIS WORKSHOP IS TO DESCRIBE THE PROCEDURE FOR RESOLVING COMPLAINTS & GRIEVANCES.

Personal Workshop #26
Complaints and Grievances

Draft a policy describing the procedure for airing complaints and grievances below.

Pegasus Computer Systems is committed to responding promptly to your questions and concerns. If you should have a question or complaint about your job or the company, feel free to discuss it with your supervisor. Supervisors will be able to handle a majority of these kinds of problems.

However, if you do not receive satisfaction from your supervisor, the next step is to appeal to the owner. It is a good idea at this time to put your concerns in writing to eliminate any possible misunderstandings. The company is very earnest in its conviction that all legitimate grievances be heard.

Personal Workshop #26
Complaints and Grievances

Draft a policy describing the procedure for airing complaints and grievances below.

Workshop Follow-Up

Some companies believe that including a policy on complaints and grievances is like an invitation to employees to complain. Again, if the company is small enough, you may not need such a policy. But once there are several employees, including such a policy in your handbook can avoid confusion and frustration for both employees and their supervisors.

Resignation Notices

In some cases, a company may request that employees notify them in advance and in writing if they intend to leave employment. This policy might describe the minimum number of days notice requested and the procedure for notification.

Exit Interview

No matter the reason for an employee leaving the organization, many companies like to conduct an exit interview. The exit interview gives the company an opportunity to wrap up final matters with the employee. This policy would describe that interview. Exit interviews might simply involve turning in keys and identification cards; or they can involve asking employees for feedback on their employment experiences.

Follow-Up to Discipline and Termination Policies

Policies regarding discipline and termination need to be checked by an attorney and carried out with consistency—otherwise your company might face a charge of discrimination or other unfair discharge. Have these policies carefully reviewed.

VII. Employee Acknowledgment

The purpose of the employee acknowledgment is to assure that each employee has received his or her copy of the employee handbook and understands that he/she is responsible for reading the policies in it.

The employee acknowledgment provides you with a great opportunity to reinforce your position as an at-will employer and to repeat disclaimers regarding insurance coverage and implied contracts.

Personal Workshop Preparation #27: Employee Acknowledgment

You want to design an employee acknowledgment that will protect the company in the event an employee claims he or she didn't know about a certain policy or procedure. Write an acknowledgment form that does the following things:

- places the responsibility for reading and understanding the policies on the employee;

- reinforces your status as an "at will" employer; and

- reinforces your right to change any and all policies at any time without notice.

NEIGHBORHOOD
MEDICAL CLINIC

Neighborhood Medical Clinic/Dr. Carole Stein: We developed an employee acknowledgment form that covers all the points in the workshop preparation. We attach it to the front of the employee handbook with a paperclip, and we let the employee know that he or she has one week to read through things, ask any questions, and return the signed form to us.

NEIGHBORHOOD
MEDICAL CLINIC

Personal Workshop #27
Employee Acknowledgment

Draft an employee acknowledgment form below which covers each of the following points:

- places the responsibility for reading and understanding the policies on the employee;

- reinforces your status as an "at will" employer; and

- reinforces your right to change any and all policies at any time without notice.

This is your personal copy of the Neighborhood Medical Clinic Employee Handbook. It has been prepared as a general statement of company policy and as a guide to set forth those matters which affect you and your job. Please take time to review its contents. We ask you to sign this form saying that you have received a copy of the guidelines and that you understand the policies and procedures outlined.

As a guideline, this handbook is not intended to become expressly or implicitly a part of any agreement or contract of employment. Where reference is made to insurance policies and coverages, the express language of those insurance policies prevails. The statements contained in this handbook do not limit the right of either the clinic or the employee to terminate the employee's employment with or without cause at any time. The clinic reserves the right to change any and all policies, rules, and methods of operations and doing business at any time.

Employee Signature _____

Date _____

THE PURPOSE OF THIS WORKSHOP IS TO WRITE AN ACKNOWLEDGMENT STATEMENT TO ACCOMPANY YOUR EMPLOYEE HANDBOOK.

Personal Workshop #27
Employee Acknowledgment

Draft an employee acknowledgment form below which covers each of the following points:

- places the responsibility for reading and understanding the policies on the employee;

- reinforces your status as an "at will" employer; and

- reinforces your right to change any and all policies at any time without notice.

Follow-Up to Employee Acknowledgment

While the employee acknowledgment may sound a little unfriendly or like legal jargon, it is important that it be clear. If you are the least bit wishy-washy about your "at will" status or your right to change policies, you could be setting yourself up for trouble in the event of a legal challenge by a disgruntled employee. Also, if you are going to require an employee acknowledgment, then you must develop a system for collecting and filing the acknowledgment forms. This is critical, once again, in case of a legal challenge.

A Final Follow-Up

Go back to the checklist you prepared in the first workshop—have you covered each topic you identified in some way? As you begin to pull all of the policies you have written together into an employee handbook, you are likely to think of other points or policies that need to be added. Be selective in what you put in your employee handbook—too much information can be overwhelming to employees. Remember that your employee handbook should provide guidelines, but not be the all-inclusive guide to every single situation that might come up. That's why you have managers. Keep your employee handbook functional for everyone.

Be sure to have all written policies reviewed by an attorney. Because of concerns over employment contracts and the ever-changing employment legislation handed down by state and federal law-makers, what is correct and legal today may not be tomorrow. Also ask your attorney to check your employee acknowledgment form—you want to be sure the disclaimers are clear and will protect you in the event of litigation.

Pulling It All Together

Congratulations! You have just worked your way through a series of Personal Workshops designed to help you write clear personnel policies. Hopefully you will now feel comfortable tackling any other policies you might need, but were not covered in this Challenge. The review and revision process lies ahead, as well as having your policies checked by an attorney. The policies will then need to be distributed and explained to employees. And then ongoing review and revisions . . .

Writing good personnel policies and keeping those policies up-to-date is a formidable and ongoing process—but remember that it is a critical one. It will help to protect your company and your employees.

You Have Completed Challenge 3

You were asked at the beginning of this Challenge whether you could imagine ever going to court against one of your employees. By now, your imagination is probably running wild! That certainly wasn't the intent of this Challenge.

The intent was to make you aware of the importance of having written personnel policies, of communicating those policies to your employees, and of keeping those policies current. By completing this Challenge, you have taken the first step toward developing an employee handbook for your company and in designing a system to assure that handbook is useful, legal and current.

You Leave Challenge 3 with the Following

Information: This Challenge has modeled a system for personnel policy management in your small business. You have learned how to identify and organize the types of policies you will need for an employee handbook, and you have practiced writing some of those policies. You have undoubtedly gained an appreciation for the possible legal pitfalls of personnel policies, and you have learned the importance of developing carefully written and reviewed policies to avoid those pitfalls. Finally, you have been given the opportunity to learn by seeing how other companies have written their policies. What you have learned in this Challenge should help you develop personnel policies that will be useful to both your employees and your company.

Tools: The **Employee Handbook Checklist** which you developed in the first Personal Workshop is a tool that can be used to outline your employee handbook. You were also given a **Model for Developing Personnel Policies.** The steps described in this model will help you accomplish the chore of developing a good employee handbook—"eating the elephant" one bite at a time. You have also been provided with many samples and templates for developing your own personnel policies. The most significant tool is the one you are developing—the **Employee Handbook,** which is now full of personnel policies that will help your employees know what is expected of them and what they can expect from you.

Learning: This Challenge has been designed to give you the basic information needed to develop useful and legal personnel policies and to communicate those policies to your employees. Several "red flags" have been raised to get your attention. Specifically, you now know about the importance of protecting your rights as an "at-will" employer. You know that you must avoid any language which might imply the existence of an employment contract or a promise of future employment. You also know the types of personnel policies you should consider including in your employee handbook, and you have been given many practical tips and examples to help you write those policies.

Keeping a current employee handbook is an ongoing process. It usually involves the work of many people over several months. But you now have the basic knowledge and tools to lead that process for your small business.

Networking: You have been encouraged to involve other people in the development process of your employee handbook. Take advantage of the knowledge your employees have in establishing policies and procedures. Involve them, at the very least, in the discussion and review process for those policies which may be negotiable. You have also been encouraged to involve an attorney in the review of your personnel policies. Few employers can keep track of all laws and regulations that apply to their operations. Hiring an attorney to review policies now may save your company significant money in the future.

Challenge 3 Self-Assessment

After completing this Challenge you should be able to develop reasonable and legal personnel policies for your small business, and you should have the tools to communicate those policies to your employees. Check your understanding of the concepts and the process for developing an employee handbook by using the following checklist. If needed, go back and review the areas where you feel you need more practice.

**Pages
113 - 114**

Establishing a System for Developing and Regularly Reviewing Personnel Policies:

( ) I have selected an individual to coordinate the development and distribution of an employee manual.

( ) I have involved other employees in the process.

( ) I have developed a process for reviewing and revising personnel policies.

**Pages
114 - 120**

Outlining the Types of Policies Needed in Your Small Business:

( ) I have used the Checklist to identify the types of policies my business needs.

( ) I have organized those policies into a format that will be most useful for employees and the company.

**Pages
110 - 113
121 - 181**

Developing Personnel Policies and an Employee Handbook which do not Threaten Employment-at-will Status:

( ) I have explored the laws in my state and understand my rights as an "at will" employer.

( ) I have carefully written or reviewed each personnel policy to be sure the language used does not imply the existence of an employment contract or a promise of future employment.

( ) I have carefully considered the possible operational implications of each personnel policy.

Developing Means for Effectively Communicating Personnel Policies to all Employees:

( ) I have developed an employee handbook and a system for ensuring that every employee receives and reads it.

( ) I understand the need for training supervisors regarding personnel policies and procedures.

( ) I have developed an acknowledgment form which all employees will be required to sign and that will be kept in their personnel files.

**Pages
181 - 184**

Minimizing the Risk of Litigation in Personnel Issues:

( ) I am alert to the possible legal implications of personnel policies, and I have made every effort to word policies so as to minimize the risk to my company.

( ) I understand that personnel law changes frequently and I have developed a system for the regular review and revision of policies in response to those changes.

( ) I understand that I should have my employee handbook reviewed by an attorney.

**Pages
109 - 184**

Take Another Look

Review the results of your self-assessment. It may actually take a long time to feel confident enough to check off each statement—after all, this Challenge is only the beginning in the development of your personnel policies. You probably won't have a completed document for several months, assuming you are using the model for developing an employee handbook that was presented to you early in this Challenge. As you continue to make progress on the development of your employee handbook, go through the self-assessment periodically, and review those sections of the Challenge where you need more help.

Record anything from Challenge 3, your Personal Workshops, or your personal reflections that you want to remember.

Challenge 4

Managing for Peak Performance

"So much of what we call management consists in making it difficult for people to work..."

—Peter Drucker

The term "performance management" gets a lot of use in today's business world. "We need to do a better job with performance management." "This problem can be resolved with performance management." "We need to manage the performance of our employees." As often as those words are used, one would think performance management is a common and consistently applied process. In truth, many business owners are confused about performance management, its purpose and its application. And very few managers, whether in a large or small business, consistently manage for peak performance.

The purpose of Challenge 4 is to teach you how to manage for peak performance—so you can be absolutely sure that every employee is an asset, not a liability to your small business. Use the case studies and Personal Workshops in this Challenge to help you develop a comprehensive performance management system that will work for your management style and will allow your employees to perform their very best.

Upon completion of Challenge 4 you will be able to:

- State the benefits of performance management for your small business.

- Communicate the vision, values and goals of your business to your employees.

- Set goals and action plan for the overall performance of your business.

- Apply the tools for managing team performance in your company.

- Implement the Eight Steps of Individual Performance Management.

- Develop a comprehensive performance management program for your business.

What Is Performance Management?

Frequently, business owner/managers use the term **performance management** to describe something they "do to employees," such as an annual performance review. True performance management, though, has a much broader meaning—it

Key Word

189

> *"When it gets down to it, it's about performance. Employees either make you money or lose you money. They're either an asset or a liability."*
>
> —Ingrid Wallace

applies not only to individual employees, but also to the teams or work groups in your business, and to your business as a whole.

Performance management is the process of planning, organizing and using your company's resources to achieve its goals and fulfill its customers' expectations. The more judiciously these resources are used, the better the performance of the business will be. Good performance management also applies measurement as a means of knowing if the company is fulfilling customer expectations.

Performance Management and Your Business

Performance management offers as many benefits to small companies as it does to large corporations. Here are some examples of those benefits:

- Performance management can help you monitor the direction in which your business is headed.

- It can spell out how a business is performing, with respect to sales, production levels, quality control, or customer satisfaction.

- It can give you the information you need to make well-advised strategic management decisions.

- It can help create an environment where strong teams work together to get the product or service out faster and with a higher level of quality.

- It can help your employees achieve peak performance, because each employee will know what the performance expectations are. Employees will also know how to get the resources and support they need to do the job right.

- It can encourage the continuous improvement of processes in your business.

- It can give you the information you need to develop a system of compensation and rewards which is equitable and motivational.

No matter what your management style, you will benefit from performance management in your business.

Levels of Performance Management

To be as effective as possible, you should implement performance management at three levels: for your overall business; for work groups or teams within your business; and for individual employees. A model for a comprehensive

FYI

The thinking and philosophy behind performance management has changed greatly in recent management history. Because many businesses still practice traditional performance management techniques, this guide explores both traditional and contemporary practices. Select and apply the performance management techniques that best fit your organization.

performance management system is shown in Table 4.1. Start by building your performance management system at the overall business level, since the decisions you make about performance at this level should guide both team and individual performance.

Table 4.1: A Model for a Comprehensive Performance Management System

Overall Business Performance	Team Performance	Individual Performance
1. Communicate vision and values	1. Set ground rules	1. Hire right people
2. Develop goals and action plans	2. Set team mission and goals	2. Start employees right
3. Monitor performance through measurement	3. Measure results	3. Training and coaching
	4. Offer team rewards	4. Motivate employees
		5. Build autonomy
		6. Manage problems
		7. Provide feedback
		8. Appropriate rewards

Success at every level will be dependent upon your ability to manage performance at the overall business level and to communicate those standards to the work groups and individual employees in your business.

Level 1: Overall Business Performance

Performance management for your business will provide employees and teams with the big picture. It helps to identify and communicate the overall performance expectations of the business. Furthermore, by managing the performance of your business, you serve as a role model for work teams and individual employees. You will demonstrate to them how to create goals, manage according to those goals and measure results. These skills will help both you and your employees achieve peak performance.

Performance management for the overall business needs to focus on two key areas:

Delivering What the Customer Wants

In any business, the ultimate indicator of performance comes from the customers. Successful business owners learn what their customers want and then manage the performance of their businesses to deliver just that. For example, if a retailer learns that its customers want courteous sales people, courtesy should be a performance standard for everyone in the business. If a manufacturing company discovers that even a low rate of defects turns customers away, then it had better make product quality a key performance standard.

Maintaining Financial Viability

Whether or not a business is for profit, a key to its success is financial viability. Businesses that neglect sound financial management practices are destined for difficulty. Smart business owner/managers include financial management in their performance management plan. They establish budgetary, expense and other financial guidelines and manage within the constraints of those guidelines. They measure such key financial indicators as profitability, sales, and expense control and reduction.

Level 2: Team Performance

Performance management at the team level can help your employees work together to accomplish common goals. Frequently in organizations, employees compete with one another. They strive to be outstanding performers, but they do so at each other's expense. If you develop a comprehensive performance management system for your business, work groups are more likely to pool their resources and use them wisely to achieve the common goal.

To manage team performance, you should focus on two important areas:

Working Together for the Customer

> *"There is no limit to what can be accomplished if no one cares who gets the credit."*
>
> —Anonymous

Just as the overall business must manage performance based on customer needs, so must teams. Everything a group or team does should be to fulfill this objective: to meet or exceed customer expectations.

Your job, as owner/manager, is to help teams understand customer expectations in your business, and to manage their performance to meet those expectations.

Treating Fellow Team Members like Customers

Not every employee in a business has face-to-face contact with customers, but even workers without direct contact have an impact on customer service. Those employees who do directly serve customers depend on co-workers to create or deliver the product. For example, a shipping clerk may never see or talk to customers, but sales people rely on the clerk to ship the product on time. If fast delivery is a performance standard for this team, the shipping clerk and the sales people must work together to achieve fast delivery. To accomplish that goal, they must treat each other like customers. The sales people should ensure that the orders they submit are neat, complete and accurate. The shipping clerk should handle every order with promptness and efficiency.

Level 3: Individual Performance

When you manage performance at the individual level, your goal should be to create an environment where each employee is responsible for his or her own performance.

You need to be sure that employees know what they are to do, and that they have the skills, information and resources needed to do it. You also need to emphasize that everything they do should be done to satisfy the customer. Then, you need to step back and let each individual employee find the most effective way to achieve the work goals that have been established. Teach your employees how to evaluate their progress and strive for continuous improvement. Encourage each individual to achieve peak performance by providing strong leadership, by modeling performance excellence, and by applying appropriate motivational strategies.

Be sure the goals and values of the company stay in the forefront—in other words, be sure that employees have incentives to meet the needs of the customer. Help employees understand their relationship with customers and encourage employees to build rapport with customers and work with customers to solve their problems. Finally, build reward systems that will assure that the customer is always "number one" in the employee's mind.

How to Manage Performance

To ensure the success of your business, you should develop and implement performance management strategies at all three levels. Start with the overall business, and then communicate that information to your employees, so that performance management strategies can be implemented at the team and individual levels. Performance management goals and criteria at all levels should be tied to the mission, vision and values of your company—otherwise you may have individual employees or work groups putting their energy and your money into meaningless endeavors.

The Overall Business

In order to effectively manage the performance of your business, you must do the following:

1. Create a vision and communicate that vision and the values of your company to every employee.

2. Set performance goals for your company and communicate those goals and your plan of action for achieving those goals to every employee.

3. Monitor performance through the measurement of certain key indicators.

A unit on quality titled *Quality Management: Mastering Your Small Business* will be available in fall 1996 from Upstart Publishing Company, Chicago, IL. It is part of the Small Business Mastery Certification Series, and you can order it by calling 1-800-235-8866.

FYI

Communicating the Vision and Values of Your Business

Your company's vision and values are at the core of performance management at all levels. **Vision** provides employees with a picture of where the business is going. A good vision always puts the customer in that picture. Beyond that, though, your vision might include any number of quantitative elements, such as growth in sales or profits or market share, or qualitative elements, such as a level of customer satisfaction or product safety.

Key Words

Values describe the deeply-held beliefs of the company, and they give employees a framework for decision-making. For example, if a business values producing products of the highest quality, employees will know to purchase the highest quality raw materials to go into that product. Other examples of business values might include integrity, friendliness, always pleasing the customer, prompt turnaround time, convenience, etc.

When employees share a common vision and values, they are more likely to consistently meet your performance expectations, and that performance should lead to success for both the employees and the company.

Personal Workshop Preparation #28: Vision Statement and Company Values

The following workshop requires some serious contemplation. The vision and values you describe in this workshop should guide every future business decision you make, so consider them carefully. If you already have vision and value statements written down for your company, pull those documents and work through this exercise to see if they are still relevant. If your vision is only in your dreams, and the values are there, but have never been written down, this workshop gives you the opportunity for some clarity. You should seriously consider involving other people in this exercise—your employees, an advisory board, or other trusted associates. These people might have a better sense of what your customer needs are, or they might come up with some creative ideas about what the ideal business should look like. Employee involvement is also important because it will help build their commitment to the vision and values they create. In preparation of this workshop, observe how Dr. Carole Stein completed this exercise.

FYI

The Disney Corporation is well known for its focus on customer service. According to one former employee, new employees are carefully trained in how to treat customers, and one performance expectation is clearly spelled out:

"Our common language is a smile. Every product and every service must be delivered with a smile. That is not an option. If you don't speak that language, you don't belong here."

A smile, then, represents a minimum level of performance expected of all employees—and judging from the success of Disney, that expectation has had a profound effect.

Neighborhood Medical Clinic/Dr. Carole Stein: I've always had an idea in my head about what I want this clinic to be some day, but because we're growing so fast and need to take on so many new employees, I decided it was time to get my ideas on paper. After all, I want all the people we hire to know how they fit into our vision for the future and how important their commitment is for getting us there. This workshop helped me get my ideas on paper.

> *"There is no right way to do a wrong thing."*
> —Anonymous

THE PURPOSE OF THIS WORKSHOP IS TO CREATE A WRITTEN VISION STATEMENT AND IDENTIFY COMPANY VALUES.

Personal Workshop #28
Vision Statement and Company Values

1. Using 30 words or less, describe the purpose or mission of your company.

The mission of Neighborhood Medical Clinic is to help patients and their families develop healthy lifestyles and maintain good health.

2. Who are your primary external customers, and what are their needs?
Customer

Families throughout the community
Elderly (at facility next door)

Needs

General health maintenance care for all ages; sick care; health care education; referrals; and compassion
General health maintenance care; sick care; medication monitoring and education; referrals; and compassion

3. Why should these customers want to come to you? In other words, what things do you have to offer (or want to offer) that are better than the competition?

A truly caring environment, top doctors who are willing to take time with patients, association with the best hospital, participation in the major health plans, emphasis on health care maintenance through education.

Steve Jobs, one of the founders of Apple Computer, communicated a vision when he challenged his company to create a computer that operated just like an office. He wanted Apple's customers to have a computer that did everything they wanted it to do—easily. Employees understood how their work was tied to that vision—and the result was the Macintosh.

FYI

4. Describe what your ideal business would look like:

Neighborhood Medical Clinic would be the primary health care provider for the county, offering a full array of wellness and sick care services to its patients. Every doctor, physician assistant, nurse, and employee at NMC would be totally committed to giving every patient the care and personal attention they deserve. Patients would never have to wait more than 15 minutes to see a health care professional, and they would be able to handle all their business affairs with the clinic in five minutes or less. The size of the clinic and staff would be adequate to serve the county, but every effort would be made to keep the clinic environment inviting, clean, and caring.

5. Consider your answers to the previous questions, and write a vision statement for your business using no more than 30 words:

Our vision is to be the best health care facility in the county, providing top quality wellness and sick care services to every patient in a sensitive and caring environment.

6. In order to achieve this vision, what values do you believe every employee must have? In other words, what are the guiding principles for work in your business?

Professional expertise (whether medical or business) , compassion, a commitment to good health maintenance and wellness education, respect for others, a helpful and friendly demeanor, and community involvement.

THE PURPOSE OF THIS WORKSHOP IS TO CREATE A WRITTEN VISION STATEMENT AND IDENTIFY COMPANY VALUES.

Personal Workshop #28
Vision Statement and Company Values

1. Using 30 words or less, describe the purpose or mission of your company.

2. Who are your primary external customers, and what are their needs?
Customer

Needs

3. Why should these customers want to come to you? In other words, what things do you have to offer (or want to offer) that are better than the competition?

4. Describe what your ideal business would look like:

5. Consider your answers to the previous questions, and write a vision statement for your business using no more than 30 words:

6. In order to achieve this vision, what values do you believe every employee must have? In other words, what are the guiding principles for work in your business?

Workshop Follow-Up

✔ Every employee in your business, at every level, should be able to tell any stranger on the street exactly what your business is. Does your mission statement make it clear? And every employee in your business needs to know what the vision and values of your business are. Does your vision statement clearly describe what you want the business to become? Will the values you identified help guide employees in their work life? If you are satisfied that the vision and values you have described are right for your business, you must now communicate them to every employee. This might be done through an orientation or training session, at a staff meeting, in a memo, or simply in everyday workplace conversation. Perhaps you want to print and frame your mission, vision and/or a statement about company values and post it in the work facility. This way every employee will have the opportunity to read the mission statement over and over again—which is what you want. Your goal is to make your vision and values the guiding force for your business decision-making every single day.

> *"If you can dream it, you can do it!"*
> —Walt Disney

Set Organizational Goals and Action Plans

Now that you have a clear vision for your business, you need to set organizational goals to help assure movement in the right direction, and you need to decide on a plan of action for achieving those goals. Set goals for your organization in each of the major functional areas: human resources, financial resources, physical resources, political resources, administrative systems, and communication/marketing. But first, it may be helpful for you to identify the major issues or problems your business is likely to face in the near future.

Personal Workshop Preparation #29: Key Issues

Throughout its lifespan, your company will face different problems and have different issues to deal with. Many of the issues you face will be driven by the needs and expectations of your customers. Before you begin to set goals, you need to identify and prioritize those issues. This exercise is best done with a representative group (or all) of your employees. Contributions from your employees will offer additional insight into company issues.

Neighborhood Medical Clinic/Dr. Carole Stein: We have a diverse group of clients, and their problems are just as diverse. I decided to pull together all of the employees of the clinic for a brainstorming session about what major issues are facing our customers, and consequently our clinic, in the near future.

Personal Notes

_____

_____

_____

_____

_____

_____

Personal Workshop #29
Key Issues

NEIGHBORHOOD
MEDICAL CLINIC

1. What are the major issues facing your customers/clients for the next five years?

- Rising health care costs and lack of adequate insurance coverage
- Lack of commitment to personal wellness; i.e., nutrition, exercise, life style
- High quality short- and long-term health care
- Accessible and convenient health care for the entire family

2. What are the major issues facing your company for the next five years?

- Hiring top quality health care providers who share our clinic values
- Expanding our services and space to meet increasing demand
- Educating our clients regarding personal wellness
- Keeping our services affordable and accessible to people in our county in spite of rising costs
- Streamlining our business systems to better serve customers

3. Prioritize the issues your organization should work on for the next five years:

1. Keeping services affordable and accessible
2. Expanding our services and space
3. Hiring top quality health care professionals
4. Streamlining our business system
5. Educating our clients

Personal Workshop #29
Key Issues

1. What are the major issues facing your customers/clients for the next five years?

2. What are the major issues facing your company for the next five years?

3. Prioritize the issues your organization should work on for the next five years:

Workshop Follow-Up

The major issues you have identified in Personal Workshop #29 should help guide your goal-setting process. Don't be alarmed if the major issues of your company don't exactly match the major issues of your customers. Unfortunately, you won't be able to solve all of their problems or meet all of their needs. But your awareness of the issues they face will help you keep your customers in the forefront as you set your own organizational goals, which is the next task before you.

Personal Workshop Preparation #30: Organizational Goals

As you write performance goals for your overall business, keep your vision and values in front of you. Set goals for each of the functional areas, keeping in mind the major issues you just identified in the last workshop. For each goal you set, briefly describe your plan and timetable for getting it done.

As you set goals and develop action plans, you may want to get very specific, describing exactly who will do what, when and how. Or you may want to keep your organizational action plans more vague, and let the individuals or work groups involved decide exactly how and when each plan will be carried out. Use whichever methods seems most appropriate for your management style and for the situation. Before you begin on this workshop, take a look at how Dr. Carole Stein completed this exercise.

Neighborhood Medical Clinic/Dr. Carole Stein: As a clinic, we decided that we want to control our growth as much as possible, but we don't want to turn away anyone in need of health care. We also agreed, though, that we didn't want to pack our appointments in so tightly that we wouldn't have the time needed to give personal attention to every client—after all, that's what we're all about. We came up with the following goals for the coming year—but we realize that we might have to adjust those goals if demand continues to grow at the rate it has for the past year.

Tips for Effective Goal Setting   *FYI*

1. Be as specific as possible. Goals should be measurable, and so think in terms of what specifically you want the outcome to be.
2. Make your goals challenging, yet achievable. If goals are too far out-of-reach, employees will figure it is useless to try.
3. Do not approach goal setting as "quota setting." Goals should be motivational, not threatening.
4. Don't set so many goals that it is impossible to achieve them. Prioritize, and save some things for next year. It is better to accomplish one or two really important things than a number of trivial things.
5. Remain flexible. Be ready and willing to adjust goals or change priorities as dictated by environmental changes or the needs of your customers.

NEIGHBORHOOD
MEDICAL CLINIC

THE PURPOSE OF THIS WORKSHOP IS TO SET GOALS AND ACTION PLANS FOR YOUR BUSINESS.

Personal Workshop #30
Organizational Goals

HUMAN RESOURCES

Goals	Action Plans
1. Hire one physician	Begin search immediately for physician to begin work in six months
2. Hire one physician assistant	Begin search immediately—start date ASAP
3. Hire one nurse	Begin search as soon as new physician starts work
4. Conduct total quality training	Begin weekly meetings on Friday mornings; bi-weekly with consultant

FINANCIAL RESOURCES

Goals	Action Plans
1. Find new accountant	Begin interviewing in September, hire in October
2. Acquire capital improvements line of credit	Meet w/banker in January
3. Develop a foundation for health care funds for the marginalized	Meet with area service clubs to determine their interest; meet w/banker re: setting up; check on tax implications

PHYSICAL RESOURCES

Goals	Action Plan
1. Prepare empty examining room for new doctor and physician assistant	Clean out storage boxes; purchase new furniture
2. Build addition for future expansion	Meet with architects in July, begin building in March, grand opening in September

POLITICAL RESOURCES

Goals	Action Plans
1. Improve client follow-up	Research software for appointment follow-up system
2. Explore better use of office staff for extended hours	Track patients/hour clinic usage to determine if office staff can be better utilized
3. Plan for support staff for increased size of clinic	Conduct job analysis and realign positions

COMMUNICATIONS AND MARKETING

Goals	Action Plans
1. Join chamber of commerce	Contact chamber; ask about professional affiliation
2. Conduct 4 public education events	Contact county agencies regarding co-sponsorship, community needs, etc.
3. Advertise new hours, new doctors, and upcoming expansion	Radio and newspaper ads, press releases, host "Business after Five" event, attend service club meetings.

Personal Workshop #30
Organizational Goals

HUMAN RESOURCES

Goals   **Action Plans**

FINANCIAL RESOURCES

Goals   **Action Plans**

PHYSICAL RESOURCES

Goals   Action Plans

POLITICAL RESOURCES

Goals   Action Plans

COMMUNICATIONS AND MARKETING

Goals   Action Plans

Workshop Follow-Up

✔ Don't make the mistake that so many business managers do by filing away your goals until some later date. Use them! Your goals and the action plans you have sketched out are a tool which should help guide you and your employees throughout the next year. Share them with your employees, since the goals of each individual or team in your company need to be tied to your goals and vision. You cannot expect your employees to help move the business in the right direction, unless they know what that direction is.

Monitor Your Performance through Measurement

> *"What gets measured gets done."*
> —Tom Peters

Your business may be performing at an acceptable level—or maybe it's not. Unless you evaluate overall performance, you may not know how your business is functioning—or you may find out when it's too late to fix. Measurement is the tool businesses use to determine how well they are performing. There are many different types of measures that can be useful in understanding how productive your business is as a whole, as well as its work groups and individual employees. Here are some ways to measure results in your small business:

- **Existing Data:** Existing data provide quantitative measures such as sales, units produced, customers served, percentage increases or decreases, averages and ratios. This data can be collected in-house, allowing for comparisons from week-to-week, month-to-month, or year-to-year. And the data can be compared to industry or geographic averages.

- **Surveys or Interviews:** You can survey customers, individual employees, teams, or any other relevant person or group to get information about performance. Surveys may be written or oral (as in telephone surveys), complex, or as simple as asking new customers how they learned about your business.

- **Observation:** By simply observing people at work or customers in your business, you can better understand how your systems are performing. For example, observing checkout lines in a grocery store at certain times of the day can give you valuable information about that process and how to improve it.

- **Critical Incidents:** Tracking critical incidents or events, such as receiving letters of complaint from angry customers—or letters of praise from happy ones—can be useful in measuring performance.

The trick to effective ongoing measurement is to identify and track a set of key indicators. The key indicators you choose to use should measure those things that best reveal how your business is doing. For example, if sales are a good indicator of the overall performance of your business for any period of time, then you need to track and carefully study sales (whether it be gross sales volume, sales revenue, sales growth, or type of sales—the possibilities are many). If productivity measures are a better indicator of how your business is doing, use those. Key indicators might include customer satisfaction, quality, turnaround time, cycle time, inventory turns, profit, financial ratios, or any other number of measurable factors.

Champy Athletic Products/Terry Rawl: Since all of our sales representatives now enter their own orders using their laptop computers in the field, it has become relatively simple for me to check how we are doing overall. And since all orders are entered within 24 hours, I can find out exactly where we stand day-by-day, if I want. I usually check our sales figures on the last day of each month. I look at total orders placed, average order size in dollars, volume by category of product, and total gross revenue. This information tells me whether we're on target in terms of our sales goals, and it shows me which products are selling and which are not, so that I can make decisions about what to put on clearance. We believe at Champy that our success tomorrow depends on how happy our customers are today, so I also look at some key indicators for customer satisfaction. For example, I check the figures for merchandise returns each month, both in dollars and by category of product. Also, each sales rep keeps a record of customer complaints. A combination of these key indicators gives us a pretty good picture of how things are going, and tracking this data regularly has really helped us make better business decisions along the way.

Team Performance Management

If you have work groups or teams operating in your business, whether for a single project or on an ongoing basis, you need to manage their performance for maximum productivity. Building dynamic work groups and teams isn't simple—after all, most people are not accustomed to working in teams or being rewarded for team work. And most don't really know how a dynamic team operates.

Characteristics of a Dynamic Team

- A clearly stated mission

- Goals which are tied to the overall goals of the business

- A focus on results

- Well-defined roles and responsibilities for every team member, which build upon their individual strengths

---

FYI

When to Measure

There is such a thing as too much control—you don't want to spend so much time measuring and tracking performance that you cut your own productivity. You should measure:

- At regular intervals, which can serve as milestones or steps to total performance. That might be quarterly, monthly, or annually—only do it as often as necessary.

- In time to take corrective action, if needed.

- Whenever needed—for example, if you suspect there might be a problem.

- Synergism—team members can do more by working together than the total of what they can do individually

- The team evaluates its own performance

If the concept of teams or work groups is new to your business, you may want to do a little research to find out more about how a team concept can enhance your business. Go to your local bookstore or library and look through the titles in the management section—you should find several books on managing teams.

At the team level, four elements contribute to excellent performance management:

1. The establishment of ground rules

2. Clarity of the team's mission and goals

3. Team performance measurement

4. Team rewards

Establish Ground Rules

Key Word

Ground rules are performance guidelines that address how employees in the work group can best get the job done. Ground rules define business protocol and identify specific operating procedures. They are the backbone of a team's performance because they delineate in writing the best procedures and behavior for the team.

Ground rules can address a variety of issues that affect performance. They can help resolve questions like these:

- How can we ensure that all employees will treat customers fairly and consistently?

- How can we ensure that our efforts will be productive and cost-effective?

- What guidelines can we establish to ensure that everyone makes a fair contribution to the team?

- What decision-making guidelines should we follow?

- How can we ensure that we will listen to each other?

- How can we ensure that we will respect one another's opinions?

Ground rules don't have to be formal. They can be a mixture of behavioral and operational rules. And ground rules don't need to sound official or fancy—they simply exist to help a team enhance its performance.

FYI

Although computer systems can make tracking key indicators much easier than it used to be, it can also be done by hand. For example, totaling and tracking daily sales receipts might be helpful; or simply counting the number of customers served.

Pegasus Computer Systems/Jean Watson: An area where we feel we've been weak for a long time is in customer follow-up. We all know how important follow-up is to customer satisfaction and future sales— but it just seemed like we were all too busy to get a system set up for consistent customer follow-up. We decided to put together a team of people—some from sales and some from service—whose mission was to establish a system for regular customer follow-up. At the first team meeting, the group came up with a set of ground rules to guide their activity.

Pegasus Team for Customer Follow-Up
Ground Rules

- We will attend and be prepared for all team meetings.

- We will operate within our written customer service philosophy guidelines.

- We will begin and end our meetings on time, and every meeting will have an agenda.

- Every team member should contribute to team discussions. Assertive team members should not dominate the discussion.

- We will not interrupt each other when we are speaking.

- We will respect each other's point of view.

Clarify the Team's Mission and Goals

Just as the vision shows where the business is going, a clear team mission and goals help members share a common purpose and direction. The most effective team goals are those that focus on the customer, the company's vision, and the goals of the company as a whole. When a team has a clear mission and well-stated goals, it is more likely to have dynamic results and a **synergy** that enhances overall performance.

Key Word

Personal Workshop Preparation #31: Setting Team Goals

Use this workshop to help a team or work group in your company get focused on its mission and goals. In some cases, you, as owner/manager, may need to clarify the mission and let the team know your performance expectations for its work. (For example, you might tell a team that you want a final report with its recommendations by December 31.) If the team has a complex task, or you aren't yet sure what performance expectations are reasonable, try to provide a timetable for moving in the right direction. For example, ask them to assess the situation for the first three months and then bring to you their recommendations for moving ahead

---

Some ground rules may be established in your employee handbook—others might not be written down or communicated outside the particular team. Whenever a work team first forms, it is important to talk about the ground rules to be sure everyone understands how the team is going to operate. Often, team members will develop their own set of ground rules at their first meeting.

FYI

as a team to solve the problem. Remember that a dynamic team needs to be focused on results; this exercise should be shared by each member of the team in order to help them get focused. For each goal, draft an action plan for achieving that goal, including what needs to be done, when and by whom. In preparation for this workshop, observe how Jean Watson completed this exercise.

Pegasus Computer Systems/Jean Watson: I met with the customer follow-up team to be sure the members were clear about their purpose and to help them develop some goals. The workshop that follows was helpful in that exercise.

THE PURPOSE OF THIS WORKSHOP IS TO DEFINE THE TEAM'S MISSION AND GOALS.

Personal Workshop #31
Setting Team Goals

Name/Description of Team: Customer Follow-up team

State the purpose, or mission, of this team:
Our mission is to establish a system for regular customer follow-up.

Team Goals	Action Plans
1. Increase customer loyalty to Pegasus by 10% per year (repeat business).	1. Establish criteria for effective follow-up system: February
2. Increase software sales by 20%.	2. Research and rate software for customer follow-up: 1 per team member, March
3. Increase enrollment in training classes by 20%.	3. Explore follow-up systems being used in-house: March
4. No customer left dissatisfied	4. Select and install systems: April
	5. Conduct training and implement systems: April
	6. Evaluate results: after six months, one year

THE PURPOSE OF THIS WORKSHOP IS TO DEFINE THE TEAM'S MISSION AND GOALS.

Personal Workshop #31
Setting Team Goals

Name/Description of Team:

State the purpose, or mission, of this team:

Team Goals	**Action Plans**

Workshop Follow-Up

The goals and action plans you have established should guide the team and keep its members results-oriented. Keep in mind, however, that simply having a clear mission and goals does not guarantee the work group will develop into a "dynamic" team, where every member contributes and no one person dominates the decision-making process. These goals will help set the stage for measuring the results of the team's work, but if you are also interested in measuring how effectively the group functioned as a team, additional measures may be needed.

Team Performance Measurement

All teams should establish measurements that tell them how effectively they are accomplishing their goals. Good goals will be measurable. For example, if a team's goal is to reduce manufacturing time, it should begin by measuring how long it takes to manufacture an item and then repeat that measurement after enacting procedures designed to cut production time. Without a baseline and subsequent measurement, the team can only guess whether performance has improved.

In addition, team members may want to evaluate how effectively they are functioning as a team. By asking themselves certain questions, a team can improve the overall dynamics and productivity of the group. Those questions might center on whether each participant is committed to and involved in the group process, how effectively the group communicates or uses individual talents, whether there is consensus decision-making, etc.

Earlier in this Challenge, you learned several techniques for measuring performance, including tracking existing data, conducting surveys or interviews, observation, or measuring critical incidents. Each of these data sources could also be appropriate for measuring team performance. For example, team members might be interviewed regarding the effectiveness of their work group; the group might be observed in action, to check for ineffective communication dynamics; or existing data could help measure what impact the team's work has had on organizational success.

Pegasus Computer Systems/Jean Watson: The team for customer follow-up did a great job of setting measurable goals for their work. As a result, they had no trouble coming up with ways to evaluate whether customer follow-up really makes a difference. They agreed to look at the following data after six months on the new system, and then again after one year:

1. Number of repeat customers within the previous six month period (existing data).

2. Software sales in dollars (existing data).

3. Enrollment in training classes (existing data).

4. Number of dissatisfied customer (to be measured by survey).

Team Rewards

Rewards are an important part of performance management. When a team achieves a stated goal or milestone towards its overall goal, its members should celebrate that accomplishment. Rewards recognize achievement and encourage continued effort. Employers should reward the team with congratulations and other expressions of pride. Team members might receive a bonus; but even if a monetary reward isn't possible in your company, a pizza party or a bonus day off might be an appropriate alternative.

> "There are no simple, cookbook formulas for working with people."
>
> —Keith Davis

As business owner/manager, you should not be the only one who congratulates a successful team. Try to create an environment in which employees celebrate their own successes as well as the successes of others.

Individual Performance Management

Once your company has performance management in place for the overall business and teams, the foundation for managing individual performance has been laid. Employees should now clearly see the overall goals for the business and for teams and that these goals can be monitored and measured. They also have a better understanding of how the process applies to them. But all of this does not guarantee peak or even acceptable performance.

As a small business owner/manager, you will face a variety of challenges in managing individual performance. Although "there are no simple, cookbook formulas," you can help increase the odds that your employees will achieve peak performance if you take the following steps:

Eight Steps for Individual Performance Management

1. Hire the right people.
2. Start employees off on the right foot.
3. Provide ongoing training and development.
4. Understand and apply motivation theory.
5. Provide leadership that builds autonomy.
6. Analyze and manage individual performance problems.
7. Provide performance feedback.
8. Use recognition, compensation and rewards.

Step 1: Hire the Right People

Excellent performance management begins with the hiring process. When you carefully plan and manage the hiring process, and when you take the time to get to know a prospective employee, you are more likely to find an employee with values and abilities that match those of your company. Each of these factors plays a crucial role in performance management.

When a job candidate's values match the company's values, he or she is more likely to meet or exceed the performance standards of the business. For example, assume your company rates customer service as a top performance standard. If you hire people who also place a high value on customer service, you can expect them to take care of customers without much additional training or motivation.

Even if there is a match in values, individual performance suffers if employees don't have the skills to do the job. During the hiring process, you need to determine what skills are needed for the job and whether you want to hire people who already have those skills or train the new employees. Hiring or equipping people with necessary skills is an important part of individual performance management. With the required skills, the employee can perform. Without the skills or the aptitude to learn them, performance suffers. As a small business owner/manager, take care to hire people who have the ability to learn needed job skills.

Challenge 1 of this series, "Hiring the Right Employees," takes you through the hiring process, step-by-step. If you choose to use that process, you can greatly increase your chances of hiring the right person for your business.

FYI

The Hidden Reasons for Employee Non-Performance

1. They don't know why they should do it.
2. They don't know how to do it.
3. They don't know what they are supposed to do.
4. They think your way will not work.
5. They think their way is better.
6. They think something else is more important.
7. There is no positive consequence to them for doing it.
8. They think they are doing it.
9. They are rewarded for not doing it.
10. They are punished for doing what they are supposed to do.
11. They anticipate a negative consequence for doing it.
12. There is no negative consequence to them for poor performance.
13. There are obstacles beyond their control.
14. Their personal limits prevent them from performing.
15. Their personal problems prevent them from performing.
16. No one could do it.

Reprinted from *Why Employees Don't Do What They're Supposed to Do and What to Do About It*, F. F. Fournies, Liberty Hall Press, NY 1988. Used by permission of Ferdinand F. Fournies.

Step 2: Start Employees Off on the Right Foot

Even when employees have the right values, skills and abilities, they still need to know how they fit into the organization. New employees need confirmation that their behaviors are appropriate for the job, they need guidance and direction on how to apply their specific skills to the job, and they need to learn this information early in their jobs. You can offer this guidance and information during new employee orientation and in early coaching sessions with supervisors.

During new employee orientation, workers can learn the vision and values of the business. They should be told who the customers are and what customers' expectations are. They also should learn the overall business performance expectations at this point. For more information on employee orientation and training, review Challenge 2 of this series, "Developing Your Employees through Education and Training."

In addition to orientation, each of your employees should set individual performance goals, with the help of his or her supervisor. Supervisors should begin the process by making sure employees understand the organization's vision and goals. Then they should discuss how the vision and goals apply to individual jobs. The goals any individual employee comes up with, then, should relate directly or indirectly to the organization's goals and the performance expectations established by the supervisor.

> *"By failing to prepare, you are preparing to fail."*
> —Anonymous

Personal Workshop Preparation #32: Goals for Individual Employees

Review the vision and goals of the company with the employee. Also review the employee's position description and performance expectations. Use this information to help the employee understand how his or her work is important to the company as a whole; and then use this workshop to help the employee develop performance goals for the coming year.

To review the process for developing a position description which includes performance expectations, go back to Challenge 1, "Hiring the Right Employees." Before you begin the next workshop, observe how Dr. Carole Stein completed the exercise.

Neighborhood Medical Clinic/Dr. Carole Stein: Once we had our goals set for the clinic for the coming year, it was time for each employee to develop a set of individual performance goals. I started this process by sitting down with the Office Manager, because I knew he would be critical to our success in keeping the searches and building addition goals on target. We went over the organizational goals and talked about how he would be involved in reaching each of those goals. Then we looked over his job description to review his other responsibilities. We used the Personal Workshop that follows to identify some goals for the coming year.

NEIGHBORHOOD
MEDICAL CLINIC

Personal Workshop #32
Goals for Individual Employees

Position: Office Manager

Performance Goals	**Action Plans**
1. Keep all searches on schedule	• Prepare timetable for all search-related tasks (January)
	• Coordinate all correspondence, meetings, and interviews on timely basis (February to December)
2. Keep accountant search on schedule	• Research accounting firms (July/August)
	• Schedule interviews (September)
3. Keep building project on schedule	• Prepare timetable (March)
	• Coordinate meetings, etc. on timely basis (March - end of project)
4. Facility ready for new doctor and P.A.	• Order new furniture (February)
	• Coordinate cleanup and preparation of examining rooms & offices (February to April)
5. Implement new patient follow-up	• Research and test available software and make recommendation (May)
	• Order and arrange for system installation (June)
	• Schedule training for staff (June/July)
6. Revamp work schedules to accommodate new hours and staff	• Track patients/hour in clinic to determine if office staff can be better utilized (January to April)

	• Meet with each staff member regarding their preferred schedules, desire to work additional hours, etc. (May to June)
	• Develop, test, and implement revised schedule (July to October)
7. Learn how to implement TQM	• Participate in clinic training (January to December)

THE PURPOSE OF THIS WORKSHOP IS TO SET INDIVIDUAL PERFORMANCE GOALS.

Personal Workshop #32
Goals for Individual Employees

Position:

Performance Goals   **Action Plan**

Workshop Follow-Up

Each employee in your company should have a set of individual performance goals to guide his or her work activity. Those goals need not be complicated. In fact, it might be reasonable for an employee to have only one goal: a one percent increase in productivity, for example. The important thing is that the employee participates in the goal setting and knows where he or she is heading and why. Remember, though, that to keep goals motivational, they should not be viewed as quotas. Otherwise, an employee who might otherwise shoot for a 10 percent increase in productivity will set a goal of one percent, just to be sure he or she makes the goal.

Step 3: Provide Ongoing Training and Coaching

> *"Haves and have nots are the second stage. The first stage is did and did nots."*
>
> —Anonymous

The demands of doing business and the needs of customers change over time. A successful business keeps track of customers' changing needs and responds to them. As the owner/manager of your business, you must ensure that employees have the skills required to effectively respond to the changing needs of your customers.

Ongoing training can give employees these skills. It may take the form of technical training to teach employees how to operate new equipment or special training to help workers understand a new vision or philosophy. Employees may need training in such basic management processes as problem solving, project management, planning and decision making.

Training is only one method of developing employee skills. In many cases a company will select an employee—a supervisor or a more experienced person—to coach another employee. A coach can help teach new skills and encourage self-learning. Coaching supports the management of employee performance several ways:

- Coaches can confirm that employees understand company vision and goals.

- Employees and their coaches can set goals together.

- Coaches can diagnose any performance problems early and take corrective action.

- Coaching can be motivational. Employees typically respond positively when a coach takes the time to work with them. Daily coaching can go a long way to keeping employee performance on track.

Coaching and training are two techniques which can help your employees perform their best. For more detail on ongoing training and coaching, refer to Challenge 2, "Developing Your Employees through Education and Training."

FYI

Setting individual goals for performance should always be a "joint venture"—both the employee and the supervisor should work together. Then, and only then, can you expect the employee to be committed to achieving those goals.

Step 4: Understand and Apply Motivation Theory

Motivation is "the set of forces that cause people to behave in certain ways."[1] There are many theories about what motivates employees. Some of those theories suggest that leaders or managers might be able to influence how motivated an employee is by the rewards they offer or the way they treat those individuals. Other theories suggest that all people are self-motivated and employers will have little influence on them. As a business owner, it might be helpful for you to have a basic understanding of motivational theory. What follows is a brief overview of the more popular theories of motivation which have influenced management for many years. You are encouraged to select elements of these theories that make sense to you in your business.

Maslow's Hierarchy of Needs

Abraham Maslow's Hierarchy of Needs is a motivation model based on the belief that all people have basic needs which drive their behavior.[2] Maslow placed these needs in a hierarchy of importance, from the most basic physiological needs, to the most spiritual, the need for self-actualization. Maslow's model is illustrated in Figure 4.1 on p. 220.

Maslow defined **physiological needs** as food, air, shelter, rest and the absence of pain. These needs are the most basic: they enable individuals to function normally, and they are shared by all human beings. If any of these physiological needs are unmet, the person will be "motivated" to meet that need. At the second level of the hierarchy are **security and safety needs**, which keep individuals free from harm or threat. At work, these basic needs might be met by safe working conditions, benefit programs, and a sense of security in the job.

Social needs make up the next level of needs, according to Maslow, and might be satisfied in the workplace through work group affiliations, company-sponsored social events, and ongoing support and feedback from supervisors. The fourth level is **ego needs**, a person's needs for self-respect and the respect of others. An employee's ego needs might be met at work by an important title, a special assignment or an employee recognition reward.

The need for **self-actualization** is at the highest level of the hierarchy. Self-actualization has to do with spiritual and intellectual development, and Maslow believed that people concerned themselves with self-actualization only if all other levels of needs were satisfied. The work setting might provide individuals with opportunities to use their intellectual or creative abilities, achieve career advancement and enjoy professional growth.

Every time a company offers training, it enhances employee performance in two important ways. Training provides a new set of skills that helps employees do their jobs more effectively. And it nurtures a positive work environment by demonstrating that the company is willing to invest in employee growth and development.

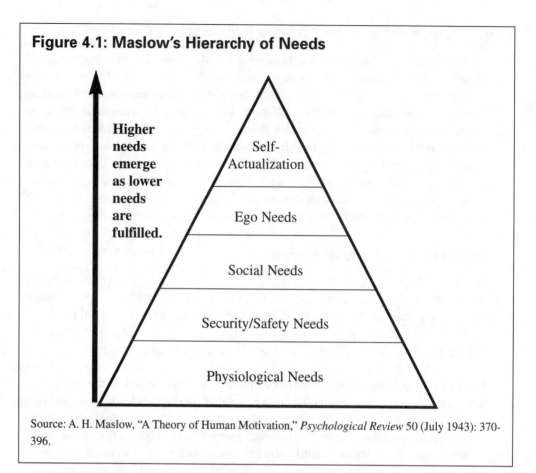

Figure 4.1: Maslow's Hierarchy of Needs

Higher needs emerge as lower needs are fulfilled.

Self-Actualization

Ego Needs

Social Needs

Security/Safety Needs

Physiological Needs

Source: A. H. Maslow, "A Theory of Human Motivation," *Psychological Review* 50 (July 1943): 370-396.

Maslow had three theories related to this model. The first was that people are motivated to do things that fulfill their unsatisfied needs. The second theory was that, once people have met their needs at the lowest level, they then become motivated to fulfill their needs at the next lowest level, and so on. The third theory was that as long as people have unfulfilled needs at a lower level they will not be motivated by higher level factors. For example, people who have unfulfilled needs for income and security will not be motivated by an exciting work project.

Although there are many arguments against Maslow's Hierarchy of Needs Theory, it has been most useful for understanding that individuals are motivated by a number of diverse factors. For managers, Maslow's theory simply suggests that what motivates one person may not motivate another.

Herzberg's Two-Factor Theory

Frederick Herzberg's two-factor theory is similar to the hierarchy of needs.[3] Herzberg identified two levels of motivation. The first contained what Herzberg called **dissatisfiers**, or **maintenance factors**, which are those factors most often mentioned by dissatisfied employees. Examples of maintenance factors are job security, wages, benefits, working conditions, supervision, status, and company policy. Note that maintenance factors are similar to Maslow's physiological, safety and social needs. Herzberg theorized that the absence of maintenance factors tends to create employee unrest and dissatisfaction. However, their presence does not necessarily create a motivated work force.

Herzberg's second level of motivation contained what he referred to as **satisfiers**, or **motivators**—those factors mentioned most often by satisfied employees. These motivators, including achievement, recognition, the work itself, responsibility, advancement and growth, tend to build self-esteem and help people reach their potential. Herzberg's motivational factors are similar to Maslow's ego and self-actualization needs.

Herzberg believed that motivators increase satisfaction and performance in the work force. He theorized that their absence would not cause dissatisfaction, although their presence would create a positive and energetic work environment. Herzberg's Two-Factor Theory suggests that to motivate individuals in the workplace, managers must appeal to their higher level needs, rather than basic needs.

McGregor's Theory "X" And "Y"[4]

Douglas McGregor formed his theory of management by studying the fundamental beliefs managers have about employees and deducing the impact these beliefs have on employee motivation. McGregor identified two basic types of leaders. The first, the Theory X leader, believes that people are by nature lazy and will avoid work. Leaders who hold this pessimistic view believe the way to motivate their employees is to be directing, controlling and coercing. The Theory Y leader, on the other hand, believes that people by nature enjoy work, are creative and seek out responsibility. They view employees as self-directed and committed to objectives. Leaders who share this more optimistic view motivate their employees by creating an environment in which workers are free to set and implement their own goals.

Citing Maslow's hierarchy of needs, McGregor suggested that a Theory X style of management might be effective in motivating employees who have lower level needs. For example, employees might be motivated by coercion if they need their jobs and fear losing them. However, McGregor argued that only a Theory Y style of management can motivate employees at the higher needs levels.

Although McGregor knew that managers could not actually *give* employees self-actualization or self-respect, he did believe they could provide an environment in which it was possible for employees to achieve these needs. McGregor's Theory Y suggests that overall business performance can be influenced by employee needs. When business owner/managers demonstrate how important employees are to company performance, they can help employees meet their social and self-actualization needs.

Vroom's Expectancy Theory

Victor H. Vroom believed that employees choose, consciously or unconsciously, to perform or not to perform at work based on three specific factors.[5] The first fac-

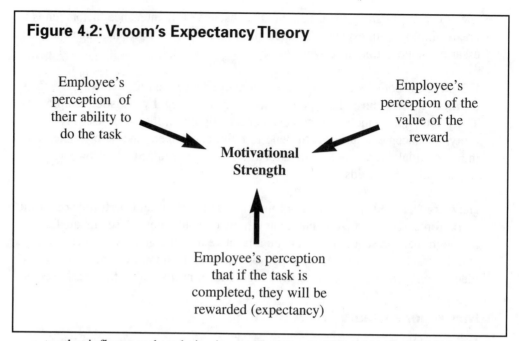

Figure 4.2: Vroom's Expectancy Theory

Employee's perception of their ability to do the task

Employee's perception of the value of the reward

Motivational Strength

Employee's perception that if the task is completed, they will be rewarded (expectancy)

tor that influences that choice is a person's perception of his or her ability to perform a given task. If an employee believes he or she can do it, motivation is strong. If an employee doesn't think he or she can, motivation will be less.

The second factor is the employee's belief (or expectancy) that if he or she does something, a certain result will occur. In other words, if the employee believes that performing a task will lead to a desired outcome, the motivation to do that task will be strong. If, on the other hand, the employee believes completing the task will not produce desirable results, motivation will be weak or neutral.

The third factor is the employee's preference for a certain outcome. If an employee really wants a pay increase, a promotion or some other outcome, motivation may be strong. But if the employee expects a negative outcome—such as additional stress, longer hours or jealous co-workers—he or she may not be motivated.

According to Vroom, an employee's motivation is dependent upon all three factors. This concept is illustrated in Figure 4.2. In other words, motivation depends upon whether the employee thinks they can achieve an outcome, whether a reward is expected for that achievement, and whether the employee values that reward. If evaluation is high on all three factors, motivation likely will be high. But if the employee views even one factor without enthusiasm, motivation may be low or neutral. This theory suggests that managers should be sure that employees have the ability to do what they are asked, that they are rewarded for their accomplishments, and that those rewards are valued by the employee.

Equity Theory

J. Stacy Adams developed his equity theory to explain how employees' views of fairness in their work influence their behaviors.[6] Employees make two comparisons,

Adams found. First, they compare the investment they make in their jobs with the rewards they receive. Their investment may include level of effort, educational background and experience; rewards might be pay, benefits, career advancement and job "perks." According to Adams, if employees perceive an inequity between their investment and the reward, they will direct their energy toward correcting the inequity—not toward their jobs.

Employees also compare their investment and rewards with those of co-workers. If they believe that other employees receive higher rewards for less investment, they will direct their energy toward balancing the perceived inequity.

Attempts to gain equity may take several forms. An employee might increase or decrease their effort. If the employee feels he or she is under-rewarded, they may try to improve their compensation package or some other element of the reward system. Or the employee might try to alter his or her perception of the inequitable relationship. If none of these methods works, the employee might choose to leave the company. This "leaving" can be mental—no further commitment to the job, or physical— the employee quits.

Equity theory may help explain why some employees lose their motivation. This theory suggests the need to be aware of actual or perceived inequities and to maintain a work environment that employees perceive as fair.

Reinforcement Theory

B.F. Skinner's Reinforcement Theory focuses on changing behavior by using positive and negative consequences.[7] Skinner believed that people experience needs or drives that cause them to behave in a certain way. Those behaviors have consequences. The resulting consequences influence whether individuals will repeat behaviors.

If a behavior results in a positive consequence, individuals are likely to be motivated to repeat it. Skinner referred to this as **positive reinforcement**. If the behavior doesn't result in negative consequences, individuals may repeat it. He called this **negative reinforcement**. On the other hand, if a behavior results in negative consequences or punishment, individuals are likely to decrease it. If a behavior doesn't result in positive consequences, people might decide not to do it again, a choice which Skinner dubbed extinction.

Skinner believed that applying positive and negative consequences can influence people's behavior. This is called **behavior modification**. For the consequences to be effective, they must be applied shortly after the behavior occurs. Here's a workplace illustration: A manager asks an employee to do something, but forgets to thank the employee even though the job was done well. The lack of instant positive reinforcement may discourage the employee from accepting future assignments (extinction). Or if the employee does a poor job with the assignment, but the manager neglects to address the poor performance right away, the employee is likely to believe the work was satisfactory and continue to produce at the same level (negative reinforcement).

Key Word

Skinner's theory has some drawbacks. It implies that employees do not think, but simply respond to stimuli. It doesn't give employees credit for understanding their own needs or having the ability to communicate these needs to their supervisors. Furthermore, Skinner's theory doesn't address a person's higher level needs, such as ego and self-actualization. Even with these drawbacks, though, Skinner's theory illustrates the relationship between behavior and the positive or negative reinforcement of that behavior.

From Theory to the "Real World"

All of these theories have helped shape the way businesses try to motivate their employees today, through the use of rewards and managerial style. Following are some examples of how you might apply motivation theory to your small business.

Employee Compensation

Maslow and Herzberg made it clear that money isn't the only thing that motivates employees. At the same time, money does play a role in fulfilling needs at every level. It can buy food and shelter, it can be invested to build a secure future, and it can enable employees to partake in social groups and buy those things that improve a person's status or image. Money can also support the freedom required to pursue a state of "self-actualization." Whether money motivates employees or not will always be a great debate—however, it is safe to say that there are very few people who would be willing to work for your business if you don't pay them.

At the same time, equity theory has shown that employees must believe they are being paid fairly with respect to others, and with respect to the investment they have made in the job. With this knowledge, be careful to develop pay systems that are fair. To help know what is fair, you might conduct salary surveys to learn the fair market value of jobs, and you should periodically analyze jobs to ensure that the compensation fits the position.

The job analysis process is fully described in Challenge 1, "Hiring the Right Employees." Take another look at this process when you are ready to conduct job analysis.

Expectancy theory also plays a role in compensation. Employees must believe that compensation is tied to performance, and they must value money as a positive reward. As odd as this sounds, if an employee sees more money as causing tax problems or the "root of all evil," he or she might not value a raise as much as a different reward. As an owner/manager, then, you need to be sure that your employees know the connection between their performance and their rewards, and you need to understand the limits of compensation as a reward. Finally, commissions, profit sharing, bonuses and merit increase programs might all be viewed as ways to "positively reinforce" performance.

Employee Benefits

Many of the needs identified by Maslow and Herzberg can be met in one way or another with employee benefits. Your business probably fulfills some of the physiological needs of your employees with minimum wages and minimum safety standards. You might offer some security with health care benefits, a retirement plan or a commitment to seniority. The higher level needs of your employees might be satisfied by your sponsorship of events that bring employees together socially, (such as company picnics and parties, company-sponsored sports teams/leagues), or programs that help people grow, like mentoring, training, and professional development programs.

Expectancy theory has helped managers understand the importance of having benefits that employees value. You might want to conduct a survey to learn what kinds of benefits your employees want. Or, you might consider offering a cafeteria benefit plan, which gives your employees a choice of benefits up to a certain dollar amount. This way, employees can select those benefits which best meet their personal needs.

Employee Participation

These programs are a direct result of motivation theory. McGregor's theory in particular had a strong influence on the movement toward participatory management. Managers have learned the value of involving employees in planning, goal setting, problem solving and decision making. This involvement meets some of the higher level motivational needs. Social needs are met when employees work with others to plan and solve problems. Ego needs are met when employees know they are important to the organization. Self-actualization needs are met when employees become excited about their work and their contributions.

This does not mean that you need to involve every employee in every decision you make in your company. It does suggest, however, that you seriously consider how you can get your employees more deeply involved in every aspect of your business. Involved employees tend to be better informed and more committed to the success of the business as a whole.

Feedback and Coaching

Motivation theory has changed the way managers relate to employees. Instead of simply directing them to do the work, managers now provide feedback and coaching. Immediate and positive feedback can reinforce good work habits and increase

Be cautious in using compensation to "motivate" your employees. There is a body of literature that supports the notion that such extrinsic rewards have only a temporary effect on employee performance.

FYI

the likelihood that those habits will continue. Feedback and coaching can contribute strongly to an employee's achievement and desire to reach peak performance. When employees know that you are interested personally in their success, their self-esteem increases.

Step 5: Provide Leadership that Builds Autonomy

As helpful as motivation theory is, those who apply it can be successful only if they also have strong leadership skills. Providing leadership that builds autonomy is the fifth and possibly the most important step in individual performance management.

Research has shown time and again that high performing organizations also have the best leaders. One of the things these leaders consistently do is develop a high degree of autonomy in their employees. They insist that decisions be left to the people who must implement and live with them. They don't require multiple layers of managerial approval. They give employees the power to make decisions, encourage them to take risks and support them when they make mistakes or "fail."

> *"Motivation does not produce success. But success produces motivation. So if you create opportunities for success, employees will be motivated."*
>
> —Ingrid Wallace

This freedom enhances employee performance in a number of ways. It makes employees accountable for their jobs and decisions. With this accountability comes an increased sense of responsibility to do a good job. It also speeds up decision making by stripping away several rounds of approval. And it helps employees develop managerial skills. The better developed these skills become, the more able employees are to make good decisions. As a bonus, they improve their performance as well.

Principle-Centered Leadership

It takes a special leadership approach to create this kind of autonomy in employees. Stephen R. Covey's book entitled *Principle-Centered Leadership* describes such an approach. Covey proposes that successful leaders are those who live by a set of simple and natural principles. They use these principles to help them make decisions. In particular, Covey identifies seven principles for building high performance in organizations.[8]

Covey's Principles for Building High Performance

1. Specify desired results, but don't supervise methods and means.
2. Ensure that the desired results are reinforced by your business vision and values.
3. Go heavy on guidelines, light on procedures.
4. Tell employees about the available resources.
5. Involve people in setting performance standards.
6. Agree on the consequences of achieving (or not achieving) specified results.
7. Trust and believe in people.

Developing Employee Autonomy

Small business managers can use Covey's principles as guidelines to develop autonomy in employees. In a coaching or training session, specify your desired results and explain how these results are consistent with the company's vision. Find out your employees' current level of technical competence and determine their confidence in their ability to do the job. If an employee's competence and confidence levels are high—and if you have confidence in the employee's judgment—allow him or her complete autonomy to determine the methods and means to get the job done. If either the competence or confidence level is low, work with the employee to increase that level. The higher the level of competence and confidence, the higher the level of autonomy the employee should be given. Your goal always should be to get every employee's competence and confidence levels as high as possible.

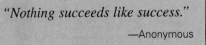

Once you have specified your desired results, give the employee some guidelines for getting the job done. The employee needs to know what and where the resources are. In addition, you and the employee should work together to set performance standards, and to agree on the rewards for meeting or consequences for failing to meet those standards.

> *"Nothing succeeds like success."*
> —Anonymous

When the coaching session is over and your employee begins work, the most important thing you can do is trust and believe in his or her ability to do the job. Leave your employee alone to do the job. If the employee fails, help him or her learn from the mistakes. Placing blame serves no purpose. Instead, ask questions about the problem and help the employee correct the situation. Ask what caused it. How would the employee like to fix it? What would they do differently the next time? If you trust in your employees, you will find that they will freely seek help and advice when they need it.

Step 6: Analyze and Manage Individual Performance Problems

No matter how good your leadership is, eventually you are likely to encounter an employee who does not perform as well as he or she should. In fact, studies consistently show that 10 to 25 percent of the people on any given work team will develop performance problems at some point. The sixth step of individual performance management is to analyze and manage performance problems.

FYI

In order to help every employee meet their personal needs, try to be as creative and flexible as possible in offering benefits. Obviously, your average 50-year-old female employee isn't going to be thrilled to know that you offer paid maternity leave as a benefit—but she might be very thrilled at the possibility of a flexible work schedule. A well thought-out cafeteria plan can provide the flexibility that makes employees happy, while keeping the value of benefits equitable, which is another important consideration.

Your failure to handle performance problems quickly and constructively can have both personal and organizational consequences: morale suffers, products or service can become shoddy, errors and accidents can increase, and your credibility as an effective manager may be at stake. One employee's performance problem can affect the performance, behavior and stress levels of many other people.

Robert F. Mager suggests a six-step process for managing performance problems[9]:

Analyzing and Managing Performance Problems

1. Identify the performance discrepancy.
2. Decide if the discrepancy is important.
3. Determine if there is a skill deficiency.
4. If there is a skill deficiency, determine if you should provide training, practice or feedback.
5. If there is not a skill deficiency, apply motivation principles to encourage performance.
6. If all else fails, determine whether to change the job requirements, transfer the employee or terminate the employee.

> *"I think the one lesson I have learned is that there is no substitute for paying attention."*
>
> —Diane Sawyer

Although these steps can be useful in analyzing and managing performance problems, keep in mind that all performance issues are different—in handling problems, you must adapt to the individual situation to be effective.

Identifying a performance problem requires specific information. Before taking action, you need to consider the following questions:

- Which job requirement has not been fulfilled?
- What is being done that shouldn't be done?
- What isn't being done that should?

Take the time to analyze the problem carefully and write down your observations. You can refer back to those notes as you continue your analysis.

Once you have identified the problem, you need to determine if the problem is serious. Don't get caught in the trap of correcting something simply because it is

FYI

There is a story told about an IBM executive who turned in his resignation after making a major booboo—a $6,000,000 mistake. Apparently the new product he was in charge of developing didn't work. To his surprise, though, his boss rejected his resignation saying, "What's this resignation? I just spent six million dollars training you!"

being done differently than you would do it. Remember that Covey recommends leaving the method and means to the employee. If an employee's different approach results in no negative outcomes, it may be better to ignore it.

If you decide the problem must be addressed, the next step is to determine whether the employee lacks a skill needed to do the job right. This might be accomplished by talking to the employee, observing the employee, or assessing the employee's skills in some other way, such as testing. If you decide the employee has a skill deficiency, you have three options:

- **Train the employee**, especially if he or she has never received training on this skill before.

- **Offer feedback** about the skill deficiency if it appears that the employee has neglected to use a skill learned in previous training.

- **Offer periodic practice** to build a skill. This is a logical choice if the employee has been trained to use the skill, but doesn't have much opportunity to use it on the job. Occasional practice should help the employee fine-tune the skill—that is why police officers have regular target practice.

If a lack of skills is not causing the problem, you must find out why the employee is not motivated to perform up to standard. Consider the following:

- **Does the employee feel punished for completing a task at the desired level of performance?** For example, if the employee who performed well on an assignment he or she considered undesirable (like taking meeting notes), is always asked to do that job in the future, the employee may feel that he or she is being punished for doing a good job.

- **Are there adequate consequences for non-performance?** If you find it difficult to confront problems or give negative feedback to employees, or if you ignore poor performance, your employees will have little incentive to change.

- **Are there any obstacles to performing the job?** For example, is the employee having difficulty getting the information from other employees that he or she needs to complete a report on time? In such cases, you must do what you can to remove those obstacles.

Sometimes, all these attempts at correction may fail. Maybe the employee just can't learn the required skills, or maybe he or she simply doesn't want to do the job. The options then are to change the requirements of the job, transfer the employee to another job or terminate the employee.

According to a study by the Society for Human Resources, the biggest complaint from employees today is not about pay or security, but rather that someone isn't doing his or her share of the work.

FYI

Terminating employees may be one of the toughest jobs you face. Nothing will make it an enjoyable experience, but a little planning can be very helpful and can result in a better experience for both you and the employee.

Tips for Terminating an Employee

- Try to put yourself in the employee's position. How would you feel? What questions would you want answered? How would you like to be treated? Prepare yourself accordingly.

- Always conduct a termination meeting face-to-face in a private place on company premises.

- Keep the termination meeting brief, and give the employee a clear reason for the termination. Let the employee know that your decision is irreversible and that it is supported by management. Avoid any long discussion—by this point it is not necessary and may only lead to an argument.

- Be firm and honest throughout the meeting. Allow the employee to express feelings and be empathetic in your response.

- Clearly define the next steps after the meeting is over. Address what the employee should do immediately following the meeting, what the procedure is for returning company property, removing personal property, and other housekeeping issues.

Step 7: Provide Performance Feedback

Key Word

All employees need feedback. Good performers need to hear that they are doing a good job just as much as poor performers need to hear how they must improve. Traditionally, performance feedback is given only during annual or semi-annual **performance appraisals**. But business management specialists these days are questioning whether formal performance appraisals should be the only feedback mechanism, or whether they should be used at all.

The Traditional Performance Appraisal

"If you have to swallow a frog, don't look at it too long."

—Ulysses S. Grant

Historically, performance appraisals have been used to let employees know how they are doing on the job. Managers have traditionally set standards for employees and, after a set period of time, met with employees to conduct a performance review. In theory, these ratings told employees how they performed against their supervisor's standards. This process presented several interrelated problems. Standards set by supervisors were not always clear. That lack of clarity produced subjective and inconsistent evaluations. And, because employees usually did not participate in setting the standards, they often lacked a commitment to meet them.

Over time, performance appraisals evolved to become management cure-alls. They were used as the basis for merit increases and promotions. Performance meetings grew to have many purposes. In one or two hour meetings, managers were expected to give employees feedback on their performance, identify their developmental needs, create a plan for improvement, discuss career interests and create objectives for the next performance period. In that same meeting, employees were expected to offer self-evaluations and give their managers feedback.

> *"Evaluation should be developmental, not just judgmental."*
>
> —Elaine Estervig Beaubian

Of course, it is impossible to complete all those tasks in so short a time. As a result, performance appraisals often yield little value for either managers or employees and produce little enthusiasm among anyone. The performance appraisal, in many cases, is used as a written justification for merit increases or disciplinary action, rather than a tool to promote continuous improvement.

Today, performance appraisals are commonly used in organizations of all sizes, in spite of their drawbacks and limits. Performance review processes take many different forms. Many involve having the supervisor rate performance by putting check marks in boxes on a standard form. Others require that both the supervisor and the employee rate the employee's performance, and then meet to discuss it. Other performance reviews may simply involve an informal meeting between the supervisor and the employee every so often, or a narrative description of the employee's performance by the supervisor. Each system has its plusses and minuses.

If you choose to use a traditional performance review process, usually done annually, be careful to develop a process that promotes positive performance development and continuous improvement. Performance review can be a useful tool for helping employees achieve peak performance, but only if it is known to be tied to the future development of employees rather than to punishing them for their past mistakes.

You should be able to locate samples of traditional performance review rating forms in your library in any book related to human resources management. Or, you can purchase software which will help you develop your own performance review system using "court-tested" language. Software is available for both Windows and Macintosh. Two sources of performance review software are Austin-Hayne Corporation ("Employee Appraiser") at (800) 809-9920, and KnowledgePoint ("Performance Now!") at (800) 727-1133.

Legal Note

There are many ways you can get into legal difficulties by improperly discharging employees. Don't wait until you need to fire someone to learn about the possible legal implications, since firing should be considered a long-range process. One good reference is the article, "Firing 101: Before, During and After" by Milton Bordwin in the *Small Business Forum*, Winter 1994-95. To order a reprint of this article, call the University of Wisconsin Small Business Development Center at (608) 263-7843 or fax (608) 262-3878.

Alternative Feedback Methods

Key Word

Cross Organizational Feedback: What are the alternatives to traditional performance appraisals? Many businesses are experimenting with simpler, more flexible feedback models and finding them to be effective. One such model is giving **cross-organizational feedback** (also called 360-degree feedback). In this model, feedback occurs throughout a business, not just between a supervisor and employee. For example, a company's new product development team would seek feedback from everyone who has a hand in helping to develop, produce and distribute new products. Feedback does not "point fingers" or place blame. Its main purpose is to provide ideas for improvement.

Pegasus Computer Systems/Jean Watson: Once the Team for Customer Follow-up had pretty well decided on a new system, team members approached everyone in the company to get their feedback about the system and the process they went through to select it. The team decided to conduct the following survey.

Customer Follow-up System Survey

Please answer the questions below from the perspective of your position at Pegasus. Return your survey to the office by Friday. We appreciate your feedback—it will help us implement the best possible customer follow-up system for everyone. Thank you for taking the time to answer these questions.

1. What do you believe is the ideal follow-up time after a sale and why?

2. What do you believe is the ideal follow-up time after a service call and why?

3. What concerns or suggestions do you have about coordinating follow-up call among sales and service representatives?

4. What do you think is the greatest benefit of the follow-up system we have tentatively selected?

5. What do you think is the greatest weakness of the follow-up system we have tentatively selected?

6. Will this weakness prevent you from providing good service to our customers, and, if so, how?

7. What suggestions do you have for overcoming this weakness?

8. Do you feel you had adequate input into the system selection process?

9. What recommendations do you have for improving the process next time?

Key Word

Peer or Team Review: Another alternative feedback model is **peer or team review**. Successful teams have clear goals and are committed to results. Any team's effectiveness in reaching its business goals depends largely upon the dynamics of the team. How team members interrelate, communicate and cooperate with one another affects that dynamic. In a peer review, team members evaluate their performance as a team and each other as team members. The team members might evaluate their structure, their problem-solving and conflict-management skills, their use of team resources, their clarity of objectives, and/or their achievements as a team. Team members might evaluate each other in terms of communication skills (listening, speaking, etc.), team leadership skills, and individual cooperation in moving the team forward. Once again, feedback is given in the spirit of improvement and making the team more effective.

Personal Workshop Preparation #33: Peer or Team Feedback

The workshop feedback form that follows has been developed for all employees to give meaningful, yet sensitive feedback to their peers. Try this feedback form with a small group of employees to see how it works. Be sure the employees understand that the purpose of the feedback is to help the team work more effectively together. It may take some employees a little while to feel comfortable offering feedback to other employees or talking openly about how they feel the group functioned as a team. With a little practice, though, employees should become more comfortable with the process and less threatened by the possibility of being critiqued by their peers.

Observe how Candace and Tony Washington from PCB Corporation completed Personal Workshop #33.

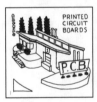

PCB Corporation/Candace and Tony Washington: We have been looking for a feedback system that will be developmental, not just critical. We wanted something that was fairly simple, yet required some serious thought; and we wanted something that would help promote the quality/team concept we are trying to instill in our employees. Following a recent team effort to reduce the number of defects in our printed circuit boards, we used the following feedback form. Each team member completed a feedback form for every other individual in the group, management or not. After everyone had a chance to read over the feedback from their peers, we got together as a group again to process what we had learned and to talk about how we could improve our performance, both as individuals and as a team. This was done in a non-confrontational way—no placing of blame—and the results were, we believe, very gratifying.

Personal Notes

_____

_____

_____

THE PURPOSE OF THIS WORKSHOP IS TO FACILITATE PEER OR TEAM FEEDBACK.

Personal Workshop #33
Peer or Team Feedback

Employee: Adam Wayne

I see that you have contributed to our work in the following way(s):
1. Knowledge from years of assembler experience
2. Several creative ideas about improving the process
3. Helped keep everyone open-minded

I admire these strength(s) in you:
1. Open to change
2. Very patient
3. Very creative

I think we could work better together if I:
1. Would quit interrupting you
2. Understood the assembly process better

I think we could work better together if you:
1. Would explain things in a non-technical way
2. Would arrive at meetings on time

Additional comments and concerns:

I'm sharing this with you in the interest of improving our work relationship. Please let me know what I can do to improve that relationship.

Peer Evaluator: Kate Butler

Date: January 10

THE PURPOSE OF THIS WORKSHOP IS TO FACILITATE PEER OR TEAM FEEDBACK.

Personal Workshop #33
Peer or Team Feedback

Employee:

I see that you have contributed to our work in the following way(s):

I admire these strength(s) in you:

I think we could work better together if I:

I think we could work better together if you:

Additional comments and concerns:

I'm sharing this with you in the interest of improving our work relationship. Please let me know what I can do to improve that relationship.

Peer Evaluator:

Date:

Workshop Follow-Up

✔ This feedback format described in the previous workshop could actually be used by a supervisor in evaluating the performance of an employee, not just in the instance of peer feedback. You may want to change the questions to meet the needs of your particular situation. But read over the questions to be sure they are developmental, not judgmental, since that should be your goal in any performance evaluation. Use this form as your guide while you and your employee work together to accomplish what needs to be accomplished—reaching peak performance.

Customer Feedback

Customer feedback is a crucial component of measuring performance. Businesses can ask customers what they think in several ways. They can send out "feedback cards," postage-paid cards with preprinted questionnaires. The questions seek to learn how customers feel generally about the business and specifically about their last encounter with the business. When customers offer feedback, they provide valuable information about what is important to them and how the business and its employees can improve.

How you obtain customer feedback depends entirely upon who and where your customers are. If you own a retail establishment, it might be easiest to ask customers to fill out a very short questionnaire at the time of purchase. Participation, of course, would be strictly voluntary, but if you keep the questions short and to the point, many customers should be willing to fill it out while you are putting their goods in a package. Some restaurants leave customer feedback cards on the table for clients to fill out. If you have a service business, it might be easiest to simply ask your customers a few questions at your initial meeting. For example, you might ask how they learned about your services or what they are looking for in a service provider. Another option would be to send a customer feedback card along with your invoice and ask the client to include it when he or she sends a check. Whatever method you use for customer feedback, remember to keep your questions short and friendly—otherwise the customer won't bother to answer. Also, keep in mind that many customers often won't send in a customer feedback form unless they are either ecstatic or disgusted with your product or service. Still,

FYI

It has been said that technology is a great equalizer. What does that mean to your business? It means that, sooner or later, someone will have a product just as good as yours, with all the fancy bells and whistles that customers want. When that happens, your customers will go to the company that offers something more than a topnotch product—they will go to the company that makes them *feel good* about their purchase.

They will go where they can get the best price, the quickest service, or the friendliest smile. With the advent of technology, how you treat your customers will make the difference in whether or not your business survives.

as unbalanced as your responses may be, this information can be very important to your future success.

Personal Workshop Preparation #34: Customer Feedback Form

The following workshop gives you the opportunity to design a customer feedback form for use in your small business. To encourage maximum participation by your customers, keep your feedback form friendly and easy to answer.

Champy Athletic Products/Terry Rawl: Since our customers are spread out over four states, we decided that sending them a postcard size Customer Feedback Form was the best way to get in better touch with their needs. We include a card in the invoice and ask that they return it when they pay their bill.

THE PURPOSE OF THIS WORKSHOP IS TO DEVELOP A CUSTOMER FEEDBACK FORM FOR YOUR BUSINESS.

Personal Workshop #34
Customer Feedback Form

Revise this card to meet the specific needs of your company for feedback from customers.

To our customers:
Our goal is to offer the best possible service. To help us serve you better, please take a few minutes to complete and return this form.

1. How many times have you used purchased our products in the past year?
   (circle one)   none   1   2   3   4+

2. How often did we provide services to your satisfaction?
   always   usually   sometimes   never

3. If you had a question or problem, how quickly did we resolve it?
   immediately   same day   within a week   more than a week

4. How would you rate our service?
   excellent   good   fair   poor

5. Please offer additional comments or suggestions here:

Thanks and it is our pleasure to serve you! *Champy Athletic Products*

Personal Workshop #34
Customer Feedback Form

Revise this card to meet the specific needs of your company for feedback from customers.

To our customers:
Our goal is to offer the best possible service. To help us serve you better, please take a few minutes to complete and return this form.

1.

2.

3.

4.

5. Please offer additional comments or suggestions here:

Thanks and it is our pleasure to serve you!

Workshop Follow-Up

You can either mail this card to customers who have recently used your services, hand it to them at the end of a service transaction or include it with your product packaging. If you expect your customers to return the form by mail, have it pre-posted.

Characteristics of Effective Feedback

With traditional performance appraisals, managers and supervisors were the only ones who needed to give feedback. New approaches require that *everyone* in a company give and receive feedback to and from people in their 360-degree circle. Managers and employees alike need good feedback skills.

Feedback requires clear communications. People giving feedback need to articulate their thoughts well. They also need to be good listeners because the best feedback sessions involve a 50/50 exchange between individuals. Although feedback often relates to past behavior, it should focus on how to handle the future. Because feedback is so essential for improvement, it should be a continuous process.

Feedback can be delivered in many ways. It can be formal, in which case two or more people plan a meeting and give each other structured feedback. Or it can be informal, with employees and/or managers spontaneously sharing their views. No matter how it is delivered, to be effective, feedback should be:

- Based on performance

- Specific to the circumstances. For example, don't just say, "good job!" Instead say, "you did a good job in clearing up the confusion on that order!"

- Equitable—be sure that every employee gets feedback when it is deserved

- As immediate as possible

- Honest and sincere

Tips for Giving Effective Feedback

Giving feedback doesn't have to be difficult. The key is to remember a few simple principles:

- Don't procrastinate. People need to hear what they have done shortly after they do it. Otherwise, they may not even remember the circumstances. And, if the feedback is good, the person wants to hear about it right away.

- Reserve feedback for issues within a person's control. It is frustrating to be criticized when you cannot control the circumstances that caused the problem. Ask yourself before you offer feedback whether it is appropriate.

- Offer feedback in an appropriate environment. If the issue is difficult, find a private place to talk. Praise should often be given publicly, but employees and managers should remember to dole out praise equitably. If one employee is praised for something others have done as well, the motivation of the other employees may suffer.

- Make sure the timing is right. Offering feedback when an employee is busy or distracted may not have much impact. If the feedback concerns a problem and the employee is having a bad day, it might be better to wait for another day.

- Before you offer any feedback, begin by creating a comfortable environment. Explain the purpose of the feedback: to improve and to explore better ways to work together. Make every attempt to keep the feedback developmental rather than blaming. If an employee begins to feel defensive, you are both less likely to come up with a positive and creative solution. Negative feedback should always be offered calmly with an explanation of the concerns and consequences of the problem. Specific examples can clarify the issue. And people should only speak on their own behalf; no one should deliver feedback for other people.

- Give the person receiving the feedback a chance to respond. Both sides need to listen carefully. Try to understand the other person's perspective and the circumstances which affected the performance. The person giving feedback should be supportive of the recipient.

After both people have aired their views, you can begin working together on a resolution. The key is to focus on the future and find a solution that both sides can accept. Try to answer some key questions. What can be done to prevent the problem from happening again? How can you do a better job the next time you are in a similar situation? The discussion should be mutual and non-confrontive. The spirit should be one of change, not blame. When an agreement is reached, the decisions should be summarized in writing to make sure both participants concur.

Receiving Feedback

As difficult as it is to give criticism, it is usually harder to receive it. However, the ability to gracefully accept criticism is important in individual performance management. Once again, as the business owner/manager, you must take the lead.

Business owner/managers need to be role models for both giving and receiving feedback. You can begin by making feedback a part of your business culture. That requires building an environment of trust. Employees must feel confident that they can say what they think without a member of management becoming defensive or placing blame. If you will seek out feedback to learn more about yourself, your employees will follow that lead.

Personal Workshop Preparation #35: Leadership Survey

This workshop will allow you to assess your leadership skills in your business, as well as to demonstrate to your employees how to seek out and gracefully receive feedback. Change the questions, if necessary, to get the information you need to develop your leadership skills. First, complete the Leadership Quiz on your own. Try to be as honest as you possibly can. Then, ask your employees for their honest feedback. Although this exercise can be pretty scary, it could be the first step to developing a more honest and productive work environment—and it could be an important step in helping you, as owner/manager, achieve peak performance.

 **Champy Athletic Products/Terry Rawl:** I can hardly expect my employees to be motivated to reach their peak performance if I don't model my own desire to do the best that I can do. That's why I decided to subject myself to this leadership quiz. I think I am pretty aware of what my weaknesses are, but I guess the employees' feedback will really show me what I need to work on. I have decided to do this in the spirit in which it is intended—to become the best possible leader/manager for Champy Athletic Products and its employees.

THE PURPOSE OF THIS WORKSHOP IS TO IDENTIFY YOUR LEADERSHIP STRENGTHS AND WEAKNESSES.

Personal Workshop #35
Leadership Survey

CHAMPY ATHLETIC CO.

Periodically consider these questions to assess your leadership in your business. Ask your employees to answer them as well.

YES	NO	
X		Do I specify results and allow employees the freedom to determine their own methods and means?
X		Do the results I request match the vision and values of the business?
	X	Do I always let employees know what resources they will need and where to find them?
X		Do I encourage employees to participate in setting their own performance standards?
	X	Do I work with employees to create appropriate consequences for achieving (or not achieving) specified results?
X		Do I trust and believe in my employees, knowing that they will do the best job possible?

"I can sum up what is happening in the American workforce today in a single phrase: a growing mismatch between incentives and motivations."

—Daniel Yankelovich

Personal Workshop #35
Leadership Survey

Periodically consider these questions to assess your leadership in your business. Ask your employees to answer them as well.

YES   NO

Do I specify results and allow employees the freedom to determine their own methods and means?

Do the results I request match the vision and values of the business?

Do I always let employees know what resources they will need and where to find them?

Do I encourage employees to participate in setting their own performance standards?

Do I work with employees to create appropriate consequences for achieving (or not achieving) specified results?

Do I trust and believe in my employees, knowing that they will do the best job possible?

Workshop Follow-Up

✔ If you participated in this workshop, you have invited your employees to give you constructive criticism. Pay attention to the results—listen to your employees without interruption, excuses or defensiveness. Ask employees what you can do to improve. Work with them to come up with a plan, and then stick to it. If you don't follow the plan, you can't expect your employees to see the value of feedback. When you demonstrate that you can accept feedback and put it to good use, it is easier to encourage employees to follow your lead with each other and, more importantly, with customers.

Step 8: Use Recognition, Compensation and Rewards

The final step in managing individual performance is to provide appropriate recognition, compensation and rewards. When employees work hard to achieve desired performance, they deserve some recognition for their efforts. Unfortunately, compensation and rewards are not always used effectively. In some instances, managers administer them unfairly; in others, they reward the wrong things. The total quality approach to management has changed the way managers view these incentives.

Traditional Thinking about Recognition, Compensation and Rewards

Compensation and rewards have long been tied to performance appraisals. Merit increases, promotions, bonuses and other incentives have traditionally been based on an employee's rating on the performance appraisal. The higher the rating, the larger the merit increase; the better the work, the faster the promotion.

There are two problems with this system. The first is that it is inherently inconsistent and, therefore, unfair. Two employees, Jack and Jill, can be used as examples. Although Jack and Jill have identical jobs, they work for different bosses. They perform their jobs at about the same level, but Jack gets higher performance ratings than Jill. Why? Because Jill's boss is a tougher evaluator. Jill's boss practices the philosophy that employees should never get the highest rating, that they should always have something to strive for. Jack's boss, on the other hand, believes in giving high ratings to keep people motivated. Because the company gives merit increases based on performance appraisal ratings, Jill is punished not for her performance, but by a subjective difference in rating philosophy.

The other inherent problem is that the traditional system ignores team effort. If, for example, Jill falls behind in her work and Jack helps her out, under the traditional reward system, Jack is not likely to be recognized for his team contribution. The system also discourages Jill from speaking out on Jack's behalf because she is rewarded for her individual efforts. Two more performance problems now exist: Jack may not be motivated to work hard and pitch in, and Jack and Jill are not encouraged to work as a team.

Contemporary Thinking about Recognition, Compensation and Rewards

The total quality philosophy seeks ways to overcome the problems of traditional incentives. Two important philosophies have emerged:

- Businesses need to rethink the assumptions they use in administering incentives.

- Businesses need to change what they reward.

Key Word

Alfie Kohn, a noted author and management expert, suggests that traditional incentive plans cannot work because they use the wrong assumptions about what motivates employees.[10] Rewards and incentive plans rely too heavily on behaviorist theory (such as B. F. Skinner's reinforcement theory), and do not recognize the importance of **intrinsic motivation**, Kohn says. Intrinsic motivation comes from within the individual, not from the traditional rewards of compensation and benefits. As a result, Kohn theorizes, businesses get temporary compliance when employees are chasing after rewards, but once rewards are given, employee performance diminishes.

Peter Scholtes, a noted quality expert, believes that traditional compensation and reward systems can't work because they focus on the wrong performance.[11] Scholtes sees businesses pitting employees against each other when they offer rewards and compensation based on individual performance. Instead of working together to accomplish something of value for the customer, employees compete with each other to "win" the money or the promotion.

Scholtes cites an additional problem. Businesses often don't reward behavior that will produce the desired performance. A practice at an insurance company illustrates this point. The company sets an organizational performance goal to pay claims within 10 days. To accomplish this goal, the company offers employees incentives for the number of claims they process. The more claims, the bigger the reward. At first it appears the carrot-and-rabbit approach is working. The number of claims more than 10 days old decreases significantly. However, the company finds, over time, that the number of claims more than 30 days old is on the rise. Employees are processing only *easy* claims so they can earn the incentives. The more difficult claims, the ones that take longer to process, are set aside. The company discovers another problem when it tries to process those older claims in a unit with a high number of them. Managers encourage employees from other units to pitch in and help the troubled unit, but they aren't interested because there is no incentive for team work. Eventually, the company discovers that a couple of employees have thrown out their oldest claims. The focus on customer service is completely lost!

Potential Alternatives

A first step toward overcoming the problems posed by traditional reward and compensation practices is to balance intrinsic and extrinsic motivators. Business owner/managers should take the time to instill in employees a genuine pride and interest in their jobs. Employees want to be trusted and given the authority to do the right thing at the right time without having to run to their supervisor for permission. If you empower your employees in such a way, they will begin to focus on the customer, not on the incentives and rewards. And if your company is going to achieve its vision, you will need the commitment, not just the participation, of every single person in your organization.

One way to shift employee interest from personal compensation is to begin offering incentives for organizational performance rather than just individual performance. Here are some suggestions for shifting the focus in your company:

- Pay employees at or above market rate.

- Pay employees extra when they learn new job skills or take on increased responsibility. That encourages employees to acquire new skills.

- Don't establish classes of employees. Avoid a pay structure in which the lowest paid employee's salary is a tiny fraction of the highest paid employee's salary. To use a famous example, Ben and Jerry's ice cream has a policy that no one will earn more than seven times the salary of any other employee.

- Share the company's success and wealth. When employees work together as a team to create a profit for the business, they should share the profit on an equal basis.

- Celebrate team work. Throw a party or make a big announcement recognizing group successes. Let the team know everyone is happy and proud of their efforts.

- Encourage employees to recognize and reward each other. The company could establish a reward budget, which is a discretionary sum of money all employees have. They can spend it any way they want, as long as they use it to recognize and reward their fellow employees.

By taking a more contemporary approach to recognition, compensation and rewards, you can promote high performance and help employees focus on the needs of the customer.

You Have Completed Challenge 4

Helping your employees and work teams achieve peak performance is critical to helping your business achieve peak performance. It all has to start with a clear vision and goals—once those are set and communicated to employees, then you can concentrate on creating an environment that allows employees to center their work activities on meeting the needs of your customers and the company as a whole. By completing this Challenge, you have developed the skills to establish a system for effective performance management at every level in your small business.

FYI

Commitment is a different concept than participation. It has been said that "an egg represents participation by the chicken, while bacon represents commitment by the pig." You don't want your employees to die for your business—but the more committed they are to what you are doing and the vision before them, the more likely they are to achieve peak performance.

You Leave Challenge 4 with the Following

Information: This Challenge has been designed to give you a wealth of information about performance management at every level. Several tips are included to help you apply the theory to your business. You should leave this Challenge with some basic knowledge about motivating performance, but an understanding that there are no easy solutions when it comes to dealing with people. You know that having and communicating a clear vision, values, and goals to your employees is key to their performance success. Beyond that, it will take an environment of mutual respect and trust to stimulate your employees to perform—and that is your responsibility.

Tools: The Personal Workshops in Challenge 4 have helped you develop several tools that will be useful in implementing a comprehensive performance management system in your small business. You have developed a vision statement and company values, which should be the basis not only for performance management, but for every decision you and your employees make. You have identified key issues for your customers and your company. You have set goals and action plans to guide performance at every level. You have been given several tools to help you gather feedback from both your customers and your employees. Finally, Challenge 4 has provided you with a six-step process for analyzing and managing performance problems in your business.

Learning: You have learned the benefits of applying performance management to your business, and the importance of managing performance at every level: for the overall company, for teams or work groups, and for individual employees. This Challenge has taken you through the steps for managing performance at every level, showing you how to make goals and measurement an integral part of any system. You have learned the fundamentals of motivation theory and how to apply that theory to your business, by offering rewards which are meaningful to your employees and help to the company as it moves towards its vision through excellent service to your customers.

Networking: Several resource tips have been included in Challenge 4, including sources for software and additional reading materials. As with most topics in management, there is a lot of help available to you—you don't need to re-invent the wheel. Challenge 4 offers several subtle and not-so-subtle suggestions that you can use to rethink the way you have traditionally managed performance in your business, if you are sincerely interested in achieving peak performance at every level. Networking is essential to achieving peak performance—both with your employees and your customers.

Challenge 4 Self-Assessment

After completing this Challenge you should be able to design and implement a comprehensive performance management system for your small business. Check your understanding of the concepts and performance management process by using the following checklist. If needed, go back and review the process where you feel you need more practice.

Stating the Benefits of Performance Management to Your Small Business

( ) I have identified several ways that performance management will help my business.

Pages 189 - 193

Communicating the Vision, Values and Goals of Your Business

( ) I have a vision statement for my company, and it has been shared with every employee.

( ) I know who my primary external customers are and have identified their needs.

( ) I have a set of guiding principles, or values, for this business, and I have communicated them to every employee.

( ) I have established a system for keeping employees informed about overall performance goals.

Pages 194 - 201

Setting Goals and Planning Action for the Overall Performance of Your Business

( ) I know the key issues for my customers and my business, and I have used that information to set overall business goals.

( ) I have established goals and action plans for the overall business in each of the functional areas: human resources, financial resources, etc.

( ) I have communicated those goals and action plans to every employee.

( ) I have identified key indicators for my business, and have set up a system for measuring those indicators to monitor performance.

Pages 201 - 206

Applying the Tools for Managing Team Performance in Your Company

( ) I have involved work teams in setting up their own performance management system.

( ) Those teams have established ground rules for their activities.

( ) Those teams have clear missions, goals and action plans.

Pages 207 - 213

( ) Those teams are involved in measuring their own team performance and rewarding that performance.

**Pages
213 - 245**

Implementing the Eight Steps of Individual Performance Management

( ) I understand that my company has a diverse group of employees and that there are many possible reasons why employees may or may not achieve peak performance.

( ) I know how to hire the right people and start those people off on the right foot through orientation and training.

( ) I understand the basic concepts of motivation theory, and I have applied some of those concepts to my performance management system.

( ) I have developed a work environment that allows employees to work autonomously and in teams for peak performance.

( ) I am able to analyze and handle performance problems in my company with sensitivity.

( ) I am comfortable receiving feedback, and I have established a non-threatening work environment where every employee freely gives and seeks developmental feedback.

( ) I have implemented a reward system that furthers the goals and vision of the company.

**Pages
189 - 245**

Developing a Comprehensive Performance Management Program for Your Business

( ) I have developed a performance management system for the overall business, for team or work groups, and for individual employees in my business.

( ) Performance management in my business focuses on delivering what our customers want while maintaining financial viability.

Take Another Look

Record anything from Challenge 4, your Personal Workshops, or your personal reflections that you want to remember.

Review the results of your checklist above. If you feel you need more work in some areas, go back into the text and challenge yourself again. Developing a comprehensive performance management system is not an overnight task, so don't be discouraged if you aren't totally clear on what makes sense for your business at this time. On the other hand, failing to manage performance at every level of your company is a potential waste of your most valuable resources—your human resources. Continue to use Challenge 4 to guide your development of a performance management system over the next several months.

Endnotes

1. Richard M. Steers and Lyman W. Porter, *Motivation and Work Behavior*, 4th ed. (New York: McGraw-Hill, 1987).

2. Abraham H. Maslow, *Motivation and Personality* (New York: Harper & Brothers, 1954).

3. Frederick Herzberg, B. Mausner and B. Snyderman, *The Motivation to Work* (New York: Wiley, 1959).

4. Douglas McGregor, *The Human Side of Enterprise* (New York: McGraw-Hill, 1985).

5. Victor H. Vroom, *Work and Motivation* (New York: Wiley, 1964).

6. J. Stacy Adams, "Toward an Understanding of Inequity," *Journal of Abnormal and Social Psychology* (November 1963): 422-36.

7. B. F. Skinner, *Contingencies of Reinforcement* (New York: Appleton-Century-Crofts, 1969).

8. Stephen R. Covey, *Principle-Centered Leadership* (New York: Simon & Schuster, 1991).

9. Robert F. Mager and Peter Pipe, *Analyzing Performance Problems* (Belmont, CA: Lake Publishing Co., 1984).

10. Alfie Kohn, "Why Incentive Plans Cannot Work," *Harvard Business Review* (September-October 1993): 54-63.

11. Peter R. Scholtes, "An Elaboration on Deming's Teachings on Performance Appraisal," (Madison, WI: Joiner Associates, 1987).

You Have Mastered
Human Resources Management

Congratulations! By actively participating in the four Challenges in this guide, you have gained knowledge, learned how to use various tools, and mastered many of the skills needed to effectively manage your most important resource—your employees.

By mastering Challenge 1, you have developed the skills needed to hire the right employees for your small business. From assessing your need for a new employee to making an offer to the top candidate, you now know the steps and can implement the tools which will help take the fear and guesswork out of the hiring process. In Challenge 2, you learned how to develop and implement orientation and training programs in your company. By assessing the training needs of your employees and providing ongoing training and development opportunities, you can build a successful company with a vital and effective work force. Challenge 3 took you through the process of developing and communicating personnel policies to your employees. While developing policies and a useful employee handbook may seem tedious, your efforts will help your employees become more effective and informed; and your company will have some protection in the event of a legal challenge to your management or operating procedures. Finally, in Challenge 4, you learned several techniques for managing the performance of your employees and work teams. With a clear vision and goals for your company, you can build a work environment which will enable employees to make good decisions about their work activities and to meet the needs of your customers.

Your mastery of the human resources management concepts in this book will help you build a stronger business and better employees. But keep in mind that human resources management is a tricky business. No matter how much you know about hiring, developing employees, writing personnel policies, or managing performance, it will always be an ominous task to keep up with government regulations and the other possible legal pitfalls that could result from your personnel decisions. Remember that being a master at human resources management does not mean you know every answer to every question. The truly wise business owner/manager also knows when to get expert help.

Your employees can make your business efficient, profitable, and everything you ever dreamed it would be. They can serve your customers with confidence, help identify and solve problems, and be a joy to work with as you achieve common goals. Use and continue to develop your human resource management skills on your way to success!

Appendix I
Employee Handbook Template

The following template can help you put together your employee handbook. You can also pick and choose sections of the handbook and add to them to construct your own version.

Writing the Introduction

Introduction

Welcome to _____**company name**_____! As an employee of this company, you become part of a team dedicated to giving its customers _____**business goals**_____

_____

___. Every employee at _____**company name**_____ has the unique opportunity to enhance our image and spread goodwill among our customers and our community. This makes your job one of the most important in the company—and _____**company name**_____ wants to do whatever it can to help you succeed and grow in your position.

This is your handbook. It is meant to be an informative guide to the policies and benefits of our company. By acquainting yourself with this information, you will have a better understanding of our operations and management style—what you may expect from us and what we expect of you. If you don't understand something, please ask. We want you to feel comfortable as a member of the _____**company name**_____ team. You are now a part of an organization that has prospered through the wholehearted efforts of every employee.

In addition to this handbook, you will be trained in your job by
_____**company name**_____. The policies in
this handbook are subject to revision by the company at any time. Business
conditions can change and, therefore, these policies may also change at the
discretion of the company. You will be promptly notified in writing of any
policy changes. The contents of this book (as a whole or in any part) in no
way imply an employment contract or guaranteed employment.

Length of Service

Length of service is defined as the length of time you have been continuously employed with _____**company name**_____
_____. Your length of service will be based on your most recent hire date.
When skill and ability levels are equal, length of service will be considered
with respect to promotions, training opportunities and vacation priorities.

Length of service will be broken by these events:

❏ Voluntary resignation

❏ Termination for any reason

❏ Failure to report for work without notification for ____**#**____ consecutive days

❏ Lay-off in excess of your length of service or ____**#**____ months, whichever is less

Sexual Harassment

Sexual Harassment by or of employees of _____**company name**_____
_____ will not be tolerated. Such conduct may result in disciplinary
actions up to and including termination of employment. Unwelcome sexual
advances, requests for sexual favors, and other verbal or physical conduct of
a sexual nature constitute sexual harassment when:

❏ Submission to such conduct is made either explicitly or implicitly a term or
condition of employment;

❏ Submission to or rejection of such conduct is used as the basis for employment decisions;

❑ Such conduct has the purpose or effect of unreasonably interfering with an individual's work performance; or

❑ Such conduct creates an intimidating, hostile or offensive working environment.

If you encounter such conduct from supervisors, other employees, or clients, you should contact any of the following as you think appropriate:

❑ _____

❑ _____

❑ _____

Complaints will be investigated in a confidential manner. Please do not assume that management is aware of an activity prohibited by this policy. It is your responsibility to bring your complaints and concerns to management's attention so that they can be addressed.

_____**company name**_____ wants employees to know that they can work in a secure environment and be treated with dignity. Insulting, degrading, or exploitative treatment of any employee will not be tolerated.

Personal Appearance

Emphasis at _____**company name**_____ is to maintain a neat, clean appearance. We expect employees to exercise good sense in determining what to wear to work. Appropriate attire depends on the employee's job within these guidelines:

- _____

- _____

- _____

In cases where good taste is not demonstrated, supervisors have the responsibility to point out what is considered inappropriate attire for _____**company name**_____.

Personnel Records

_____company name_____ maintains personnel files on each employee. Your personnel file contains documentation regarding all aspects of your tenure with the company. All material in the file is strictly confidential. Access to the file is restricted to __person(s) responsible__ _____. The only information that will be released in the event of an employer's reference request is your name, dates of employment, and job title. Other employment data or credit information will be released only with your written approval.

The company allows you to view your personnel file upon written request. File access will be allowed during normal business hours and only in the presence of an authorized representative.

It is your responsibility to make sure that all your employment records are kept current. Any change in name, address, etc., should be reported to _____ **person(s) responsible** _____. Any change in marital or dependency status or in beneficiary should also be reported so that necessary changes in deductions or benefit plans can be made.

Personal Property

_____company name_____ does not assume responsibility for your personal property. Personal items and property of value should not be left in the building. If you find it necessary to leave valuables in the office, lock them up and take the key with you. Valuables should not be left unattended at your work station at any time.

Telephone Use

When answering the telephone, identify _____**company name**_____ _____ and yourself. If answering someone else's phone, always offer to help or take a message. Remember to obtain the caller's name, place of business, if applicable, phone number, and the date and time of the call. If you plan to be away from your phone, let someone know when you expect to return.

It is good business practice to restrict personal phone calls during regular business hours to emergencies only. If it is necessary to make a personal call, please do so _____ **recommended times** _____; any personal long distance calls should be put on your personal calling card. All personal calls should be kept as brief as possible.

Bulletin Boards

Information of general interest to all employees appears on the bulletin boards located _____ **names of designated areas** _____ _____. You (may/may not) have personal material posted on the bulletin boards after it has been submitted and approved by the _____. All notices will be dated and removed after _____ **specific time limit** _____.

Open Door Policy

_____ **company name** _____ has an open door policy which encourages any employee to discuss his/her work-related problems with management. You are encouraged to take any issues you wish to discuss to _____ **person(s) responsible** _____ first. _____ **person(s) responsible** _____ will treat your complaint or problem with respect. If _____ **person(s) responsible** _____ cannot resolve the problem or if you feel uncomfortable discussing the issue with _____ **person(s) responsible** ___, you should request a meeting with _____ **person(s) responsible** _____.

These individuals will try to work out a satisfactory resolution to the problem, or will direct you to someone else who can help.

Regular Work Hours

_____**company name**_____ is open from
_____**hours of operation**_____. Work schedules for
employees will be set by _____**person(s) responsible**_____on a
_____**time frame**_____ basis and in consideration of advanced approval
for vacations or other personal time off. Employees will normally work no
more than ___**#**___ hours per week.

Management reserves the right to change work schedules as needed to meet
customer demand.

Attendance Policy

When you are absent, it means extra work for someone else; and in turn
when others are absent, it means more work for you. You should be interested in and responsible for holding absenteeism to an absolute minimum.
When you know you are going to be absent from work, or unavoidably late,
it is your responsibility to notify your supervisor before or by
_____**hours**_____ a.m./p.m. If you cannot notify your supervisor, you are
expected to have your family or a friend call for you. Failure to do so may
result in dismissal. Failure to notify or report for ___**#**___consecutive workdays shall be deemed to be a voluntary termination.

Absence and tardiness become a part of your work record and are reviewed
before promotions and salary increases are considered. Absences that are not
approved by your supervisor can result in disciplinary action up to and
including termination.

Compensation/Wages

Be sure to include in your policy, if applicable:

• information about pay periods and paydays;

- special instructions for getting on the payroll or recording hours worked;
- information about deductions from a paycheck; and
- information about how pay rates or salaries are determined.

Payday is ____ **day(s)** ____. For full-time employees, your check will reflect payment of regular hours through _____ (date or day of the current pay period). However, since each payroll is prepared several days in advance, any exceptions to a normal pay period, such as overtime or leave without pay that is submitted on an individual time card, may be reflected on a later paycheck. If payday falls on a holiday, you will receive your pay _____(before or after) the holiday. You may receive your paycheck _____(in person, by mail, and/or have your pay deposited directly to a checking or savings account).

Time cards for part-time and on-call employees are due ____ **day(s)** ____ by _____ A.M./P.M. and must reflect the hours worked in the prior ____ **#** ____ week(s). Your check will be issued _____ **time frame** _____.

Certain deductions from your pay are required by law, such as federal and state income taxes, Social Security taxes, and any local taxes, if applicable. Other payroll deductions may be authorized by you and may include such items as _____(list the more common types of deductions). Your paycheck stub will reflect all information about your pay and deductions including current and year-to-date figures. If you have any questions concerning your paycheck, see _____ **person(s) responsible** _____.

Your rate of pay is determined by the job you are doing, the market rate for similar work and your performance. Your rate of pay will also be reviewed _____ (semi-annually, annually, or as needed). Based on company performance and your individual performance, your rate of pay may be adjusted.

Overtime Pay and "Comp" Time

If you are eligible for overtime, you will be paid straight time for any hours you work under ___**#**__ hours a week. You will be paid __**amount of time**__ for the time you work over ___**#**__ hours. Whenever possible, employees are _____ (required/encouraged) to take compensatory time off for hours worked beyond their normal schedule. "Comp" time must be taken within ____**#**____ week of the overtime worked.

If you are considered "nonexempt", you must receive prior approval to work overtime. If you are considered "exempt" under the Federal Wage & Hour Law, these policies of overtime pay and compensatory time do not apply. If there is any question as to your exempt or nonexempt status, please contact __**person(s) responsible**__.

Paid Holidays

_____**company name**_____ observes___**#**__ scheduled paid holidays each year as follows: (list holidays and dates below)

Holiday   Date

Holidays falling on Saturday will be observed on _____ (Friday or Monday) .

Holidays falling on Sunday will be observed on _____ (Monday or Friday).

If full-time employees are required to work on a holiday, they will be paid _____**rate**_____. Part-time employees are eligible for _____**rate**_____.

Vacation

All regular full-time employees will receive vacation with pay based on their length of service with the company as follows:

Length of Employment   Vacation Earned

___**#**___ years   ___**#**___ days

___**#**___ years   ___**#**___ days

___**#**___ years   ___**#**___ days

___**#**___ years   ___**#**___ days

Employees accumulate 1/12 of their annual vacation each month. Vacation leave must be earned before it can be taken. New employees are eligible for vacation after ___**#**___ months of full-time employment. Vacation leave must be scheduled with _____ to ensure the smooth operation of the company. When a company-observed holiday falls within a vacation period, it _____(does/does not) count as a day of vacation. Up to ___**#**___ days of vacation may be carried over from one year into the next year. All remaining unused days each year will be forfeited. Any unused vacation at date of termination, retirement, or permanent disability will be _____ (paid/not paid) upon such occurrence.

_____(Part-time and/or temporary employees) _____(are/are not) eligible for paid vacation. Vacation leave for _____(part-time and/or temporary) employees is pro-rated, based on hours worked per week, and cannot be used until after

___#___ months of service. If a temporary or part-time employee changes to continuous full-time status, the effective date of the change is used to compute the vacation benefit.

Sick Leave

Full-time employees accumulate ___#___ sick day(s) per full month of employment for a maximum of ___#___ days per year. You must have completed ___#___ months of continuous, full-time service to be eligible to use your sick leave. Unused sick leave _____(can/cannot) be carried into future years and accumulated to a maximum of _____ days. You _____ (may/may not) convert any unused vacation if your sick day accumulation is exhausted. _____(Part-time and/or temporary) employees _____ (are/are not) eligible for sick leave, which is pro-rated based on hours worked per week.

Jury Duty

_____(full-time, part-time, and/or temporary) employees who are called for jury duty during regular work hours will be granted time off, provided proper verification of the days of service is furnished by the Clerk of Courts. The company _____(will /will not) continue to pay the employee's salary as follows: _____

_____

(Make up the difference between the regular rate of pay and the jury duty pay for up to ___#___ days per year or pay the employee's regular salary for up to ___#___ days upon surrender of jury duty pay to the company). You are expected to report for work if a reasonable amount of time remains in the regular workday. After ___#___ days, employees may take an unpaid leave of absence until their jury duty obligation is fulfilled.

Funeral/Bereavement Leave

When a death occurs in your family, notify __**person(s) responsible**__ to request time off. If you are a full-time employee and a death occurs in your immediate family _____**list of approved relatives**_____, time off _____(with/without) pay will be permitted at the discretion of _____. This is generally limited to _____ _____ (specify time limits). In the event circumstances require additional time off, use of vacation days or general leave of absence should be requested.

For close relatives _____**list of approved relatives**_____, or co-workers, the company generally _____ (allows/does not allow) time off to attend the funeral. Part-time employees _____ (are/are not) paid for time off as a result of a funeral.

Leave of Absence

Pick and choose what you want from this template to write a leave of absence policy for your company, or create your own policy.

A general leave of absence is defined as authorized time off from work without pay for a specified period which exceeds __#__ consecutive workdays but does not exceed __#__ months duration, without loss of employment status. Employees must have completed at least __#__ months of continuous full-time service to request a leave.

Employee requests for leave are to be submitted in writing to __**person(s) responsible**__ and should include the beginning date of the leave, the return to work date, and the specific reason for the leave. The following criteria will be considered by management in deciding whether or not to grant leave: _____ (list all that apply: return to work after the leave; work performance and attendance record; ability of remaining staff to cover duties during the leave; the total length of the requested leave; etc.).

The company _____ (will/will not) pay its portion of all insurance and retirement expenses which occur during an approved leave period. The employee must pay or authorize payment for all deductions for which the employee is responsible. Failure to pay deductions will result in cancellation of the benefits for nonpayment of premium. Employees on approved leave of absence _____ (will/will not) continue to accrue vacation and sick leave, (but these benefits can be used only after the employee returns to work on a continuous, full-time basis). Any office or holiday closing occurring during a leave _____ (is/is not) considered as part of the leave time and _____ (is/is not) compensable. Any change in salary _____ (will/will not) become effective for an employee on leave until the employee returns to work on a continuous, full-time basis.

Employees who are granted leaves are to contact __**person(s) responsible**__ at least ___**#**___ weeks prior to the return to work date and confirm their return as scheduled. Failure to confirm and/or return to work on the approved return to work date could result in termination of employment. You _____ (may/may not) return to work earlier than the approved return to work date with the approval of ___**person(s) responsible**___ and, in the case of medical leave, a release to return to work from the attending physician. Such a release must detail any or all work restrictions. The company will try to accommodate these restrictions, but cannot guarantee a job if the employee is unable to perform the essential functions of the job.

If you are unable to return to work as scheduled because of a disability, you must notify ___**person(s) responsible**___ and submit written proof of disability from the attending physician. Failure to notify the company, submit written proof of disability, or promptly return to work may result in denial of benefits and/or termination of employment.

Failure to return to work at the end of the leave of absence will be considered a voluntary resignation. _____**company name**_____ will attempt to place an employee returning from leave in the same or equivalent job, but does not guarantee return to the same job as held before commencement of the leave.

Accidents

____company name____ is dedicated to maintaining a safe work environment at all times. As an employee, you are required to be familiar with safety regulations and accident procedures, and you should practice caution at all times. Follow safety rules, use safe equipment, and report any unsafe conditions. If you should suffer an accident during working hours, notify __person(s) responsible__ immediately and obtain any necessary first aid. If the accident or injury is severe, professional help should be obtained immediately. Supervisors should complete a First Report of Injury form on all accidents or injuries that occur at the workplace and forward it to ____person(s) responsible____.

First Aid and Emergencies

Emergency procedures for _____(fire, tornado, hurricane, earthquake, etc.) are posted on the company bulletin board located ____designated location____. It is each employee's responsibility to review those procedures and emergency exits and to be prepared to evacuate in the event of such a disaster. Emergency telephone numbers for fire and police are to be displayed on all telephones in the building. Fire extinguishers are located ____designated location____ _____. A first aid kit is located ____designated location____.

Standards of Conduct

____company name____ is confident that all employees will conduct themselves in a businesslike and professional manner. No written list of company rules can be complete or substitute for the good judgment and cooperation of employees. However, for the protection of employees and the company, we have established some rules and regulations. Some of these rules are outlined below. These rules do not limit the company's right to impose discipline for other conduct detrimental to the interests of the company, its customers and other employees.

The actions listed here will result in disciplinary action. This list is not all-inclusive. The severity of the disciplinary action will be assessed on an individual basis; it may, but need not include warning, suspension and termination. Management reserves the right to determine disciplinary action for each violation. Termination may occur without previous warning.

These actions or behaviors are prohibited (list the actions or behaviors prohibited in your company below):

❑ _____

❑ _____

❑ _____

❑ _____

Complaints and Grievances

___**company name**___ is committed to responding promptly to your questions and concerns. If you should have a question or complaint about your job or the company, feel free to discuss it with your supervisor. Supervisors will be able to handle a majority of these kinds of problems.

However, if you do not receive satisfaction from your supervisor, the next step is to appeal to ___**person(s) responsible**___. It is a good idea at this time to put your concerns in writing to eliminate any possible misunderstandings. The company is very earnest in its conviction that all legitimate grievances be heard.

Employee Acknowledgment

Draft an employee acknowledgment form that covers each of the following points:

- places the responsibility for reading and understanding the policies on the employee;

- reinforces your status as an "at will" employer; and

- reinforces your right to change any and all policies at any time without notice.

This is your personal copy of the _____**company name**_____ _____ Employee Handbook. It has been prepared as a general statement of company policy and as a guide to set forth those matters which affect you and your job. Please take time to review its contents. We ask you to sign this form saying that you have received a copy of the guidelines and that you understand the policies and procedures outlined.

As a guideline, this handbook is not intended to become expressly or implicitly a part of any agreement or contract of employment. Where reference is made to insurance policies and coverages, the express language of those insurance policies thereto control. The statements contained in this handbook do not limit the right of either the company or the employee to terminate the employee's employment with or without cause at any time. _____**company name**_____ reserves the right to change any and all policies, rules, and methods of operations and doing business at any time.

Employee Signature _____

Date _____

Appendix II

Application for Employment Form

The following is a standard application for employment you may feel free to photocopy for use in your business.

Application for Employment

An Equal Employment Opportunity Employer

NAME: _____

ADDRESS: _____

TELEPHONE NO.: _____ SOCIAL SECURITY NO.: _____

DRIVER'S LICENSE NO.: _____ STATE: _____

FRIENDS/RELATIVES WORKING WITH COMPANY: _____

MILITARY SERVICE:YES _____ NO _____ BRANCH _____

EDUCATION: HIGH SCHOOL DEGREE   YES _____ NO_____
List the names of all educational institutions attended after high school; state what academic degrees have been attained: _____

_____

_____

WORK EXPERIENCE: PRIOR EMPLOYMENT   YES _____ NO _____
List the names and addresses of your last five (5) employers; state your position and work duties/responsibilities; provide the name of your supervisor and state the reason you left each employer:

_____

_____

_____

_____

_____

_____

_____

_____

_____

Is there a criminal charge, felony or misdemeanor, currently pending against you which would substantially relate to the position you are applying for: Yes _____ No _____

If you checked "yes," please give a brief description of the pending charge:

_____

_____

Have you ever been convicted of a crime, felony or misdemeanor, which would substantially relate to the position you are applying for, or which would affect your ability to be bonded?

Yes _____ No _____ If you checked "yes," please give a brief explanatory statement:

_____

_____

_____

REFERENCES: (NAME, ADDRESS, TELEPHONE NUMBER)

_____

_____

_____

_____

_____   _____

Date   Signature

Acceptance, retention or review of this application for employment does not guarantee that an applicant will be offered a job. If an employment offer is made, any position, unless otherwise agreed to in writing, is for no specified period of time, and is at the will of the employee and the employer. If an applicant is employed, separation from employment may occur at any time, for any reason, with or without prior notice, either by action of the employee or the employer.

Key Resources

The following is a suggested resources and reading list for additional research. Reprints of articles from the *Small Business Forum* can be ordered from the Wisconsin Small Business Development Center. Call (608) 263-7843 for a complete reprint list and ordering information.

Customer Satisfaction

Hayes, Bob E., *Measuring Customer Satisfaction* (Milwaukee, WI: ASQC Press, 1992).

Discipline and Termination

Bordwin, Milton, "Firing 101: Before, During and After," in *Small Business Forum* (Winter 1994/1995).

General Human Resources Management

Bangs, David H., *The Personnel Planning Guide*, Third Edition (Chicago, IL: Upstart Publishing Company, Inc., 1990).

Group/Team Processes

Auvine, Brian; Densmore, Betsy; Extrom, Mary; Poole, Scott; and Shanklin, Michael; *A Manual for Group Facilitators* (Madison, WI: Center for Conflict Resolution, 1978).

Bader, Gloria; Bloom, Audrey and Chang, Richard *Measuring Team Performance* (Irvine, CA: Richard Chang Associates, 1994).

Chang, Richard Y., *Building a Dynamic Team* (Irvine, CA: Richard Chang Associates, 1994).

Scholtes, Peter R., *The Team Handbook* (Madison, WI: Joiner Associates, 1988).

Varney, Glen H., *Building Productive Teams* (San Francisco: Jossey-Bass, 1989).

Hiring

Pinsker, Richard J., "Hiring Winners," in *Small Business Forum*, (Fall 1994).

Stover, Catherine. "Case Study: 'I Want to Hire a Top-Level Employee. How Do I Go about It?'," in *Small Business Forum* (Fall 1994).

Stover, Catherine. "Case Study: 'Where Can I Get Good Employees?'," in *Small Business Forum* (Fall 1990).

University of Wisconsin-Madison Small Business Development Center, *Hiring an Employee*, 1989.

Job Analysis and Design

Campion, Michael A. and Paul W. Thayer. "How Do You Design A Job?" in *Small Business Forum* (Fall 1990).

Leadership and General Management

Block, Peter, *The Empowered Manager* (San Francisco: Jossey-Bass, 1987).

Covey, Stephen R., *Principle-Centered Leadership* (New York: Simon & Schuster, 1991).

McGregor, Douglas, *The Human Side of Enterprise* (New York: McGraw-Hill, 1985).

Senge, Peter M., *The Fifth Discipline* (New York: Currency Doubleday, 1990).

Motivation and Performance

Adams, J. Stacy, "Toward an Understanding of Inequity," *Journal of Abnormal and Social Psychology* (November 1963, 422-36).

Herzberg, Frederick; Mausner, B. and Snyderman, B., *The Motivation to Work* (New York: Wiley, 1959).

Kohn, Alfie, "Why Incentive Plans Cannot Work," *Harvard Business Review* (September-October 1993): 54-63.

Lawler, Edward E., *Motivation in Work Organizations* (Belmont, CA: Brooks/Cole, 1973).

Mager, Robert F.; and Pipe, Peter, *Analyzing Performance Problems* (Belmont, CA: Lake Publishing Company, 1984).

Mager, Robert G., and Pipe, Peter, *Analyzing Performance Problems* (Belmont, CA: Lake Publishing Company, 1984).

Maslow, Abraham H., *Motivation and Personality* (New York: Harper & Brothers, 1954).

Ryan, Kathleen D. and Oestreich, Daniel K., *Driving Fear Out of the Workplace* (San Francisco: Jossey-Bass, 1991).

Scholtes, Peter R., "An Elaboration on Deming's Teachings on Performance Appraisal" (Madison, WI: Joiner Associates, 1987).

Skinner, B.F., *Contingencies of Reinforcement* (New York: Appleton-Century-Crofts, 1969).

Vroom, Victor H., *Work and Motivation* (New York: Wiley, 1964).

Orientation

Cadwell, Charles M., *New Employee Orientation* (Menlo Park, CA: Crisp Publications, 1988).

Training and Development

Cantor, Jeffrey A., *Delivering Instruction to Adults* (Middletown, Ohio: Wall and Emerson, 1992).

Carnevale, Anthony; Gainer, Leila; and Meltzer, Ann. *Workplace Basics Training Manual* (San Francisco: Jossey-Bass Publishers; 1990).

EQW National Employer Survey, sponsored by the Office of Educational Research and Improvement, U.S. Department of Education, 1995.

Geber, Beverly., "Does training make a difference? Prove it!" in *Training* (March 1995).

Mager, Robert F., *Measuring Instructional Results* (Belmont, CA: Lake Publishing Company, 1984).

Mager, Robert F., *Preparing Instructional Objectives* (Belmont, CA: Lake Publishing Company, 1984).

Newstrom, John W., and Scannell, Edward E., *Games Trainers Play* (New York: McGraw-Hill, Inc., 1980).

Pfieffer & Company, *The Encyclopedia of Group Activities* (San Diego, CA: CMA Publishing, 1989).

Pfieffer & Company, *The Encyclopedia of Icebreakers* (San Diego, CA: CMA Publishing, 1983).

Steinback, Bob, *The Adult Learner* (Menlo Park, CA: Crisp Publications, 1993).

Zaccarelli, Herman E., *Training Managers to Train* (Menlo Park, CA: Crisp Publications, 1988).

In addition to these resources, the American Society for Training and Development (ASTD) publishes Info-Line, a series of publications dedicated to topics related to training. Call ASTD at 703-683-8129. Specific topics that may be of interest are:

#841110	Great Games and How to Use Them
#8412	Get Results From Simulation and Role Play
#8501	Computer-Based Learning: What, Why and How
#8502	Be a Better Needs Analyst
#8507	Write, Design, and Produce Effective Training Materials
#8601	Essentials for Evaluation
#8602	Alternatives to Lecture
#8610	Find the Right Consultant
#8703	Get Results from the Case Method
#8708	Successful Orientation Programs
#8803	Basics of Instructional Systems Development
#8808	Basic Training for Trainers

#8810   Make or Buy: How to Decide

#8911   Icebreakers: Warm Up Your Audience

#9003   How to Train Managers to Train

Additional Resources

Books

Upstart Publishing Company, a division of Dearborn Publishing Group, Chicago, IL. Call 800-235-8866 for a free catalog. List of titles include:

Launching New Ventures: An Entrepreneurial Approach, Kathleen Allen, 1995. Innovative entrepreneurship text that enables the students to plan and start a world-class venture guide that takes the reader from the first basic steps of developing an idea to creating a detailed business and marketing plan. Instructor's manual available. 496 pp., $35.00

Strategic Planning for the New and Small Business, Fred L. Fry and Charles R. Stoner, 1995. This highly practical text guides students through the strategic planning process using case histories and examples of actual businesses. Unique in that it is a strategy book aimed specifically at small businesses. Instructor's manual available. 256 pp., $24.95

Financial Essentials for Small Business Success, Joseph Tabet and Jeffrey Slater, 1994. This text stresses the importance of common sense in overcoming the problems of poor record keeping and planning. Step-by-step guidance results in students learning to interpret financial reports and building the necessary financial tools for a profitable small business. Instructor's manual available. 272 pp., $22.95

Business Planning Guide, Seventh Edition, David H. Bangs, Jr., 1995. Designed for both beginning students and more experienced practitioners, this is a vital tool for putting together a complete and effective business plan and financing proposal. Contains three complete sample business plans. Available on CD-ROM. Instructor's manual available. 224 pp., $22.95

Anatomy of a Business Plan, Third Edition, Linda Pinson and Jerry Jinnett, 1996. The step-by-step approach assumes no prior knowledge of a business plan. This basic presentation enables the student or entrepreneur to prepare a start-up plan for a new small business or plan new strategies for an existing business. Instructor's manual available. 256 pp., $22.95

Market Planning Guide, Fourth Edition, David H. Bangs, Jr., 1995. Practical text that shows students how to create an effective marketing plan suited to the business' goals and resources. Features complete marketing plans for two actual businesses. Instructor's manual available. 257 pp., $22.95

Target Marketing, Third Edition, Linda Pinson and Jerry Jinnett, 1996. Text is a comprehensive guide to developing a marketing plan for your business. Broken into a simple three-stage marketing process of research, reach and retain. Instructor's manual available. 176 pp., $22.95

The Start Up Guide, David H. Bangs, Jr., 1994. Walks students through every phase of small business start-up. Text is based on a hypothetical one-year process. 176 pp., $22.95

Steps to Small Business Start-Up, Linda Pinson and Jerry Jinnett, 1993. One step at a time, the student learns the mechanics of business start-ups and gets started on everything from record-keeping to marketing and business planning. Contains forms, examples and worksheets. Instructor's manual available. 255 pp., $22.95

Cash Flow Control Guide, David H. Bangs, Jr., 1990. Step by step guide to learning a cash flow control process for the small business. It uses a real-life example of a company that demonstrates how cash flow planning can smooth out some of the small business's roughest spots. 88 pp., $19.95

Keeping the Books, Third Edition, Linda Pinson and Jerry Jinnett, 1996. Hands-on introduction to small business bookkeeping, which may be used with students who have no financial or accounting background. It covers all the essentials and provides numerous sample forms and worksheets. Instructor's manual available. 208 pp., $22.95

Export Profits, Jack Wolf, 1993. Comprehensive guide that simplifies the complex subject of exporting. It assumes no prior knowledge of international trade and with the aid of resources, examples and sample documents, covers all the aspects of exporting. 304 pp., $22.95

Cases in Small Business Management, John de Young, 1994. More than 50 intriguing and useful case studies focusing on typical problems faced by small business managers every day. Problem solving is encouraged through end-of-chapter questions that lead students through an analysis of possible solutions. Instructor's manual available. 288 pp., $24.95

Problems and Solutions in Small Business Management, Editors of Forum, 1995. A collection of case studies selected by the editors of the small business journal, Forum. A problem drawn from an actual business is presented and then followed by three possible solutions written by experts from a variety of areas within the field of small business management. 192 pp., $22.95

Other Titles

Small Business Source Book, Detroit, Michigan: Gale Research Co., 1995.

The Brass Tacks Entrepreneur, by Jim Schell. New York: Henry Holt and Company, Inc. 1993.

Magazines

Black Enterprise, 130 5th Avenue, 10th Floor, New York, NY 10011-4399. (212) 242-8000.

D&B Reports, 299 Park Avenue, New York, NY 10171. (212) 593-6724.

Entrepreneur Magazine, 2392 Morse Avenue, Irvine, CA 92714-6234.

In Business, J.G. Press, Inc., 419 State Street, Emmaus, PA 18049-0351. (215) 967-4135.

Inc. Magazine, Goldhirsch Group, 38 Commercial Wharf, Boston, MA 02110-3809. (617) 248-8000.

Small Business Forum, University of Wisconsin-Extension, Madison, WI 53706-1498. (608) 263-7843.

Associations

American Society of Independent Business, 777 Main Street, Suite 1600, Fort Worth, TX 76102. (817) 870-1880.

National Association for the Cottage Industry, Box 14850, Chicago, IL 60614-0850. (312) 472-8116.

National Association for the Self-Employed, 2328 Gravel Road, Fort Worth, TX 76118. (800) 232-6273.

National Small Business Association, 1155 15th Street NW, Washington, DC 20005-2706. (202) 293-8830.

On-Line Services

America Online (AOL): Call 800-827-6364 for a free trial membership.

CompuServe: Call 800-487-0588 for a free trial membership.

Prodigy: Call 1-800-PRODIGY ext. 358 for a free trial membership.

Local

SBDC: Contact your local Small Business Development Center for local publications.

Library

Check with your librarian for resource recommendations.

Key Word Glossary

Affirmative Action: designed to make up for past discrimination, affirmative action refers to a plan for seeking out, employing and developing employees who are members of protected groups (such as women and minorities).

Behavior Modification: applying positive and negative consequences with the goal of influencing behavior.

Cafeteria Plan: a strategy which allows each employee to choose the benefits to be included in his or her benefit plan.

Coaching: a management style where the supervisor provides support and encouragement to the employee, while allowing the employee to make decisions.

Cross-Organizational Feedback: a model for giving and receiving feedback from everyone in the company whose work relates to an individual's job.

Distance Learning/Distance Education: when programmed instruction is combined with some level of contact with a teacher who is not physically present with the student.

Employee Handbook/Personnel Manual: A written document used to communicate policies, procedures, and regulations to employees.

Employment-at-Will Doctrine: the historical right" of either the employer or employee to legally terminate an employment relationship at any time with or without notice and with or without cause.

Equal Employment Opportunity (EEO): designed to prevent future discrimination, EEO refers to the legal requirement of most employers to make employment and personnel decisions solely on the basis of objective criteria and without regard for race, religion, national origin, gender, color, age, or handicapped status.

Extrinsic Motivation: motivation that results from rewards given by external sources, such as compensation and benefits.

Ground Rules: performance guidelines that address how employees in a work group should behave.

Independent Study: a training method where the employee directs his or her own learning; also called self-study or self-directed learning.

Instructional Plan/Lesson Plan: a written description of what will be taught in a training session and how it will be delivered.

Intrinsic Motivation: motivation that comes from within the individual, not from the traditional rewards of compensations and benefits.

Job Analysis: the process of studying a job to understand the usual responsibilities and duties, specific tasks, reporting relationships and working conditions of the position.

Job Description: a written summary of responsibilities, duties, working conditions and performance expectations of a job.

Job Specifications: a written summary of the skills, knowledge, abilities and experiences needed to do a job.

Job Transfer: a situation when what is learned in the training session can be applied to the job.

Learning Outcome: a statement of what an employee should know, do or be like as the result of training.

Learning Style: how individual people use their perceptual strengths (auditory, visual, kinesthetic or tactile) to receive, process and remember new information.

Mission Statement: a clear and concise statement of the purpose of the company.

On-the-Job Training: learning that occurs while the employee is performing his or her work.

Orientation: a program for introducing new employees to the business, people, practices and culture of the company.

Peer Review/Team Review: a model for feedback where team members evaluate each other.

Performance Appraisal: a system for providing feedback on performance to the employee.

Performance Management: the process of planning, organizing and using your company's resources to achieve its goals and fulfill its customers' expectations.

Programmed Instruction: training materials designed specifically for self-directed learners.

Sexual Harassment: prohibited by law, sexual harassment refers to unwelcome sexual advances, requests for sexual favors, and/or verbal or physical conduct of a sexual nature which results in an intimidating, hostile or offensive work environment.

Synergy: the whole is greater than the sum of its parts (2 + 2 = 5); for example, two people working together can accomplish more than the sum of what each can accomplish working alone.

Training: a teaching and learning process in a company which gives employees the ongoing knowledge and skills needed to perform their jobs.

Training Needs Assessment: a workplace study for identifying gaps between what an employee needs to know or be able to do and what he or she actually knows and is able to do.

Values: the deeply held beliefs of the company, which give employees a framework for decision making.

Vision Statement: a statement of what the company is trying to become.

Personal Workshops

Your participation in Personal Workshops is a key factor in the success of your mastery learning experience. These workshops provide you with the opportunity to react and to respond to the information given in each lesson. As you complete each workshop, you are encouraged to apply your knowledge to your own business experience.

The Personal Workshops presented in this guide are reprinted on the following pages. While the directions needed to complete each exercise are included on each workshop page, the information necessary to prepare you for the activity is not. To fully understand each Personal Workshop, you will need to read the text and the Personal Workshop Preparations that precede each exercise.

THE PURPOSE OF THIS WORKSHOP IS TO IDENTIFY WHAT DUTIES THE PERSON IN THE JOB WILL HAVE, WHAT TASKS NEED TO BE DONE, AND TO DESCRIBE THE WORKING CONDITIONS OF THE JOB.

Personal Workshop #1
Job Analysis

Job Title:

Reports to:

Supervisory Responsibility for:

Major Duties/Responsibilities: **Percent of Total Time:**

Specific Tasks: **How Often:**

Specific Tasks: **How Often:**

Specific Tasks: **How Often:**

Specific Tasks: **How Often:**

What special equipment or tools does the person in this position use?

_____

What is the relationship of this position to other positions in the business?

Describe the working conditions for the position:

Usual hours:

Overtime required:

Travel required:

Special conditions or requirements of position:

THE PURPOSE OF THIS WORKSHOP IS TO DESCRIBE THE JOB AND YOUR PERFORMANCE EXPECTATIONS.

Personal Workshop #2
Building A Results-Oriented Job Description

Job Title:

Reports to:

Job Summary:

Major Responsibilities and Duties	Performance Expectations
(note: take this information from the job analysis worksheet)	(note: for each duty, write at least one measurable result you expect)

Supervisory Responsibilities:

Working Conditions:

Special Requirements/Other Relevant Information:

THE PURPOSE OF THIS WORKSHOP IS TO IDENTIFY THE SKILLS, KNOWLEDGE, ABILITIES AND EXPERIENCES AN INDIVIDUAL SHOULD HAVE TO FILL THIS POSITION.

Personal Workshop #3
Writing Job Specifications

Job Title:

Education:

Required:

Desired:

Experience:

Required:

Desired:

Special Skills or Abilities:

Required:

Desired:

Personal Characteristics:

Required:

Desired:

Physical Requirements:

THE PURPOSE OF THIS WORKSHOP IS TO DEVELOP AN INFORMATIVE AND ATTRACTIVE ANNOUNCEMENT OF THE AVAILABLE POSITION IN YOUR BUSINESS.

Personal Workshop #4
Writing a Position Announcement

Write an announcement for the position in the space below. As a minimum, always include the following information in the position announcement:

- ❏ The position title and a brief descriptive overview of the job
- ❏ Required qualifications
- ❏ How to apply
- ❏ Application deadline
- ❏ The name of the company
- ❏ Equal employment opportunity statement, if applicable
- ❏ Affirmative action statement, if applicable

In addition, you may choose to include the following information:

- ❏ Descriptive information about the company or organization
- ❏ Desired qualifications
- ❏ Salary and/or benefit information
- ❏ Information about working conditions, hours, etc.
- ❏ Information about the community
- ❏ Anticipated start date, or other special information
- ❏ Our business logo
- ❏ Letter and or resume required

Using the checklist as your guide, write your announcement in the space below.

Go back and review your checklist. Did you include everything in the announcement that you noted on your checklist? Is your announcement clear and easy to understand? If no, you will want to revise your copy, as necessary.

THE PURPOSE OF THIS WORKSHOP IS TO DESIGN A TOOL TO HELP YOU SCREEN APPLICANTS.

Personal Workshop #5
Developing a Screening Worksheet

Applicant Name:_____

Required Qualifications/Skills	Yes	No	Comments
1.	❑	❑	
2.	❑	❑	
3.	❑	❑	
4.	❑	❑	
5.	❑	❑	
6.	❑	❑	
7.	❑	❑	

Desired Qualifications/Skills	Yes	No	Comments
1.	❑	❑	
2.	❑	❑	
3.	❑	❑	
4.	❑	❑	
5.	❑	❑	
6.	❑	❑	
7.	❑	❑	

Notes:

Overall Impression:	*Not Qualified*	*Marginal*	*Unsure*	*Highly Qualified*
	❑	❑	❑	❑

Initials:_____**Date:**_____

THE PURPOSE OF THIS WORKSHOP IS TO DEVELOP A LIST OF LEGAL AND OPEN-ENDED INTERVIEW QUESTIONS WHICH WILL HELP YOU GAIN INFORMATION ABOUT AN APPLICANT'S SUITABILITY FOR THE JOB.

Personal Workshop #6
Developing Valid Interview Questions

Questions related to work experience:

Questions related to education and training:

Questions related to personal work characteristics, style, attitude, values, etc.:

Other Questions:

Personal Workshop #7
Step 1: My Personal Notes

Step 1—Information That Brings Employees on Board

Jot down those administrative procedures which you feel new employees should complete during their orientation.

Payroll/Payroll Information:

Benefit Information:

Tax Information/Forms:

Insurance Information/Forms:

Company Identification card, keys, etc.:

Additional Information:

THE PURPOSE OF THIS WORKSHOP IS TO JOT DOWN INFORMATION WHICH WILL HELP NEW EMPLOYEES BECOME ORIENTED TO YOUR COMPANY'S PHYSICAL LAYOUT, ITS OPERATIONS, ITS PEOPLE AND PROCESSES.

Personal Workshop #7
Step 2: My Personal Notes

Step 2—Information That Helps Employees Understand the System

Write down the information you need to provide new employees so that they will understand your company's systems and procedures:

List those areas which should be included in the company tour. (i.e.: restrooms, lunch and break rooms, mail rooms, parking, etc.)

List any business policies and procedures which you feel should be reviewed. (i.e.: customer service policies, telephone procedures, etc.)

Identify your company safety rules and evacuation procedures.

Identify your company safety rules and evacuation procedures.

Identify company health requirements.

List the people with whom your new employee should meet during the orientation process.

Basic overview of your company policies and procedures. (i.e.: your company handbook)

THE PURPOSE OF THIS WORKSHOP IS TO COME UP WITH IDEAS FOR THINGS YOU CAN DO TO MAKE A NEW EMPLOYEE FEEL WELCOME.

Personal Workshop #7
Step 3: My Personal Notes

Step 3—Information That Gives Employees a Sense of Belonging

Use the space below to brainstorm ideas that will help give new employees in your company a sense of belonging. Ideas might include: holding an open house, taking the new employee to lunch, providing the new employee with a company T-shirt or hat. The ideas are endless. Just use your imagination!

Personal Workshop #7
Step 4: My Personal Notes

Step 4—History and Philosophy of the Company

History   Assume that you have only five minutes to explain to a complete stranger what your business is, how it got started, and how it has developed into what it is today. Use the space below to jot down key words and/or events you would include in your description for a new employee.

Philosophy   What is the philosophy of your company? In other words, what are the key values and beliefs that guide the way the company operates and the way the employees conduct business? What personal characteristics do you expect every successful employee in your company to possess? Jot down your ideas in the space below.

Now, how will you share the history and/or philosophy of your company with the new employee? Will you place this information in a company handbook? Will you share this information verbally? Will you write it in the form of a letter or a handout to be given to the new employee? Write your answer below.

Personal Workshop #7
Step 5: My Personal Notes

Step 5—Business Goals and Objectives

Use your business plan and/or strategic plan to determine what your company's mission and vision statements should be.

What is the **mission** of your company?

What is the **vision** of your company?

Use your business plan and/or strategic plan as a guide to decide what every employee needs to know about the goals and objectives of your company.

What are the major goals of your company? What objectives will you use to meet each goal?

Goals   **Objectives**

How will you share your company's goals and objectives with the new employee? Will it be placed in a handbook or letter? Will it be shared verbally in a meeting? Write your ideas in the space below.

THE PURPOSE OF THIS WORKSHOP IS TO IDENTIFY NEW EMPLOYEE RESPONSIBILITIES.

Personal Workshop #7
Step 6: My Personal Notes

Step 6—Information that Acquaints Employees with their Responsibilities

Prepare for a new employee training period by answering the following questions.

What steps will the new employee take to learn the job?

Who will be responsible for training the new employee?

What is a reasonable schedule for completing the training?

Personal Workshop #7
Step 7: My Personal Notes

Step 7—Who to Involve in Orientation

List the people in your company who need to be involved in the orientation process for the new employee. Next to that person, indicate what his or her responsibilities will be.

	Contact People	Responsibilities
Owners/Managers		
Supervisors		
Payroll and Administrative Personnel		
Other Employees		

THE PURPOSE OF THIS WORKSHOP IS TO IDENTIFY THE SPECIFIC INFORMATION YOU NEED TO INCLUDE IN AN ORIENTATION, WHO SHOULD PROVIDE THAT INFORMATION AND WHEN.

Personal Workshop #8
Orientation Checklist

Position:

Orientation Information	Who	When
I. Information that Brings Employees on Board:		
II. Information About the System:		
III. Information that Gives a Sense of Belonging:		
IV. History and Philosophy of the Company:		
V. Business Goals and Objectives:		
VI. Information about Job Responsibilities:		

Personal Workshop #9
Training Needs Assessment

Position:

Staff:

List below the knowledge and skills required to successfully meet performance expectations.	List the knowledge and skills that the employee needs but seems to be lacking.	Indicate the name of the employee(s) needing training.
Skills/Knowledge Required	**Skills/Knowledge Needed**	**Employee Name**
Sales Skills:		
Service Skills:		
Administrative Skills:		

THE PURPOSE OF THIS WORKSHOP IS TO SPECIFY THE OUTCOMES YOU DESIRE FROM THE TRAINING EXPERIENCE.

Personal Workshop #10
Identify Learning Outcomes

Training Topic:

Purpose or Training Goal:

What do you want the employee to know as a result of this training?
Learning Outcome:

What do you want the employee to be able to do as a result of this training?
Learning Outcome:

What do you want the employee to be like or feel like as a result of this training?
Learning Outcome:

THE PURPOSE OF THIS WORKSHOP IS TO DESIGN AN INSTRUCTIONAL PLAN FOR TRAINING.

Personal Workshop #11
Design an Instructional Plan

Training Topic:

Purpose or Training Goal:

Learning Outcomes:

Materials:

Approximate length of training session:

Equipment::

Process and content:

Personal Workshop #12
Plan for Job Transfer

Topic of the Training Session:

1. What are some examples of real problems these employees are experiencing on the job that relate to the topic of this training?

2. What are some ways that achieving the learning outcomes will help the employees solve their problems?

3. What are some ways you can demonstrate these benefits to the employees?

4. What activities can you build into the training to help employees understand how this new information transfers to their jobs?

5. How can you get supervisors involved in the training process?

Personal Workshop #13
Employee Handbook Checklist

Place a check in the box of each topic or issue below which needs to be covered in your employee handbook. Add other topics as needed.

I. Introduction

- ❑ Welcome statement
- ❑ "At-will" statement
- ❑ Right to amend
- ❑ Company history
- ❑ Company philosophy
- ❑ Mission and vision statements
- ❑ How to use the employee handbook
- ❑ _____
- ❑ _____

II. General Employment/Management Policies

- ❑ Employee classifications
- ❑ Length of service
- ❑ EEO statement
- ❑ Sexual harassment
- ❑ Hiring policies: hiring of relatives
- ❑ Promotion policies
- ❑ Physical examinations
- ❑ Accommodation for disabilities and compliance with ADA
- ❑ Immigration issues
- ❑ Probation
- ❑ Orientation and training
- ❑ Non-compete policy/ trade secrets
- ❑ Confidentiality
- ❑ Outside employment
- ❑ Personal appearance/dress code
- ❑ Gifts and gratuities
- ❑ Solicitations and distributions
- ❑ Personnel records (access and privacy)
- ❑ Smoking

❑ Alcoholism and drug abuse
❑ Travel policies
❑ Personal property
❑ Telephone usage
❑ Parking
❑ Keys and identification cards
❑ Bulletin boards
❑ Open door policy
❑ _____
❑ _____

III. Policies about Work Schedules

❑ Regular work hours and schedule setting
❑ Breaks
❑ Attendance policy
❑ Weather
❑ _____
❑ _____

IV. Compensation and Benefits Policies

❑ Compensation/wages/salaries
❑ Overtime pay and compensatory ("comp") time
❑ "On-call" employee pay
❑ Garnishment
❑ Legally-required benefits (workers' compensation insurance, Unemployment insurance, FICA)
❑ Leave policies
  ❑ Holidays
  ❑ Vacation
  ❑ Sick leave and personal leave
  ❑ Jury duty
  ❑ Funeral/bereavement leave
  ❑ Military duty
  ❑ Leave of absence
❑ Health and life insurance
❑ Short- or long-term disability insurance
❑ Retirement benefits and annuity options
❑ Educational assistance programs
❑ _____
❑ _____

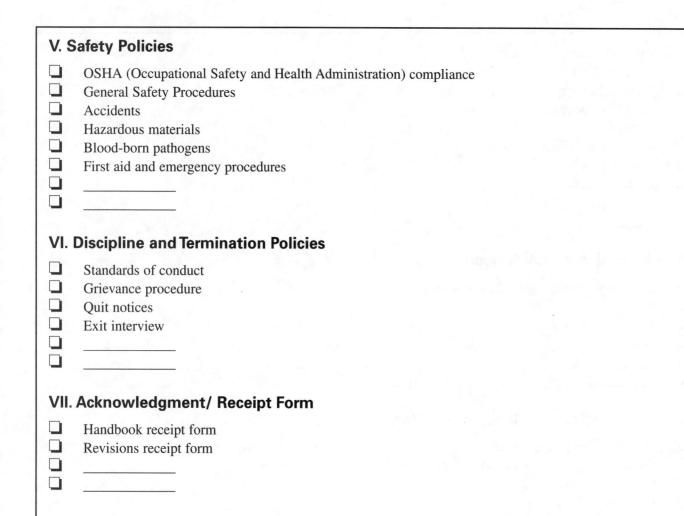

V. Safety Policies

❑   OSHA (Occupational Safety and Health Administration) compliance
❑   General Safety Procedures
❑   Accidents
❑   Hazardous materials
❑   Blood-born pathogens
❑   First aid and emergency procedures
❑   _____
❑   _____

VI. Discipline and Termination Policies

❑   Standards of conduct
❑   Grievance procedure
❑   Quit notices
❑   Exit interview
❑   _____
❑   _____

VII. Acknowledgment/ Receipt Form

❑   Handbook receipt form
❑   Revisions receipt form
❑   _____
❑   _____

THE PURPOSE OF THIS WORKSHOP IS TO WRITE AN INTRODUCTORY SECTION FOR YOUR EMPLOYEE HANDBOOK.

Personal Workshop #14
Writing the Introduction

Part I: Check off the items you need or want to include in your introduction.

Always include

___ welcome statement

___ "at will" statement

___ right to amend policies

___ how the handbook should be used

___ list of officers

___ other: _____

Optional items to include

___ company history

___ philosophy

___ mission and/or vision

___ organizational chart

Part II: Write an introductory statement for your company here:

Personal Workshop #15
Employee Classifications

Part I: Identify the different types of employee classifications you have in your company.

___ regular full-time   ___ temporary part-time

___ regular part-time   ___ on-call

___ temporary full-time   ___ other: _____

Part II: Write a description for each classification which includes information about:
* working conditions (such as hours, how paid, etc.)
* benefits eligibility
* the employer's "at will" status

Note: If this information is different for non-management and management, write separate descriptions for each.

Regular Full-Time	Non-Management	Management
Regular Part-Time		
Temporary		

On-Call	Non-Management	Management

Other

Personal Workshop #16
Sexual Harassment

Use this template to write a sexual harassment policy for your company, or develop your own policy.

Sexual Harassment by or of employees of _____ will not be tolerated. Such conduct may result in disciplinary actions up to and including termination of employment. Unwelcome sexual advances, requests for sexual favors, and other verbal or physical conduct of a sexual nature constitute sexual harassment when:

- Submission to such conduct is made either explicitly or implicitly a term or condition of employment.

- Submission to or rejection of such conduct is used as the basis for employment decisions.

- Such conduct has the purpose or effect of unreasonably interfering with an individual's work performance.

- Such conduct creates an intimidating, hostile or offensive working environment.

If you encounter such conduct from supervisors, other employees, or clients, you should contact any of the following as you think appropriate:

- _____

- _____

- _____

Complaints will be investigated in a confidential manner. Please do not assume that management is aware of an activity prohibited by this policy. It is your responsibility to bring your complaints and concerns to management's attention so that they can be addressed.

_____ wants employees to know that they can work in a secure environment and be treated with dignity. Insulting, degrading, or exploitative treatment of any employee will not be tolerated.

Sexual Harassment

Personal Workshop #17
Personnel Records

Instructions: Write a policy regarding the handling of your personnel records which covers each of the following points:

- what the personnel record contains;
- your policy regarding confidentiality and security of records;
- the procedure for employee access to the file; and
- the procedure for changing information in the file.

THE PURPOSE OF THIS WORKSHOP IS TO DEVELOP POLICIES FOR TELEPHONE USAGE IN YOUR COMPANY.

Personal Workshop #18
Telephone Use

Write a policy regarding telephone use in your company.

THE PURPOSE OF THIS WORKSHOP IS TO DRAFT A POLICY REGARDING REGULAR WORK HOURS AND/OR SCHEDULE SETTING FOR YOUR BUSINESS.

Personal Workshop #19
Regular Work Hours

Draft a policy regarding regular work hours and schedule setting below.

THE PURPOSE OF THIS WORKSHOP IS TO DRAFT AN ATTENDANCE POLICY.

Personal Workshop #20
Attendance Policy

Draft an attendance policy for your business in the space below.

THE PURPOSE OF THIS WORKSHOP IS TO WRITE A POLICY REGARDING EMPLOYEE COMPENSATION.

Personal Workshop #21
Compensation/Wages

Draft a policy regarding compensation and wages in the space below. Be sure to include in your policy, if applicable:

- information about pay periods and paydays;

- special instructions for getting on the payroll or recording hours worked;

- information about deductions from the paycheck; and

- information about how pay rates or salaries are determined.

THE PURPOSE OF THIS WORKSHOP IS TO WRITE A POLICY REGARDING PAID HOLIDAYS.

Personal Workshop #22
Paid Holidays

Write a policy below which lists holidays observed, whether they are paid or not, and any special information regarding eligibility or holiday pay.

THE PURPOSE OF THIS WORKSHOP IS TO WRITE A VACATION POLICY FOR YOUR COMPANY.

Personal Workshop #23
Vacation

Write a vacation policy below which describes eligibility and any special limitations for taking vacation.

THE PURPOSE OF THIS WORKSHOP IS TO WRITE A SICK LEAVE POLICY FOR YOUR COMPANY.

Personal Workshop #24
Sick Leave

Use the space below to draft a sick leave policy for your company.

Personal Workshop #25
First Aid and Emergencies

Draft a policy regarding first aid and emergencies in the space below.

THE PURPOSE OF THIS WORKSHOP IS TO DESCRIBE THE PROCEDURE FOR RESOLVING COMPLAINTS & GRIEVANCES.

Personal Workshop #26
Complaints and Grievances

Draft a policy describing the procedure for airing complaints and grievances below.

Personal Workshop #27
Employee Acknowledgment

Draft an employee acknowledgment form below which covers each of the following points:

- places the responsibility for reading and understanding the policies on the employee;

- reinforces your status as an "at will" employer; and

- reinforces your right to change any and all policies at any time without notice.

Personal Workshop #28
Vision Statement and Company Values

1. Using 30 words or less, describe the purpose or mission of your company.

2. Who are your primary external customers, and what are their needs?
   Customer

   Needs

3. Why should these customers want to come to you? In other words, what things do you have to offer (or want to offer) that are better than the competition?

4. Describe what your ideal business would look like:

5. Consider your answers to the previous questions, and write a vision statement for your business using no more than 30 words:

6. In order to achieve this vision, what values do you believe every employee must have? In other words, what are the guiding principles for work in your business?

THE PURPOSE OF THIS WORKSHOP IS TO IDENTIFY AND PRIORITIZE KEY ISSUES FACING YOUR BUSINESS.

Personal Workshop #29
Key Issues

1. What are the major issues facing your customers/clients for the next five years?

2. What are the major issues facing your company for the next five years?

3. Prioritize the issues your organization should work on for the next five years:

THE PURPOSE OF THIS WORKSHOP IS TO SET GOALS AND ACTION PLANS FOR YOUR BUSINESS.

Personal Workshop #30
Organizational Goals

HUMAN RESOURCES

Goals   Action Plans

FINANCIAL RESOURCES

Goals   Action Plans

PHYSICAL RESOURCES

Goals   Action Plans

POLITICAL RESOURCES

Goals   Action Plans

COMMUNICATIONS AND MARKETING

Goals   Action Plans

THE PURPOSE OF THIS WORKSHOP IS TO DEFINE THE TEAM'S MISSION AND GOALS.

Personal Workshop #31
Setting Team Goals

Name/Description of Team:

State the purpose, or mission, of this team:

Team Goals   **Action Plans**

THE PURPOSE OF THIS WORKSHOP IS TO SET INDIVIDUAL PERFORMANCE GOALS.

Personal Workshop #32
Goals for Individual Employees

Position:

Performance Goals   **Action Plan**

THE PURPOSE OF THIS WORKSHOP IS TO FACILITATE PEER OR TEAM FEEDBACK.

Personal Workshop #33
Peer or Team Feedback

Employee:

I see that you have contributed to our work in the following way(s):

I admire these strength(s) in you:

I think we could work better together if I:

I think we could work better together if you:

Additional comments and concerns:

I'm sharing this with you in the interest of improving our work relationship. Please let me know what I can do to improve that relationship.

Peer Evaluator:

Date:

THE PURPOSE OF THIS WORKSHOP IS TO DEVELOP A CUSTOMER FEEDBACK FORM FOR YOUR BUSINESS.

Personal Workshop #34
Customer Feedback Form

Revise this card to meet the specific needs of your company for feedback from customers.

To our customers:
Our goal is to offer the best possible service. To help us serve you better, please take a few minutes to complete and return this form.

1.

2.

3.

4.

5. Please offer additional comments or suggestions here:

Thanks and it is our pleasure to serve you!

Personal Workshop #35
Leadership Survey

Periodically consider these questions to assess your leadership in your business. Ask your employees to answer them as well.

YES   NO

Do I specify results and allow employees the freedom to determine their own methods and means?

Do the results I request match the vision and values of the business?

Do I always let employees know what resources they will need and where to find them?

Do I encourage employees to participate in setting their own performance standards?

Do I work with employees to create appropriate consequences for achieving (or not achieving) specified results?

Do I trust and believe in my employees, knowing that they will do the best job possible?

Index